THE PRACTICE TURN IN ARCHITECTURE:
BRUSSELS AFTER 1968

Ashgate Studies in Architecture Series

SERIES EDITOR: EAMONN CANNIFFE, MANCHESTER SCHOOL OF ARCHITECTURE,
MANCHESTER METROPOLITAN UNIVERSITY, UK

The discipline of Architecture is undergoing subtle transformation as design awareness permeates our visually dominated culture. Technological change, the search for sustainability and debates around the value of place and meaning of the architectural gesture are aspects which will affect the cities we inhabit. This series seeks to address such topics, both theoretically and in practice, through the publication of high-quality original research, written and visual.

Other titles in this series

The City Crown by Bruno Taut
Edited by Matthew Mindrup and Ulrike Altenmüller-Lewis
ISBN 978 1 4724 2199 9

In-Between: Architectural Drawing and Imaginative
Knowledge in Islamic and Western Traditions
Hooman Koliji
ISBN 978 1 4724 3868 3

Architectural Projects of Marco Frascari:
The Pleasure of a Demonstration
Sam Ridgway
ISBN 978 1 4724 4174 4

Phenomenologies of the City
Studies in the History and Philosophy of Architecture
Edited by Henriette Steiner and Maximilian Sternberg
ISBN 978 1 4094 5479 3

From Formalism to Weak Form: The Architecture
and Philosophy of Peter Eisenman
Stefano Corbo
ISBN 978 1 4724 4314 4

Forthcoming titles in this series

Architecture of Great Expositions 1937–1959
Messages of Peace, Images of War
Edited by Rika Devos, Alexander Ortenberg and Vladimir Paperny
ISBN 978 1 4724 3460 9

Global Perspectives on Critical Architecture
Praxis Reloaded
Edited by Gevork Hartoonian
ISBN 978 1 4724 3813 3

The Practice Turn in Architecture: Brussels after 1968

Isabelle Doucet
University of Manchester, UK

LONDON AND NEW YORK

First published 2015 by Ashgate Publishing

2 Park Square, Milton Park, Abingdon, Oxfordshire OX14 4RN
711 Third Avenue, New York, NY 10017

Routledge is an imprint of the Taylor & Francis Group, an informa business

First issued in paperback 2017

Copyright © Isabelle Doucet 2015

Isabelle Doucet has asserted her right under the Copyright, Designs and Patents Act, 1988, to be identified as the author of this work.

All rights reserved. No part of this book may be reprinted or reproduced or utilised in any form or by any electronic, mechanical, or other means, now known or hereafter invented, including photocopying and recording, or in any information storage or retrieval system, without permission in writing from the publishers.

Notice:
Product or corporate names may be trademarks or registered trademarks, and are used only for identification and explanation without intent to infringe.

British Library Cataloguing in Publication Data
A catalogue record for this book is available from the British Library.

Library of Congress Cataloging-in-Publication Data
Doucet, Isabelle.
   The practice turn in architecture: Brussels after 1968 / By Isabelle Doucet.
      pages cm. -- (Ashgate studies in architecture)
   Includes bibliographical references and index.
   ISBN 978-1-4724-3735-8 (hardback: alk. paper)
   1. Architecture and society--Belgium--Brussels--History--20th century.
2. Architecture and society--Belgium--Brussels--History--21st century. 3. Brussels (Belgium)--Social conditions--20th century. 4. Brussels (Belgium)--Social conditions--21st century. I. Title.
NA2543.S6D67 2015
720.1'03--dc23

2015019284

ISBN-13: 978-1-4724-3735-8 (hbk)
ISBN-13: 978-1-138-57231-7 (pbk)

Contents

List of Colour Plates — vii
List of Black and White Figures — ix
List of Abbreviations — xv
Acknowledgements — xvii
Preface — xix

1 Introduction: The City as a Practice — 1

2 Counter-projects — 39

3 Interstitial Activism — 79

4 Participatory Challenges — 111

5 Learning from Things — 133

6 Unsung Heroes — 155

7 Conclusions: Towards a Cautious Pragmatism — 187

Appendix: Interviews and Exchanges with Brussels Stakeholders — 193
Index — 195

List of Colour Plates

1   *La rencontre évocatrice* and *Le portique des maîtres carriers*, part of the 'Différents Projets pour la Reconstruction et l'Embellissement de la Partie de Bruxelles éventrée par la Jonction des Gares du Nord et du Midi' (Sefik Birkiye, Gilbert Busieau, Patrice Neirinck, La Cambre, 1978). Image source: A. Brauman, M. Culot, and M. Louis (eds), *La Reconstruction de Bruxelles*, Editions des AAM, 1982, p. 75. Copyright: Archives d'Architecture Moderne. Used with permission.

2   Proposal for the Carrefour de l'Europe site, by the ARAU, 1976. ARAU, ed., *Bruxelles Vu par ses Habitants, Quinze années d'action urbaine* (Brussels: Commission Française de la Culture et de l'Agglomération de Bruxelles and ARAU, 1984), 65. Copyright: Archives d'Architecture Moderne. Used with permission. Maurice Culot included it also in 'The right wing in disguise', *Lotus International* 13, 94–101, 100; where the caption states: 'the style developed for this project […] unleashed the fury of architects who hold that the use of "pastiche" is an immoral act'.

3   Lakense Straat, Brussels. Photograph by the author, 2015.

4   Benjamin Verdonck, *Barake* project near the Brussels Gare du Midi. Copyright: City Mine(d). Used with permission.

5   Location of Recyclart, Brussels, January 2015. Photograph by the author.

6   *Arabesk-Palaverboom* project, Brussels. Photograph by the author, 2015.

7   *De Roze Verspreiding* project, design by Les Saprophytes. Copyright: Les Saprophytes. Used with permission.

8   Ursulines Square / Skate Park, Brussels. Photograph by Filip Dujardin. Copyright: L'Escaut. Used with permission.

9   Ursulines Square / Skate Park, Brussels. Photograph by the author, 2015.

10 Théâtre National, Brussels, by SCA Architectes Associés, Atelier Gigogne, and L'Escaut. Photograph by the author, 2015.

11 Théâtre National, Brussels, by SCA Architectes Associés, Atelier Gigogne, and L'Escaut. Entrance foyer: used also as an informal semi-public space. Photograph by the author, 2015.

12 Wall tapestry designed for the *Jonction 4 x 4* exhibition. Photograph by Kevin Laloux and Maxime Delvaux. Copyright: Bouwmeester Maître Architecte bMa, asbl Recyclart, and asbl Congrès. Used with permission.

13 Wall tapestry designed for the *Jonction 4 x 4* exhibition. Photograph by Kevin Laloux and Maxime Delvaux. Copyright: Bouwmeester Maître Architecte bMa, asbl Recyclart, and asbl Congrès. Used with permission.

14 Les Vignes Blanches, Cergy-Pontoise, France. 1976–1979. Copyright: Lucien Kroll. Used with permission.

15 *Maison des Citoyens* by Atelier d'Architecture Pierre Hebbelinck. Photograph by Marie-Françoise Plissart. Copyright: Pierre Hebbelinck. Used with permission.

16 Signs indicating that this location is not a place for urination ('ceci n'est pas un urinoir') whilst directing towards nearby public urinals. Photograph by the author, 2015.

17 Example of a new urinal. Eight of those were installed from late 2013 onwards, replacing the original brick ones. Photograph by the author, 2015.

18 Place Flagey, Latz & Partners / D+A International. Copyright and photograph by Serge Brison. Used with permission.

19 Place Flagey, Latz & Partners / D+A International. Copyright and photograph by Bernard Capelle. Used with permission.

20 Rogier Project, Xaveer De Geyter Architects. Copyright XDGA Architects. Used with permission.

List of Black and White Figures

1.1 During a visit to Brussels in January 2015, the café called Skieven Architek turned out to have closed. Photograph by the author. — 2

1.2 The dome of the Palace of Justice can be seen on several occasions when walking through the Marolles neighbourhood. Photograph by the author, 2015. — 3

1.3 Belgium's regions. Map provided by the Brussels Agence de Développement Territorial – Agentschap voor Territoriale Ontwikkeling (ADT-ATO). Used with permission. — 7

1.4 Belgium's regions and communities. Map provided by the Brussels Agence de Développement Territorial – Agentschap voor Territoriale Ontwikkeling (ADT-ATO). Used with permission. — 8

1.5 Brussels' 19 Municipalities. Map provided by the Brussels Agence de Développement Territorial – Agentschap voor Territoriale Ontwikkeling (ADT-ATO). Used with permission. — 8

1.6 Brussels 'in action'. Marolles neighbourhood. Photograph by the author, 2015. — 9

1.7 Cover of the exhibition catalogue *bMa Man of Thoughts: 5 jaar Brussels bouwmeester – 5 ans maître-architecte à Bruxelles – 5 years Brussels head architect* (exhibition from September 12–25, 2014). Copyright: Bouwmeester Maître Architecte bMa. Used with permission. — 14

2.1 Counter-projects combining critique with alternative proposal. Proposal for the Carrefour de l'Europe site, Brussels (Sefik Birkiye, Gilbert Busieau, Patrice Neirinck, La Cambre, 1978) as part of the 'Différents Projets pour la Reconstruction et l'Embellissement de la Partie de Bruxelles éventrée par la Jonction des Gares du Nord et du Midi'.

Source: Léon Krier and Maurice Culot, *Contreprojets – Controprogetti – Counterprojects*, Brussels: AAM, 1980, no page numbers. Copyright: Archives d'Architecture Moderne. Used with permission.   46

2.2 The counter-project *les extensions des communautés Européennes à Bruxelles* (1973–1974, fifth-year students La Cambre) proposes an urban morphology based on a model of streets and squares, as an alternative to the model of towers in an open landscape as suggested by the original project (bottom page). Source: École nationale supérieure d'architecture et des arts visuels, eds, *Le Bateau d'Élie. Contributions aux luttes urbaines et projets opportunistes, La Cambre 1971–1975* (Brussels: Éditions des AAM, 1975), p. 47. Copyright: Archives d'Architecture Moderne. Used with permission.   48

2.3 *Projet d'aménagement de la vallée du Maelbeek* (La Cambre, 1971–1973). In *Wonen TA-BK* (nr. 15–16, 1975, p. 70), the project is credited to Ph. Lefèvre, in the framework of the design by Levy and Mierop. Source: École nationale supérieure d'architecture et des arts visuels, eds, *Le Bateau d'Élie. Contributions aux luttes urbaines et projets opportunistes, La Cambre 1971–1975* (Brussels: Éditions des AAM, 1975), p. 25. Copyright: Archives d'Architecture Moderne. Used with permission.   49

2.4 *L'orient est rouge* (part of the *Cinq propositions pour le Square du Bastion* project, La Cambre, 1974–1975, third-, fourth-, and fifth-year students). In Maurice Culot, 'The right wing in disguise' (*Lotus* 13 (1976): 101) the project is credited to Levy, Lenain, Lefebvre, Mierop, Louis. Source: École nationale supérieure d'architecture et des arts visuels, eds, *Le Bateau d'Élie. Contributions aux luttes urbaines et projets opportunistes, La Cambre 1971–1975* (Brussels: Éditions des AAM, 1975), p. 60. Copyright: Archives d'Architecture Moderne. Used with permission.   50

2.5 Interventions of architects were also targetted at optimising and clarifying existing drawings made by action committees. Here shown is a drawing by the ARAU (F. Joachim) as reworked by Maurice Culot: addition of street names and annotations. Source: *Wonen TA-BK*, 15–16 (1975): p. 66. Copyright: Archives d'Architecture Moderne. Used with permission.   51

2.6 *La Reconstruction des Marolles* (S. Birkiye, G. Busieau, Les AAM, 1978). Source: André Barey, ed. *Déclaration de Bruxelles: propos sur la reconstruction de la ville européenne* (Brussels: Éditions des AAM, 1980), p. 83. Copyright: Archives d'Architecture Moderne. Used with permission.   51

2.7 *Réorganisation des carrières de soignies* (Dominique Delbrouck and Jean-Pierre Majot, La Cambre, 1979). The caption in the original states 'different stages in the production of natural stone and their *mis en oeuvre* on the building site' (translated from French). Source: André Barey, ed. *Déclaration de Bruxelles: propos sur la reconstruction de la ville européenne*

(Brussels: Éditions des AAM, 1980), p. 86. Copyright: Archives d'Architecture Moderne. Used with permission. 52

2.8 *La rencontre évocatrice* and *Le portique des maîtres carriers*, part of the 'Différents Projets pour la Reconstruction et l'Embellissement de la Partie de Bruxelles éventrée par la Jonction des Gares du Nord et du Midi' (Sefik Birkiye, Gilbert Busieau, Patrice Neirinck, La Cambre, 1978). Image source: A. Brauman, M. Culot, and M. Louis (eds), *La Reconstruction de Bruxelles*, Editions des AAM, 1982, p. 75. Copyright: Archives d'Architecture Moderne. Used with permission. 53

2.9 Third project in the 'Trois projets de crèche dans les marolles'; *trompe l'oeil* applied to a roof visible from an adjacent high-rise housing block. Source: École nationale supérieure d'architecture et des arts visuels, eds, *Le Bateau d'Élie. Contributions aux luttes urbaines et projets opportunistes, La Cambre 1971–1975* (Brussels: Éditions des AAM, 1975), p. 20. Copyright: Archives d'Architecture Moderne. Used with permission. 55

2.10 Project for the Musée d'Art Moderne, Brussels, Daniel Lelubre, 1973. Source: Maurice Culot, 'La Longue Marche', *Architecture d'Aujourd'hui* 180 (July–August 1975): 18–29, 25. Copyright: Archives d'Architecture Moderne. Used with permission. 56

2.11 Project for the Musée d'Art Moderne, Brussels, Daniel Lelubre, 1974. Source: Maurice Culot, 'La Longue Marche', *Architecture d'Aujourd'hui* 180 (July–August 1975): 18–29, 25. Copyright: Archives d'Architecture Moderne. Used with permission. 56

2.12 Project for the Musée d'Art Moderne, Brussels, the ARAU, 1977. Source: ARAU, ed., *Bruxelles Vu par ses Habitants, Quinze années d'action urbaine* (Brussels: Commission Française de la Culture et de l'Agglomération de Bruxelles and ARAU, 1984), 70. Copyright: Archives d'Architecture Moderne. Used with permission. 57

2.13 Proposal for the Carrefour de l'Europe site, by the ARAU, 1976. ARAU, ed., *Bruxelles Vu par ses Habitants, Quinze années d'action urbaine* (Brussels: Commission Française de la Culture et de l'Agglomération de Bruxelles and ARAU, 1984), 65. Copyright: Archives d'Architecture Moderne. Used with permission. Maurice Culot included it also in 'The right wing in disguise', *Lotus International* 13, 94–101, 100; where the caption states: 'the style developed for this project […] unleashed the fury of architects who hold that the use of "pastiche" is an immoral act'. 58

2.14 Overview map of the Reconstruction of Brussels Centre, also called the *Différents Projets pour la Reconstruction et l'Embellissement de la Partie de Bruxelles éventrée par la Jonction des Gares du Nord et du Midi* (Sefik Birkiye, Gilbert Busieau, Patrice Neirinck, La Cambre, 1978). Carrefour de l'Europe is one of seven project-sites. The project was published in its

	entirety in *Bulletin des AAM* 16 (1979); and in *La Reconstruction de Bruxelles*. Source: Maurice Culot, 'La cambre school of architecture and anti-industrial resistance', *Lotus International*, 21, December 1978, 46–71, 58. Copyright: Archives d'Architecture Moderne. Used with permission.	60
2.15	Lakense Straat, Brussels. Photograph by the author, 2015.	65
2.16	Maurice Culot and René Schoonbrodt, eds, *Les Espaces Publics Bruxellois: analyse et projets* (Brussels: Fondation Roi Baudoin: 1980; an initiative of IEB and the AAM), 415. Copyright: Archives d'Architecture Moderne. Used with permission.	66
2.17	Marie Demanet and Jean-Pierre Majot, eds, *Handboek van de Brusselse Openbare Ruimten* (Brussels: Iris, 1995; in collaboration with the Brussels Capital Region and the AAM), 35. Copyright: Archives d'Architecture Moderne. Used with permission.	67
3.1	Benjamin Verdonck, *Barake* project near the Brussels Gare du Midi. Copyright: City Mine(d). Used with permission.	80
3.2	*PleinOPENair*. Copyright: City Mine(d). Used with permission.	80
3.3	Location of Recyclart, Brussels, January 2015. Photograph by the author.	86
3.4	The Fabrik workshop, Recyclart. Copyright: Recyclart. Used with permission.	87
3.5	*Arabesk-Palaverboom* project, Brussels. Photograph by the author, 2015.	88
3.6	*De Roze Verspreiding* project, design by Les Saprophytes. Copyright: Les Saprophytes. Used with permission.	89
3.7	Ursulines Square / Skate Park, Brussels. Photograph by Filip Dujardin. Copyright: L'Escaut. Used with permission.	90
3.8	Ursulines Square / Skate Park, Brussels. Photograph by the author, 2015.	90
3.9	Ursulines Square / Skate Park. Design timeline. Copyright: L'Escaut. Used with permission.	91
3.10	Théâtre National, Brussels, by SCA Architectes Associés, Atelier Gigogne, and L'Escaut. Photograph by the author, 2015.	97
3.11	Théâtre National, Brussels, by SCA Architectes Associés, Atelier Gigogne, and L'Escaut. Photograph by the author, 2015.	97

3.12	Théâtre National, Brussels, by SCA Architectes Associés, Atelier Gigogne, and L'Escaut. Entrance foyer: used also as an informal semi-public space. Photograph by the author, 2015.	98
3.13	Poster of the *Jonction 4 x 4* event. Copyright: Bouwmeester Maître Architecte bMa, asbl Recyc art, and asbl Congrès. Used with permission.	99
3.14 & 3.15	Wall tapestries designed for the *Jonction 4 x 4* exhibition. Photographs by Kevin Laloux and Maxime Delvaux. Copyright: Bouwmeester Maître Architecte bMa, asbl Recyc art, and asbl Congrès. Used with permission.	100
4.1	Les Vignes Blanches, Cergy-Pontoise, France. 1976–1979. Copyright: Lucien Kroll. Used with permission.	124
5.1	Engineers Without Borders campaign poster. Copyright: Engineers Without Borders, Canada division. Used with permission.	135
6.1	Model of the *Maison des Citoyens* by Atelier d'Architecture Pierre Hebbelinck. Copyright: Pierre Hebbelinck. Used with permission.	156
6.2	*Maison des Citoyens* by Atelier d'Architecture Pierre Hebbelinck. Photograph by Marie-Françoise Plissart. Copyright: Pierre Hebbelinck. Used with permission.	156
6.3	The *Maison des Citoyens* in context: outlook onto the Quartier du Nord office area, including the realised towers of the Manhattan Project. Photograph by the author, 2015.	159
6.4	Map of the area surrounding the Rue de Brabant and the Rue d'Aerschot. The map indicates new urinals that replaced the original ones in brick. Map by VOLTA. Copyright: SamenlevingsopbouwBrussel vzw. Used with permission	161
6.5	One of the two originally installed urinals. Photograph by the author, March 2007.	164
6.6	Local social workers applying signs onto the pavement aiming at directing people to the nearby urinals. Copyright: SamenlevingsopbouwBrussel vzw. Used with permission.	164
6.7	Signs indicating that this location is not a place for urination ('ceci n'est pas un urinoir') whilst directing towards nearby public urinals. Photograph by the author, 2015.	164
6.8	Example of a new urinal. Eight of those were installed from late 2013 onwards, replacing the original brick ones. Photograph by the author, 2015.	164

6.9	Place Flagey, Latz & Partners / D+A International. Copyright and photograph by Serge Brison. Used with permission.	167
6.10	Place Flagey, Latz & Partners / D+A International. Copyright and photograph by Bernard Capelle. Used with permission.	167
6.11	Rogier Project, Xaveer De Geyter Architects: context. The horizontal boulevard coincides with the municipal boundary between the City of Brussels and St. Joost-ten-Node. Copyright XDGA Architects. Used with permission.	170
6.12	Rogier Project, Xaveer De Geyter Architects. Copyright XDGA Architects. Used with permission.	171
6.13	Rogier Project, Xaveer De Geyter Architects. Copyright XDGA Architects. Used with permission.	172
6.14	Rogier Project, Xaveer De Geyter Architects: view of courtyard / entrance to underground space. Copyright XDGA Architects. Used with permission.	172
6.15	Cover of the *Brüsel* graphic novel by François Schuiten and Benoît Peeters (2008 [1992]) as displayed in the Brussels shop with the same name: promoted as 'a classic' (classique!) and 'indispensable' (indispensable!). Photograph by the author.	176
6.16	The Palace of Justice as seen from the Marolles neighbourhood. Photograph by the author, 2015.	177

List of Abbreviations

AAM	Archives d'Architecture Moderne
ADT / ATO	Agence de Développement Territorial / Agentschap voor Territoriale Ontwikkeling [Urban Development Agency of the Brussels Capital Region]
AG / AV	Assemblée Générale / Algemene Vergadering [General Assembly]
ARAU	Atelier de Recherche et d'Action Urbaines
ATO	see ADT
BIM / IBGE	Brussels Instituut voor Milieubeheer / Institut Bruxellois pour la Gestion de l'Environnement [Brussels Institute for Management of the Environment]
bMa	Bouwmeester Maître Architecte [Brussels Master Architect]
BRAL	Brusselse Raad voor het Leefmilieu
CIVA	Centre International pour la Ville, l'Architecture et le Paysage
CLDI / PCGO	Commission Locale de Développement Intégré / Plaatselijke Commissie voor Geintegreerde Ontwikkeling [Local Commission for Integrated Development LCID]
GEWOP / PRD	Gewestelijk Ontwikkelingsplan / Plan Régional de Développement [Regional Development Plan]
IBAI	Institut Bruxellois d'Architecture Brussels Architectuur Instituut [Brussels Architecture Institute]
IBGE	see BIM
IEB	Inter-Environnement Bruxelles
ISACF or La Cambre	Institut Supérieur des Arts Décoratifs de la Cambre

LCID	Local Commission for Integrated Development: *see* CLDI / PCGO
NC	Neighbourhood Contract / Contrat de Quartier / Wijkcontract
NMBS / SNCB	Nationale Maatschappij der Belgische Spoorwegen / Société nationale des Chemins de fer belges [National Railway Company of Belgium]
PCGO	*see* CLDI
PDI / PIO	Plan de Développement International de Bruxelles / Plan voor de Internationale Ontwikkeling van Brussel [Brussels International Development Plan]
PV	procès-verbal
RAC	Rijks Administratief Centrum
SNCB	*see* NMBS
SPFMT	Service Public Fédéral de la Mobilité et des Transports
UPP	Urban Pilot Project
VAI	Vlaams Architectuur Instituut [Flemish Architecture Institute]

Acknowledgements

I have received support from numerous individuals and institutions whilst researching and writing this book. These acknowledgements are written in the hope that my memory has not let me down.

This book originates in research conducted at the Sint-Lucas School of Architecture in Brussels and the Delft University of Technology in The Netherlands, where research was made possible through the generous financial support of the Institute for the Encouragement of Scientific Research and Innovation of Brussels (2004–2007) and the Delft University of Technology (2008–2009). My colleagues at Sint-Lucas, including Marc Godts, Nel Janssens, Annette Kuhk, Raf De Saeger, Dag Boutsen, Johan Verbeke, and Marc Dubois, provided input during this time. The Delft School of Design provided an intellectually stimulating environment: Tahl Kaminer, Heidi Sohn, Lukasz Stanek, Gregory Bracken, Leslie Kavanaugh, Deborah Hauptman, M. Christine Boyer, K. Michael Hays, and Patrick Healy, have, often unwittingly, been formative through comments and discussions. A very special thank you goes to Arie Graafland, supervisor of the doctoral research, for his support and encouragement throughout this adventure, and beyond. I would also like to thank the examiners and advisers Erik Swyngedouw, Margaret Crawford, Jeremy Till, Pieter Uyttenhove, Peter Kroes, Luuk Boelens, and Jean-Louis Genard, for their comments and critiques. I am grateful also for the intellectual exchanges with researchers at the Vrije Universiteit Brussel (Cosmopolis), the Université Libre de Bruxelles (GECO), and La Cambre. Eric Corijn and Benedikte Zitouni deserve a special mention.

In finalising this book, I benefitted from financial support through the Research Stimulation Fund of the School of Environment, Education, and Development (SEED), at the University of Manchester (2012), and from on-going support at the Manchester Architecture Research Centre (MARC). In addition to MARC and SEED colleagues, including Leandro Minuchin, Maria Kaika, Melanie Lombard, Andrew Karvonen, and Simon Guy, I am particularly grateful to Albena Yaneva for her invaluable and in-depth comments on several chapter drafts of this book. I would like to express my gratitude to Lieven De Cauter, Pieter Uyttenhove, Didier Debaise, and Alan Lewis, for their constructive critiques and feedback on chapters of the book. Amongst the architects, planners, policy makers, civil servants, social workers, and activists who have taken the time for interviews and for discussions, I am additionally grateful to Maurice Culot, Laurence Jenard, Geraldine Bruyneel, Françoise Deville, Sofie Van Bruystegem, and Xaveer De Geyter, for their comments and clarifications.

I would like to thank Valerie Rose, the reviewers, and production team at Ashgate; and Angela Connelly for her thorough English revision. I am grateful for the generosity and hospitality of the Archives d'Architecture Moderne and the architecture library of Sint-Lucas. In providing opportunities to present and discuss my work, I would like to thank, amongst many others, the European Architectural History Network, the Architectural Humanities Research Association, the Royal Institute of Technology Stockholm, Sheffield University, Chalmers School of Architecture, the Architectural Association, TU Delft, and the Facoltà di Architettura in Sardinia.

A very special thank you goes to Kenny Cupers who has been a friend and intellectual companion throughout the years; and with whom the long hours of side-by-side writing were pleasant and stimulating. He also provided invaluable comments on parts of the book. Continued support came from my family, and friends, with a special mention of Filip Cleynen, Yohko Mizushima, and Federico Demontis. Ben Rowley deserves a most gracious word of thanks for his unconditional patience and companionship during the final stages of this project.

Preface

I have fallen in love with Brussels, I have fallen out of love with Brussels: always, however, we have been reconciled. Throughout the highs and lows of our encounters, the city has excited, fascinated, and mesmerised me. Equally, it has, at times, intimidated me and left me feeling tricked. Now, as an *émigré*, I find myself missing this city. The overall impression that I have formed of Brussels is one of a complex city that often struggles to cope. And although, at times, it seems to stagnate, against all odds things 'get done' – both in spite of and because of Brussels' complexity. It is an appreciation of this complexity that makes me, at times, forgive its defects.

This book is about architectural theory, and its critical theory legacy. It addresses the transformations, merits, and hopes for criticality under recent debates in architectural theory; in particular, the crises of criticality that have accompanied a so-called practice turn in architecture. I set out with the ambition to study questions related to criticality in architecture through Brussels and its critical practices. In order to gain access to these practices, Brussels was to be studied through its *specificity*. Such ambitions faced a double challenge.

Firstly: how to gain access to Brussels and its architectural culture? How to find a point of entry to this complex city? I soon discovered that the simple question as to 'where to start' was not to be taken lightly. If this is the case for all cities, it is even more so in Brussels. It is multi-layered, multi-lingual, administratively complex, geographically contested, and, as a capital city, it is home to prestigious institutions as well as numerous minorities. Moreover, it became soon apparent that Brussels has a love–hate relationship with architecture, and architecture struggles to love it back. Whichever lens adopted, whichever angle chosen, Brussels seemed impenetrable, complex, unruly, and opaque. I felt, however, that I had to put up with Brussels' unruliness, its eccentricities and resistances, and to take its complexity seriously. To start such endeavour, I found methodological inspiration in pragmatist and relation perspectives, as will become clear in the first chapter of this book.

Secondly, I decided to study critical practices as found in Brussels after 1968. Each chapter in this book forms a conceptual–empirical exploration into critical architectural practices in Brussels. These explorations are not, however, disconnected from the theoretical questions of this book; they cannot be fully understood without tackling the first series of challenges as to *how* to look at Brussels? How to gain access? And to look at what? This book is an exploration into Brussels *and* criticality. More so, because it theorises Brussels and criticality through how they are *practised* rather than through external referents (as used in conventional theory), the book is also a methodological adventure. The first chapter of this book elaborates on this theoretical–methodological adventure. As well as introducing Brussels, it carefully guides the reader through the combined methodological-critical task set out by this book. Starting from the crises of criticality in recent architectural theory, I will unpack the methodological relevance, and challenges, of pragmatist perspectives for architectural theory. Only *after* the relationship between Brussels, architectural theory, and pragmatism is fully explored, can the Brussels-explorations, as represented by individual chapters, be introduced. This is why the book's chapter outline will only arrive at the end of the first chapter. Whereas the first chapter explains, theoretically, how pragmatism can be made relevant for architectural theory, the rest of the book *shows* how such approach can work in the concrete setting of a city (Brussels).

Before we start this journey, I feel committed to explain to the reader how I have dealt with a dilemma that is very specific to Brussels: language. Navigating between Brussels' two official languages, Dutch and French, is not an easy matter. For meetings, the unwritten rule applies that 'everybody speaks their own language', which presumes that participants are sufficiently bi-lingual to, if not speak, at least follow conversations in both languages. When addressing an audience, however, no such rules seem to apply. As a Dutch-speaking Belgian, fluent in French and English also, I have found myself regularly having to choose a language to deliver a public talk. I would speak in French when facing a predominantly French-speaking audience, Dutch with a predominantly Dutch-speaking audience (a rarity), or if dealing with a mixed audience (Dutch, French, and/or other-languages), I would choose English. By adapting to a given situation, it simply worked out better – admittedly, a pragmatic, rather than ideological, choice. For this book, I faced a similar dilemma. Brussels is, officially, a bilingual city. Hence, official documents, urban planning instruments, and so on, exist in both French and Dutch. For readability reasons, these terms will, where possible, be used in their English translation. Where this is not possible, for example in the case of street names which appear in both languages, the question emerges as to which language to adopt? Given the dominant language of the source material for this research, I have settled for French, unless specific cases suggest otherwise, for example an interview with a Dutch-speaking person.

Finally, numerous interviews, collaborations, discussions, and conversations in Brussels have informed my thinking when writing this book, whether explicitly or implicitly. Of the many interviewees, colleagues, collaborators, social workers, architects, and administrators, who have contributed to this book in one way or another, some may appear to be absent from the text. I have chosen, therefore, to include those less-explicit contributions as an appendix. As with language, this was a pragmatic choice, but also one informed by a great affection for my sources – and for Brussels.

1

Introduction: The City as a Practice

For a year or so, in the mid-2000s, I lived in a flat located off a well-known square in Brussels called, in Dutch, Vossenplein – so named after the nearby Vossenstraat. In French, however, it has a very different name; in reference to a ball game which was popular at the time of the square's creation in the mid-19th century, it is known as Place du Jeu de Balle.[1] The square is best known for its daily antique and flea market. I can still vividly recall the buzz amongst the tourists and vintage enthusiasts as they eagerly sought out their bounty; and the local poor searching for anything that might have been left-over as the stalls were packing up: it is telling that the public swimming pool located on this square still provides baths and showers for those without access to such facilities at home. On the square, one could also find a café called *Skieven architek* (Figure 1.1). I remember wondering what this strange name referred to; only later did it become clear. The neighbourhood surrounding the square is called the Marolles. Historically dense and working-class, it is now largely gentrified although the area still contains pockets of poverty. With its antique shops, curiosities and cobblestoned streets, it is a lovely neighbourhood for a stroll – if you do not mind a bit of topography, that is. This is, after all, a point of transition between Brussels' dense downtown area and the leafier, more affluent upper-town. Whilst strolling through the area, glimpses of a shiny golden dome occasionally appear between the outline of the buildings (Figure 1.2). This mysterious dome is quite difficult to locate, but if you take the public elevator which connects the Marolles neighbourhood with the Place Poelaert, it will be revealed in all its glory. Yet this magnificent structure is only the surface level manifestation of a much vaster building which exists underneath: the enormous, intimidating, and somewhat gloomy Brussels Palace of Justice. In a documentary about Belgium, the architectural writer Jonathan Meades described it as 'both laughable and frightening, buffo and Babylonian'.[2] Designed in the second half of the 19th century by Joseph Poelaert, its scale is so vast that part of the Marolles had to be cleared to enable its construction: its breathtaking scale is confirmed by the fact that the restoration works on the dome in the 1990s and 2000s took so long that even its scaffoldings needed renovation.[3] Whilst, for some, the Palace of Justice is a landmark building to be celebrated, to others it elicits mere derision; it s more infamous than famous. The Brussels dialect makes this clear by means of a popular insult – *architek*.

1.1 During a visit to Brussels in January 2015, the café called Skieven Architek turned out to have closed. Photograph by the author.

1.2 The dome of the Palace of Justice can be seen on several occasions when walking through the Marolles neighbourhood. Photograph by the author, 2015.

Invented by the inhabitants of the Marolles, it decries the megalomania of its architect, Poelaert. In popular Brussels culture, calling someone an *architek* is a severe insult. This is especially the case in the Marolles, and in those other inner-city neighbourhoods whose population endured repeated waves of bulldozers, cranes, modernisation fever, and hygienist measures, often at the expense of local livelihoods. Returning to the *Skieven architek*, that café off the Place du Jeu de Balle, we can now start to make sense of its name. The full understanding of the name, including the meaning of *skieven*, will become clear in the last chapter of this book. Important here is that *architek* refers to a landmark building in Brussels, namely the Palace of Justice; located in the capital city of Belgium, of Europe. And yet this is not a city that connects the profession of architecture with unbridled optimism, but rather with a derogatory word. It is a city whose population has been traumatised by architects and developers, but passionately fought back.

◐ ◐ ◐

What makes a city? What makes architecture? And, what is to be included in the discussions of architecture and the city? In Brussels, the Palace of Justice surely helps to make the city. But what about the word *architek*? Does *architek*, in this specific setting, not equally shape the city? Are the public baths not also part of the city's spatial infrastructure and, thus, contributing to the workings of the city? If so, should such buildings be included in the discussions of architecture and the city? And what about the café called *Skieven architek*? Does it, despite the café's architectural modesty, participate in Brussels' architectural culture as a material reinforcement of the insult *architek*? Can urban traumas, and the urban struggles of the inhabitants, take part in an architectural discourse? And what about language? In a French-Dutch bilingual city like Brussels, language performs an intriguing role by enacting differing references (Vossenpein / Place du Jeu de Balle) and, therefore, different ways of making-city.

Cities are fabricated through landmark buildings, but they are equally enacted by citizens, users, mind-sets, words, and all sorts of mundane infrastructures and practices. Very different in their nature and performance, these practices also make-city. In this book, we will discover how landmark buildings, *architek*, urban traumas, language, and even public urinals contribute to architectural discourses and production in the specific setting of Brussels. In doing so, the complexity, ambiguity, and social ambition of Brussels' architecture will be revealed.

Confronted with this specificity of Brussels, the theorising of cities through external referents seems odd. Are we not to take the specificity and complexity of cities more seriously, and study how they are *practised* rather than how they fit a theory's predefined categories and concepts? Would such an approach not offer a more realistic account of how a city, and its architecture, actually works? As a particularly complex city with a turbulent architectural and urban past, Brussels calls for an alternative mode of analysis. It calls for an understanding of how the city works as a consequence of, rather than in spite of, its complexity, and how its architecture emerges not just through a portfolio of important buildings, but also through a series of mundane practices.

This book is about Brussels as much as it is about architectural theory. It responds to recent debates in architectural theory related to the critical agency of architecture and the locus of critical action. Whilst criticality has for a long time been associated with theory, recent architectural debates have emphasised practice as a locus for critical action. This book puts the potential of such criticality through-practice to the empirical test. Through the study of a series of critical actions which occurred in Brussels' architectural and urban culture after 1968, this book will contribute to a better understanding of architecture's processes of critical engagement and the tools which can be mobilised for that purpose.[4]

I believe that the exploration of criticality through-practice can offer a different type of criticality – one which I call 'criticality-from-within'. Through conceptual–empirical explorations, this book will show how such a criticality allows for different understandings of how the city and its architectural production work; understandings that, ultimately, allow different theories and different cities to become possible. We will discover how an emphasis on practice does, however, not inform a dismissal of theory as a locus for criticality. On the contrary, through a specific, situated account of critical practices in Brussels, I will ask: How can theory better contribute to the formulation of a critical agenda for architecture? Can theory itself operate as a practice?

In this first chapter, I will guide the reader, step by step, through the combined methodological–critical task set-out by this book. I will start by introducing Brussels, and offer a brief history of its architectural culture. I will then turn to recent debates in architectural theory that indicate a renewed emphasis on practice and a search for alternative forms of critical action. I will elaborate on pragmatist and relation perspectives that I deem particularly relevant for revisiting criticality through practice; and discuss their relevance for architecture, but also the challenges they pose. In response to such challenges, I will introduce the notion of criticality-from-within, a reading of criticality which will inform my study of those critical practices featured in later chapters.

A SHORT INTRODUCTION TO ARCHITECTURAL CULTURE IN BRUSSELS

> *Above all, Belgium has helped me to put things in their proper perspective; to see that there is not just one universal truth, but a whole range of different truths.*[5]

Whether acting as an emancipatory force or a resistance to change, Brussels' everyday life is often associated with a strong instinct of survival. This survival requires negotiation, creativity, and tactics. In his series of Brussels-stories collected under the title *Chagrijn en Charme*, politician and former priest Staf Nimmegeers illustrates this with a story of a bucket being placed under a leaking ceiling of a subway station. Standing there for months, it became apparent that, whilst failing to repair the leak, someone must nevertheless have regularly emptied the bucket.[6]

This engrained everyday survival instinct is also termed *Belgitude*, and underpins a sense that the Belgians, and even more so the citizens of Brussels, are 'anarchists at heart'.[7] It also refers to a skill of struggling practicality described, in Dutch, by the words *plantrekkerij* and, in French, *se débrouiller*. In English, this could be translated as 'coping', 'getting by' or, even 'muddling through'. Moreover, in the context of Brussels, such skills are associated with a fondness for the absurd and surreal, and for mockery, as expressed by the word *zwanze*. The downside of this, often glorified, surrealism and pragmatism is that it applies to everyday life as much as to ambitious projects, often resulting in opaque decision-making and inventive, yet obscure, ways of getting things done. The installation of the European Union in Brussels could, in fact, be seen as one large pragmatic experiment, which used Brussels' complexity to its advantage. Despite celebrating the virtue of 'getting one's own way', Brussels struggles to implement *structural* change, which is largely due to its administrative complexity.

From the point of view of architectural culture, the Brussels situation can be entered through a couple of conversations that I had whilst visiting the exhibition *Man of Thoughts: 5 years Brussels Head Architect* in September 2014.[8] The Master Architect in Brussels is called the bMa, which stands for the Dutch-French combination *Bouwmeester Maître Architecte*. The first bMa, Olivier Bastin, was appointed in November 2009 by the Brussels Capital Region. The exhibition celebrated the achievements of the bMa, an administrative role created with the aim to 'assist commissioners in guaranteeing the architectural and spatial quality of public design projects'.[9] Yet, at the opening of the exhibition, I could sense the slight disappointment of a friend and colleague, who is also an architect and urban planner, with the absence of concrete realisations. This triggered a dialogue on the complexity and specificity of the Brussels situation, and the difficulty of evaluating, amidst such complexity, the bMa's achievements. A second conversation evolved around the bMa's resistance to simply model Brussels on other successful cities through the introduction of a star-architecture or urban-creative laboratory; as seen with Berlin, for example. Instead the bMa seemed to have opted for a more cautious approach informed by the specificity of Brussels. In this respect, the bMa represents continuity in long-standing emancipatory processes that are evident in Brussels' architectural culture. In this section, we will discover how this emancipation was piecemeal, modest, and fragmented, and how it triggered an architectural optimism that was ambitious, but also cautious and informed by an adherence to Brussels' socio-urban situation. It was, moreover, a product of Brussels' balancing act between a complex series of forces. To understand these forces, let us start with Brussels' position in the Belgian context.

Belgium is politically divided into three regions: the Walloon region in the south of the country, the Flemish region in the North, and the Brussels Capital region. It is also governed through its three language communities (Dutch-, French-, and German-speaking), these communities having distinct responsibilities from the regions. For example, education and culture are in the hands of the communities whilst planning, infrastructure, and other territorial matters are the competences of the regions. To complicate matters further, the competence areas of communities and regions are not overlapping: the Walloon region is predominantly French-speaking, but also includes a small German-speaking community; the Flemish region overlaps with the Dutch-speaking community; and, whilst the Brussels region is officially Dutch-French bilingual and geographically enclosed by the Flemish region, it is predominantly French-speaking. To deal with this odd situation, the Flemish region grants important language facilities to its French-speaking population living just outside the Brussels region.[10] Officially bilingual, Brussels reconciles the authority of French- and Dutch-speaking communities with regional power. In addition, despite being a city-region, Brussels is subdivided in 19 municipalities, each with an elected Mayor (Figures 1.3, 1.4 and 1.5). Brussels is, as such, not just governed by the Minister-President of the region and his ministers, but also by nineteen Mayors. The resultant multi-layered governance structure leads to all sorts of political intricacies that have important consequences for architectural and urban production. For example, a regional minister may also be a municipal Mayor, alderman, or community representative. Such instances of political actors occupying more than one position are known as *multiples casquettes* (many hats) syndrome. Due to the multi-layered governance structure, the simplest project tends to involve a disproportionally large amount of stakeholders. These intricacies are often experienced as undemocratic by citizens and architects alike, for they are believed to trigger a political laissez-faire mentality and an opaque decision-making process. Unsurprisingly, perhaps, Brussels (and Belgium) is often mocked as Kafkaesque or surreal (Figure 1.6).

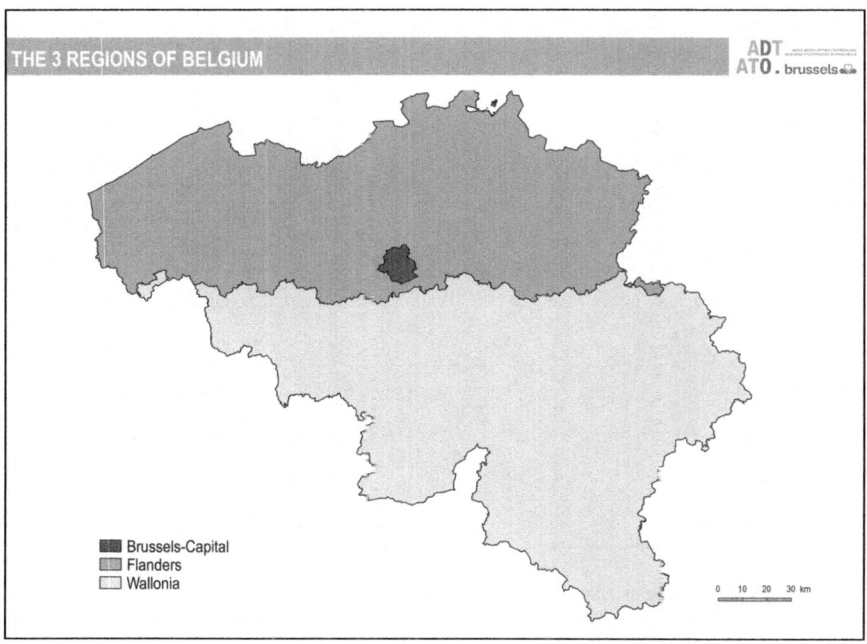

1.3 Belgium's regions. Map provided by the Brussels Agence de Développement Territorial – Agentschap voor Territoriale Ontwikkeling (ADT-ATO). Used with permission.

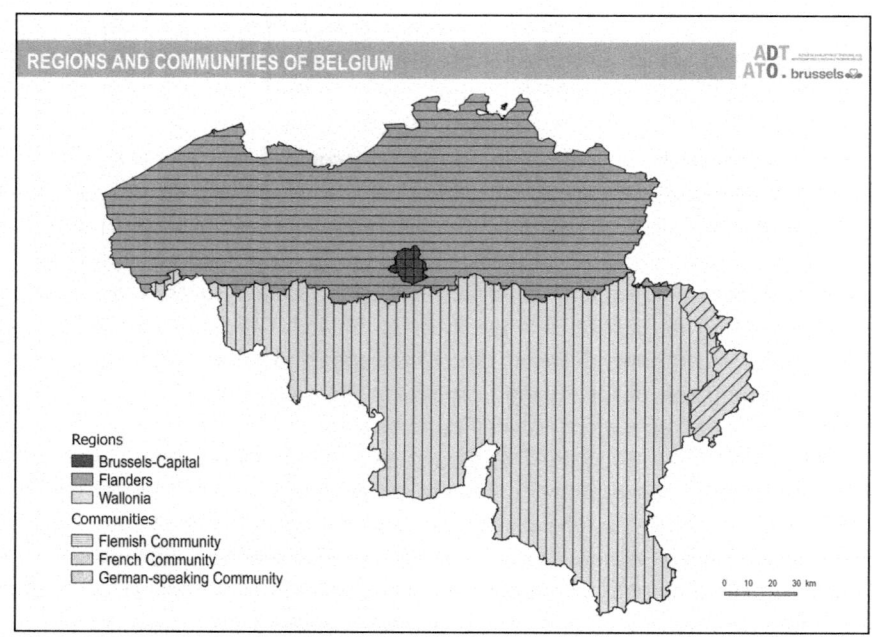

1.4 Belgium's regions and communities. Map provided by the Brussels Agence de Développement Territorial – Agentschap voor Territoriale Ontwikkeling (ADT-ATO). Used with permission.

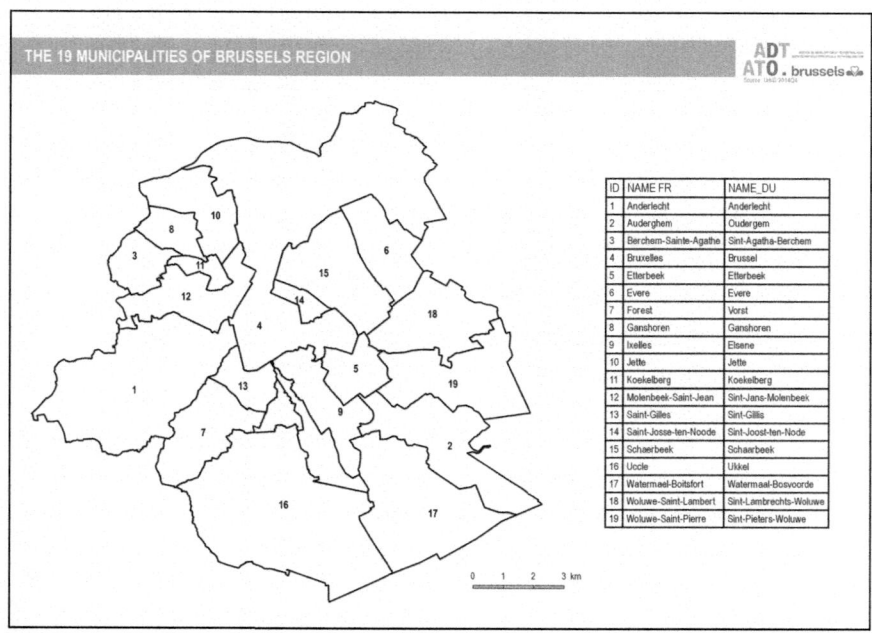

1.5 Brussels' 19 Municipalities. Map provided by the Brussels Agence de Développement Territorial – Agentschap voor Territoriale Ontwikkeling (ADT-ATO). Used with permission.

1.6 Brussels 'in action'. Marolles neighbourhood.
Photograph by the author, 2015.

To understand Brussels' architectural culture, however, we have to step outside the region and look at the architectural emancipations that have taken place elsewhere. In particular, the Flemish region underwent an important architectural emancipation during the 1980s and 1990s. Initially triggered by individual oeuvres on private housing, Flemish architecture matured within the context of large-scale urban renewal strategies, and through structural government initiatives specifically tailored towards the promotion of architecture. So, when compared to the Walloon region, the Flemish region engaged in a more structural and explicit promotion of architecture during this period.[11] These developments were particularly important because they triggered a long-awaited optimism and self-confidence that would gradually infect the Brussels architecture scene.

In the Flemish region, a Master Architect had been installed already in 1999, ten years ahead of Brussels. The Flemish Master Architect had been part of a wider architectural emancipation of the Flemish region instigated in the 1980s with the emergence of a new generation of architects which included, amongst others, Stéphane Beel, Jo Crépain, and Xaveer de Geyter.[12] With their individual architectural language, these architects received only gradual recognition as a distinct new generation or movement. Yet, despite their individual expression, architectural critics recognised commonalities: architectural critic and historian Geert Bekaert saw in this generation a shared understanding of the Belgian-Flemish everyday which, in turn, informed his work on the *gemeenplaats*;[13] whilst Francis Strauven termed this movement as *Nieuwe Eenvoud* or New Simplicity.[14] Instrumental in the emancipation of Flemish architecture was the sensitisation work of cultural foundations including the Stichting Architectuurmuseum (S/AM) and Architectuurwerking De Singel, and the subsequent policy responses. These included the publication, since 1994, of architecture yearbooks; the instalment of a Flemish Master Architect in 1999; and the creation of a Flemish Architecture Institute in 2002.[15] These initiatives were aimed at the promotion of Flemish architecture, and at the creation of procedures for securing architectural quality. The Flemish Master Architect was, through the organisation of 'open calls', pivotal in creating opportunities for young architects.

In Flanders, this architectural awareness went hand in hand with an embrace of urban regeneration strategies and new private–public development models such Urban Development Projects (UDPs). UDPs were understood as large-scale urban plans combining a qualitative vision with concrete architectural and urban projects; precedents included Baltimore Inner Harbor, London Docklands, and Euralille. Such planning initiatives forced urban planning and architecture into a position of being used as a tool for economic development through city-marketing and city-management, and raised concerns about planning and architecture's involuntary contribution to social displacement and socio-spatial segregation; both typical side-effects of such planning. This was evident in the planning discussions of the time, and was also debated in architectural circles.[16] Flanders embraced this new urban regeneration through the 1980–1982 Urban Renewal Campaign, which came in response to the European campaign of 1980, and through the Flemish Urban Renewal Act of 1988. This Act was believed to announce an important shift from neighbourhood-based social planning to large-scale renewal schemes thriving on economic attractiveness and public–private partnerships.[17]

Two initiatives which stand out are the Stad-aan-de-Stroom UDP in Antwerp, and the events of Antwerp 1993 – Cultural Capital of Europe.[18] Both demonstrate how Flanders used the new planning approach as an opportunity for promoting architecture, in both economic and cultural terms. The Stad-aan-de-Stroom team attempted to generate more qualitative spatial design through, for example, the organisation of a prestigious international architecture competition, aimed at developing a vision and urban design proposals for the 19th-century port quarters. The Antwerp 1993 initiative was an important urban regeneration effort that mobilised architecture in an attempt to promote Flanders globally. For example, the urban think-tank known as Open City organised a series of architectural-cultural events which included thematic tours, exhibitions, international lecture series, films, debates, and workshops.[19]

When returning to Brussels, it is tempting to measure the achievements of the bMa against these Flemish developments. However, it is important to remember that Brussels' architectural culture operates within very different circumstances. For example, in contrast to the Flemish embracement of UDPs as an equally urban and architectural opportunity, Brussels' UDPs were devoid of architectural debates. Instead, commissions were largely distributed amongst developers and their preferred architects. The Brussels UDP for turning the Brussels South Station into a new High Speed Train hub did not trigger an architectural competition, and was considered a planning fiasco.[20] Also, the installation of Europe in Brussels is a notorious case of planning failure, and is often perceived as a missed opportunity for architecture. Architecture considered to be international, daring, or landmark barely made it through to commissions.[21] In other words, the Brussels architectural culture operates amongst a very different set of forces than the Flemish one, namely, being at the intersection of a Flemish and French architectural culture, international ambitions reinforced by the European presence, and local socio-urban realities. It is, moreover, challenged to reconcile any new architectural optimism with a longstanding conservative stronghold.

This conservative stronghold originates in the action groups that emerged in the wake of 1968. These groups fought the perceived destruction of the city and its neighbourhoods by the developers and architects, and decried the traumatic effects of demolitions and large-scale expropriations on the inhabitants. This local activism was known through the activities of the Atelier de Recherche et d'Action Urbaines, which collaborated with the Archives d'Architecture Moderne and the architectural education at La Cambre. The resultant 'anti-industrial resistance' would become known as the Reconstruction of the European City movement, a traditionalist branch of postmodernism that was supported by Léon Krier and Maurice Culot, amongst others, and prioritised historical forms and types over formal innovations.[22] With the support of cultural foundations, the Reconstruction mind-set found resonance in Brussels: for example, the Fondation pour l'Architecture, created in 1986 (and integrated with the Centre International pour la Ville, l'Architecture et le Paysage, CIVA, in 1999) was intellectually affiliated with the Reconstruction of the City.[23] The reconstruction legacy was evident, for example, in its architectural competitions.[24] Moreover, the Reconstruction mind-set based on historical corrections, pastiche and façadism, also infiltrated mainstream architectural production in Brussels where it proved popular amongst developers (see Chapter 2).

The popularity of traditionalism can also be brought back to the fact that Brussels' population was severely traumatised by modernisation; so much so that insults were developed for depicting the devastation (see Chapter 6). The two main historical settings for this urban trauma are the 19th century hygienist urban restructurings, and the modernisation fever throughout those decades of the post-war period. In the first instance, large parts of the inner-city were radically transformed in order to turn Brussels into a *Petit Paris*.[25] From this era originates the insult *architek*. From the second instance emerges the term *Bruxellisation*, which refers to the destruction of the city by profit-driven developers and architects. The most prolific, but by no means only, symbol of this destructive episode in urban planning is the Manhattan Plan, a CIAM-inspired Central Business District and icon of progressive urbanism approved in 1967, for which a vast residential area near Brussels North Station was expropriated and demolished. Other symbols include the in 1952 inaugurated tunnel for the North–South railway junction, which left a scar throughout Brussels' historic centre; the creation of a ring road across tunnels, urban highways, and flyovers that were planned as part of the World Expo 1958; and the 1965 demolition of Victor Horta's Art Nouveau masterpiece (despite international outcry), the Maison du Peuple. It is remarkable how these traumas 'act' far beyond their historical timeframes, and influence popular urban debates until today.

Confronted with such 'active' urban trauma and traditionalist mind-sets, Brussels architects and urban designers often feel somewhat straightjacketed by Brussels' neophobia, and perceive it to have a paralysing effect on efforts towards a contemporary and innovative architecture. This is a far cry from the pre-war architectural heydays of the internationally renowned Art Nouveau architects such as Victor Horta, Paul Hankar and Henri Van de Velde, and the planning experiments of the Cité Moderne (Victor Bourgeois) and the garden cities Logis and Floréal (Louis Van der Swaelmen; Jean-Jules Eggericx). Recent years, however, have seen the return of an optimistic outlook that is triggered by modest architectural realisations rather than bold experiments, and is spread across the region, like 'floating islands'.[26] These occurred, for example, in the context of Neighbourhood Contracts (NCs), created in the mid-1990 to aid urban renewal, and in the realisations of contemporary Walloon and Flemish architects in Brussels; the latter often being small commissions such as shops or restaurants.[27] In addition, there has been a revival of public architectural competitions, notably in the Brussels municipality of Schaerbeek which through organised competitions and architectural tours is committed to innovative design. In terms of architectural reflection, important contributions include the anthologies published in Dutch, French and English, by Prisme Éditions; the research and design workshops by think-tank Studio Open City; and the activities of Brussels 2000 European Capital of Culture.[28]

Brussels 2000 was a spur for the architectural community for several reasons. With its emphasis on urban culture, it further consolidated the urban activism that had already emerged in Brussels in the mid-1990s and which will be discussed in the third chapter of this book. Moreover, Brussels 2000 reinforced the interactions between urban activism and architecture and, in doing so, placed architecture in a wider reflection on the city. The Brussels 2000 legacy was felt in architectural culture through the creation of a new book series dedicated to the work of young architects;[29] the contemporary and international architecture programming of The Museum of Fine Arts (BOZAR); and the creation of a Brussels Architecture Institute, or IBAI, French-Dutch acronym for Institut Bruxellois d'Architecture Brussels Architectuur Instituut. Through design workshops and an exhibition dedicated to young architects, called *Supernova Jonge Belgische Architectuur – Jeune Architecture Belge*, Brussels 2000 explicitly boosted young architectural talents.[30]

Calls for a contemporary architecture infiltrated Brussels not only through the legacies of Brussels 2000 and the optimism of the Flemish architectural culture, but also on account of the noticeable changes which occurred in the Francophone Brussels architecture scene from the mid-2000s. The architectural activities within the department of cultural infrastructure of the French Community, since 2007 known as the Direction de l'Architecture, focused on the promotion of architecture, and of young architects.[31] Activities included the organisation of architectural competitions and the publication of architecture manuals for public commissioners including, notably, the *Vade-Mecum*, a detailed manual for policy makers to organise architecture competitions, and the White Paper with the provocative title *Qui a peur de L'Architecture?* (who is afraid of architecture?).[32]

Regional authorities also attempted, albeit belatedly, to place Brussels on the global architecture map, through urban regeneration, city marketing, and the approval of an International Development Plan. This signalled a move away from the piecemeal regeneration of the historical central neighbourhoods towards a more radical, large-scale, and supra-regional regeneration.[33] And yet, due to its social, economic, and governance challenges, Brussels notoriously struggles to bring ambitious projects to successful realisation. Despite its relatively small size (approximately 1 million inhabitants), Brussels has a strong metropolitan feel thanks to its international function and its large immigrant population. However, this metropolitan feel is more often associated with the cosmopolitan lifestyles of the expats working with the European Institutions, NATO, and other related international functions, than with the working-class immigrants who, nevertheless, make up an important part of the Brussels population. This distracts from the fact that Brussels faces structural socio-economic challenges; a chronic shortage of social housing; and a spatial-economic segregation between the affluent suburbs in the East and the poorer city centre and Western periphery.[34] In other words, whilst Brussels *needs* structural solutions and ambitious visions, such solutions are complicated by its complex, multi-layered governance structure.

Returning to the discussions around the achievements of the bMa, it is now clear how the Master Architect triggered an optimism that was ambitious but nevertheless rooted in the Brussels complex reality. For example, on the cover of

1.7 Cover of the exhibition catalogue *bMa Man of Thoughts: 5 jaar Brussels bouwmeester – 5 ans maître-architecte à Bruxelles – 5 years Brussels head architect* (exhibition from September 12–25, 2014). Copyright: Bouwmeester Maître Architecte bMa. Used with permission.

the exhibition catalogue, the bMa states: 'A good process is a guarantee for quality, but there are other factors involved. We must leave some room for chance. We need to keep an open mind, be able to react to the unexpected, the odd nice surprise.' (Figure 1.7). This cautious optimism is appropriate for Brussels, perhaps more so than for any other city. I believe it is also instructive for exploring questions related to critical engagement which have resurfaced in recent debates on the practice turn in architecture.

THE PRACTICE TURN IN ARCHITECTURE

Since the mid-1990s, a new generation of theorists started to challenge a critical theory that had become overly intellectualised, and whose contribution to design practice had been limited to abstract and formal experimentations.[35] Questions related to architecture's critical engagement are, in architectural theory, largely associated with critical theory, which prevailed, particularly within American academia, from the mid-1960s to the mid-1990s.[36] Such questions also circulated in the counter-cultural experiments of the 1960s, and in the aftermath of 1968, when architectural criticism negotiated its modern legacy at the intersections of social critique, politics, and aesthetics. Under postmodernism, however, architecture's radical politicisation saw it gradually reduced to discussions around style.[37]

The new generation of theorists questioned the authority allocated to architectural theory as a critical reflection on, and inspiration, for design. Undergoing a crisis of criticality, architectural theory grew divided between an 'old' and a 'new' theorising. Whereas the former (critical theorists) still held onto the role of theory as a locus of critique, the latter was sceptical about the effectiveness thereof. This divide was epitomised by the publication of two readers, each representing the 'old' and the 'new' theorising in architecture: K. Michael Hays' *Architecture Theory since 1968* and Kate Nesbitt's *Theorizing a New Agenda for Architecture: An Anthology of Architectural Theory, 1965–1995*.[38] The 'new' generation of theorists grew divided between those who felt that the critical project was exhausted, such as George Baird, building on Robert Somol and Sarah Whiting's 'Notes around the Doppler Effect and Other Moods of Modernism', and Michael Speaks's 2002 essay 'Design Intelligence'. Other theorists, including Reinhold Martin and Arie Graafland, still believed in the potentials of architecture's critical programme.[39] In an architectural theory reader *Constructing a New Agenda*, A. Krista Sykes recognises in the theorists of the late-1990s, a 'pro-practice movement' that, if not strictly anti-theoretical, was 'a mandate to focus on the realities of architecture and building'.[40] This practice turn in architecture was informed by several socio-technological and economic changes that affected the profession and discipline of architecture. Sykes summarises these as technological changes (such as the use of digital technologies in architectural design); environmental concerns; attention for the everyday and the real; and the emergence, and use of, iconic architecture and the 'starchitect' for marketing purposes.[41]

This practice turn coincided with significant changes in the architectural profession. Under the impetus of neoliberal urban planning strategies, and the so-called Bilbao-effect, architects increasingly operated on a global scene. Architects were mobilised in a global market economy through their landmark buildings or starchitect status. Confronted with a 'post-political city' informing an appeased architectural practice, architectural theorists did not just search for new modes of theorising architecture through practice, but also for modes to theorise *critical* engagement through practice.[42] This is the case with the debates on 'new pragmatism' and the 'projective practice'. Whereas the first focused on the ethical performance of architecture through a focus on what architecture does rather than what it means, the latter claimed that the reality of architectural practices rendered the desires and claims of the 'old' critical theory unproductive. The 'projective practice' debate has, therefore, become associated with a post-critical debate.[43]

A renewed interest in *critical* spatial practices resonated with a wider rediscovery of the everyday and of spatial tactics in architecture; one can think of the rediscovery of Henri Lefebvre's theories of the everyday, and the revalidation of the ordinary in architecture.[44] This rediscovery informed an architectural theory that explored critical practices by studying architecture and urban design in terms of praxis, agency, or co-production, and where the designed object emanates from a collaborative effort rather than the heroism of one designer.[45] This renewed interest in collaborative design signalled a revival of community design efforts, often under the sustainability agenda, and popular taste in architectural practices.[46] Instead of formal autonomous experimentations, critical theorists had grown interested in the critical potential of spatial *practices* such as walking, appropriating, experiencing, and even skating. In the UK, theorists such as Jane Rendell, Jonathan Hill, Iain Borden, and Murray Fraser revalidated the transformative powers of the users and consumers of space next to those of the designer.[47]

In addition to the socio-technological and economic changes informing a pro-practice movement, it is important to include the intensified scholarly interest in transdisciplinary and designerly ways of knowing in the fields of design research and practice-based research. This is marked by the recognition of a shift from 'mode 1' to 'mode 2' knowledge production, or from a traditional scholarly research to an 'in-practice model' based on the knowledge gathered 'in the context of application'.[48] This shift recognises design practice as a locus for research and, thus, a source of knowledge that is perceived to be equally important as the knowledge gathered through theory and history. In a recent anthology of Design Research, Murray Fraser, for example, defines architectural design research as 'the processes and outcomes of inquiries and investigations in which architects use the creation of projects, or broader contributions towards design thinking, as the central constituent in a process which also involves the more generalized research activities of thinking, writing, testing, verifying, debating, disseminating, performing, validating, and so on'.[49]

With this book, and in response to recent debates on criticality in architectural theory, I aim to explore criticality through practice. I will study concrete instances of critical engagement, drawing upon cases taken from Brussels after 1968. But how exactly can we study criticality in, and through, practice? For such purpose I take inspiration from pragmatist and relational perspectives. In what follows, I will introduce these perspectives, their relevance, merits, and possible pitfalls in architecture.

HOW TO STUDY THINGS *IN PRACTICE*?

In my quest for studying critical architectural operations through practice, I am inspired by the fields of Science and Technology Studies (STS) and Actor-Network Theory (ANT), and pragmatist philosophy. STS and ANT both originate in the field of Science Studies: STS focuses on the cultural and social forces that are at work in sciences and technology whilst ANT, which originates in the work of STS scholars Michel Callon, Bruno Latour, and John Law, focuses on the networks and relations of the social world that are believed to be material as much as semiotic. ANT is also inspired by pragmatist philosophies, and is best known for its controversial recognition of the actions of non-humans, or 'things', and for the study of those things and their networks of making and becoming. ANT, as such, proposes a mode of inquiry that analyses things in-the-making and things as they act as part of a wider series of networks of engagement, and proposes a mode of inquiry that, with its emphasis on making, is instructive for architecture and has, therefore, become popular in architectural studies. Bruno Latour and Albena Yaneva, in particular, have been instrumental in the promotion of ANT in architectural studies. The insertion of ANT in architecture does, however, come with important challenges, and deserves meticulous attention. STS and ANT's appeal to architecture derives from their study of things, such as buildings, in terms of socio-technological assemblages. STS and ANT refuse the epistemological and ontological separation of the world between a scientific and a social part; between hard facts and empirical evidence on the one hand, and values, instinct, and social production on the other. This refusal to separate the social and material world invites one to study architecture as a product of political, social and cultural concerns as much as that of technology and engineering. In order to describe this complex tangle, STS and ANT suggest shifting attention from finished objects to things in-the-making. By studying things in-the-making, and as socio-technical assemblages, writers such as Latour and Yaneva, claim to gain insights into the workings of architecture that are more realistic than the insights gained through the abstract ideological–conceptual vehicles of theory.[50] One can think of the studies of, for example, the use and re-use of buildings (Thomas Gieryn, Stewart

Brand, Michael Guggenheim); their decay and maintenance (Jane M. Jacobs and Stephen Cairns); or the complexity of design processes and their involvement in political, social, or ecological controversies (Latour, Yaneva, Victor Buchli, Sophie Houdart, Steven A. Moore).[51]

The pragmatist interest in practices, material processes, and processes of making, has found, apart from architecture, widespread implementation in other disciplines including urban studies, cultural geography, cultural studies, philosophy, critical geography, and art history.[52] It is particularly appealing in architecture because of its suggestion of a mode of inquiry that, with its focus on processes of making and complex networks of actors, seems particularly suitable for design.[53] This affinity, nevertheless, distracts from important challenges. Firstly, in an object-centred context such as architecture, the emphasis on things risks prioritising those objects that are familiar to the discipline, such as buildings, models, and drawings, whilst underestimating those other things that matter in the making of architecture, such as words, regulations, habits, mind-sets, clients, or money. Secondly, such different, more realistic accounts are not aimed at informing a better architecture; rather, they offer a better *understanding* of architecture. Because such value-neutrality risks the dismissal of critical concern, the insertion of ANT in architecture poses specific ethical challenges that need to be treated with care.

Both challenges, the first more explicit than the second, can be traced back to the notion of the 'actant', as developed within Latour's book *Reassembling the Social: An Introduction to Actor-Network-Theory*, a work that has travelled well within architectural theory.[54] One chapter in particular, 'Third Source of Uncertainty: Objects too Have Agency', is crucial for understanding the translation of ANT into architecture. The chapter states that objects have agency, which, in architecture, is somewhat stating the obvious. Do not all architects believe, and hope, that the objects they create have an impact; that these objects 'act'? And does urban regeneration's faith in the economic agency of architectural icons not ultimately illustrate the belief in architecture as a full-blown, economic, actor? It is, however, important to remember that Latour's emphasis on the agency of things was formulated in the context of the social sciences, not architecture, where, for a long time, things were excluded from the social world, and 'action was delimited *a priori* to what "intentional", "meaningful" humans do'.[55] Objects had for a long time been considered 'humble servants, living on the margins of the social, doing most of the work, but never allowed to be represented as such'.[56] In architecture, by contrast, one finds numerous theories on the interactions of the material/physical world with the social. Often, however, such theorisation either stressed the social aspects of space whereby, under anthropological influences, material space was seen as a mere backdrop of social interaction.[57] Or, as was the case with environmental determinism, such theories emphasised material space whereby design, space, and morphology were believed to influence social behaviour.[58] In other instances, the social and material were studied as *mutually* influential, which informed the reading of architecture through the interactions between, for example, space and use, or strategies and tactics.[59]

It is tempting, but misleading, to align such studies with Latour's sociomaterial notion of the actant. The actant does not depict the *interaction* between a material and a social world, or between humans and non-humans. Instead, it depicts the fact that things can never exist in themselves, as bound objects, but can only exist through their entanglements, and through their networks. Actants are, therefore, always *both* thing *and* network. For Latour, there are no substances; only relations.[60] An actant, or thing, gathers numerous networks, whilst it is also itself enrolled in other thing-networks. It is important, therefore, to identify not what 'is' but what 'takes part' in action. Latour defines a participant in action as 'any thing that modifies a state of affairs by making a difference [...] in the course of some other agent's action'.[61] Because things only exist through their entanglements with human and non-human actors, the task at hand is to map the 'participants in action'. If one is to map *all* participants, or at least *as many as possible*, this task, thus, implies taking the complexity and multiplicity of a thing-network seriously. This, in turn, informs the need to describe those things through complex, and entangled accounts.[62]

ENTANGLED ACCOUNTS OF ARCHITECTURE

In order to describe a thing through its entanglements, a whole range of new terminologies emerged, in STS and ANT, including 'hybrid', 'quasi-object', 'assemblage', 'imbroglio', 'gathering', 'fluid object' and 'matter of concern'.[63] For architecture, these terms describe architectural projects through their networks of users, production processes, design, architects, engineers, materials, building permissions, aesthetic preferences, innovation, etc. The building does not mean anything in itself, but it becomes meaningful through its alliances. Latour, therefore, distinguishes between describing architectural projects as 'bald objects', and 'dishevelled, hairy, networky "things"', namely through their networks of fabrication.[64] Because architectural projects engage with different networks *over time*, they are not just 'hairy', they also 'move'. To describe how the entanglements of objects can change over time, Latour and Yaneva have introduced the term 'object-in-flight'.[65] They do not consider a building to be a static object; rather, it is a moving project which mobilises a variety of networks including architects, construction engineers, clients, city planners, budgetary constraints, and conflicting stakeholders. They therefore call for 'earthly accounts':

> Only by generating earthly accounts of buildings and design processes, tracing pluralities of concrete entities in the specific spaces and times of their co-existence, instead of referring to abstract theoretical frameworks outside architecture, will architectural theory become a relevant field for architects, for end users, for promoters, and for builders.[66]

One way of delivering earthly accounts is by unpacking those seemingly 'bald' objects, and to return to their networks, their construction site, and expose their processes of making. One can access things 'in the making' by studying those moments when the black-boxes of 'made' things are opened up. For example, in the case of a breakdown, one has to enter a thing's networks in order to retrace and resolve the problem. Likewise, when objects are subject to controversy, a whole series of stakes and stakeholders enters the discussion.[67] How then to study things 'in the making' outside the specific situation of a breakdown or controversy? A response to this question can be found in the Elements exhibition curated by the architect Rem Koolhaas for the 2014 Architecture Biennial in Venice. Koolhaas exhibits architecture through its composite elements, such as ceilings, windows, floors, balconies, and façades, rather than through iconic buildings and projects.[68] These elements are analysed as assemblages of technical knowledge, historical understanding, regulations, testing and experimentation, politics, cultural aspects, and ideologies. For example, the section on the façade section called Technologies of the Envelope, which is co-curated with Alejandro Zaera-Polo, studies grand themes like sustainability by unpacking the entanglement of politics, technical advancements, and typological choices in one single façade system. The most convincing example is the Deutsche Börse Façade Sample wherein Zaera-Polo recognises 'the perfect embodiment of German corporate environmental sensibilities and left-leaning politics from the 1990's'.[69] Workers unions had negotiated the right to fresh air and light, which make office windows that can open as much an embodiment of workers' rights as they are the politics of climatisation.

If objects and buildings can be approached as assemblages, the same can be said of cities. Belgian philosopher Isabelle Stengers, for example, distinguishes between *La Ville Complexe* and *La Ville Compliquée*.[70] She argues that modern urban planners opted – largely for practical reasons – for the *choix de la complication*. It is a choice whereby societies develop rules and conventions for stabilising entities in order to make them workable, as opposed to working with, and through, their complexity.[71] Stengers traces this back to the 19th-century hygienist approach to the city, with its obsession with order and rationality. She argues that the choice for *la ville compliquée* remains popular because it approaches the city as something homogeneous, legible from the outside, organised, and functional. Instead, Stengers suggests studying cities as complex entities or 'imbroglios'; complex knots of stakes, ideas, actors, and practices that are opaque from the outside, and always more of a draft than a finished product.[72] Latour too has suggested approaching the city as an assemblage. In *Paris Invisible City*, he studies Paris through a so-called 'oligoptic view'. With the oligopticon, Latour offers a new way of reading, mapping, visualising, and understanding the city. In contrast to the panoptic view or the panorama (striving to grasp the city through an all-encompassing view), the oligopticon maps *multiple* Parises including networks such as, traffic control, water distribution, and electricity. From such partial viewpoints, one does not see much – *only* electricity or *only* water. Paris emerges, as a city, through a montage of these networks; a composite of many oligoptic views.[73]

CHALLENGES OF ENTANGLED ACCOUNTS OF ARCHITECTURE

> *Architectural design embraces a complex conglomerate of many surprising agencies that are rarely taken into account by architectural theory.*[74]

The complex, networked descriptions of reality, as suggested by Latour and Stengers, are posited as more realistic accounts than the ones delivered through theory's critical method of denunciation, whereby one layer of reality is studied through a set of external referents and then used to explain the whole of reality. The merit of earthly accounts for architecture is, firstly, that it is closer to how architecture actually works. Secondly, it allows for breaking with architectural theory's habit of discussing architecture through abstract categories and unhelpful oppositional pairs, that is top-down versus bottom-up, design versus use, politics versus aesthetics, and experts versus laypeople. Complex accounts, however, do not come without methodological and ethical challenges.

One challenge relates to the requirement of becoming receptive to the numerous forces that make things, or make-city. If, as the opening quote of this section suggests, architecture embraces a 'conglomerate of many surprising agencies', then which actors deserve attention? ANT suggests looking into as many actors as possible. In architecture, this implies that researchers should avoid limiting the study of non-humans to familiar architectural artefacts such as buildings, plans, drawings or models, and to consider more mundane actors including materials, mind-sets, ideologies, regulations, conventions, and certificates. These, too, 'act'. No matter how mundane, these actors mobilise, transform, reinforce, disrupt, and manipulate networks, and because more objects 'act' than one may expect, researchers are invited to become receptive to unexpected, seemingly trivial, and surprising actors.[75] With this book, I intend to select those social and material actors that are worth following, and study how these actors equally and *together* make-city.

Giving voice to as many actors as possible evokes a second challenge. Namely, as ANT shows, actors are always 'situated'. Architectural actors such as plans and drawings demonstrate that, in addition to being situated, actors also get *re-situated* over time; they act differently in changing circumstances. For example, an architectural project mobilises different devices, including models, technical drawings, and images, depending on whether it travels through participatory settings or political negotiations; whether it intends to seduce customers in a real estate brochure; or whether it is to obtain a building permit. Because plans, maps, and models are often on the move, and because their agency transforms whilst moving, the researcher can no longer justify mobilising them as mere sources. Instead these actors are to be taken seriously as material–representational entities.

A third challenge relates to ANT's non-normativity and, thus, to the critical and transformative merit of complex and entangled descriptions of architecture. What change can such descriptions induce? ANT's ontological emphasis on *describing* situations, rather than *judging* or *changing* them, has been subject to debates around ANT's political and ethical potentials.[76] When researchers are encouraged to *describe* architectural processes, rather than make judgments with the help of external referents as to what is 'good' or 'bad', then *how* can 'good' ways of *doing* architecture or *doing* cities become possible? This challenge is, compared to the social sciences, additionally complicated in the case of *transdisciplines* such as architecture.[77] *Transdisciplines* operate at the intersections of discipline and profession, and, therefore, engage with the world in analytical, situated, *and* productive manners. As a consequence, the findings of architectural researchers potentially have effects on the profession and so, by default, make researchers implicated: as such, the architectural researcher involved in situated, relational inquiries has a 'duty of care' for the consequences of their work.[78]

CRITICALITY-FROM-WITHIN: TOWARDS SITUATED ACCOUNTS

> *A problem is always a practical problem, never a universal problem mattering for everybody.*[79]

In response to the ethico-methodological challenges posed by ANT/pragmatism and the practice turn, I have chosen to introduce criticality-from-within for studying the possibilities of criticality through practice. Inspired by Stengers' consideration of immanent critique as 'an ingredient of the assemblage, not as critically examining/dismembering the assemble itself',[80] criticality-from-within will join me throughout the adventures of this book as a conceptual companion. I chose the term, firstly, because it suggests a mode of operating from-within that is not value-neutral, but explicitly critical. Secondly, criticality-from-within suggests re-envisioning, rather than dismissing, the role of theory and the theorist. As such, 'from-within' depicts actions through practice, whilst 'criticality' denotes care for the critical project in architecture. The use of the term 'criticality' is imperative in this respect. I agree with the French sociologist Luc Boltanski that the most commonly proclaimed forms of criticality, such as the use of theory as 'metacritique', and the critical (Marxist) promises of emancipation based on the replacement of structure with agency fall short.[81] However, whilst recognising the limitations of critical theory, I believe that retaining the term criticality allows, in the face of a post-political condition, to rescue the political and ethical preoccupations of critical theory. To paraphrase Donna Haraway, the philosopher of science and technology and feminist thinker, keeping the term criticality at hand requires a willingness to work through – rather than dismiss – the contradictions of one's intellectual heritage, with its categories and taxonomies, no matter how inappropriate these may be.[82] My choice of the term criticality-from-within thus expresses affinity with ANT and pragmatism's within-ness and the feminist objectivity defined in terms of 'situated knowledges'.[83] But it is also a choice to articulate, within the context of architectural theory, the critical dimension of that within-ness.

Criticality-from-within signals a critical engagement albeit without choosing between critiques and metacritique; between agency and structure; and between the uses of analysis as a mere 'instrument of description' or a 'weapon of critique'.[84]

Instead, it suggests a mode of inquiry whereby things are studied as assemblages and through their processes of making; it suggests studying the world as a 'pluriverse in the making'.[85] There is, however, another reason for retaining the term criticality. Critique can be considered to refer to the unmasking of hidden power structures and oppressions 'from the outside', as in critical theory. Criticality, by contrast, emphasises the situatedness of things, and is embodied.[86] This 'embodied criticality' refers to 'a state from which one cannot exit or gain a critical distance [so it positions one *within*] but which rather marries our knowledge and our experience in ways that are not complimentary'.[87] It is a criticality that is preoccupied with delivering situated, embodied, partial, and, therefore, '*better* accounts of the world' than the ones offered through abstract, external viewpoints.[88]

In the pragmatist tradition, such 'better' descriptions are seen as analytical acts as much as they are future-shaping, and are, therefore, ethical: better descriptions of a current state-of-affairs are believed to allow for imagining the composition of that state-of-affairs anew and, thus, for producing a different world.[89] In order to describe the complex and networked existence of things, Stengers advises to radically slow down. Only by 'slowing down' can the complexity of things be grasped, and will space be created for hesitation, for imagining alternatives, and for surprises. Slowing down is at the heart of Stengers' 'ecology of practices', an approach whereby one thinks through practice, and encourages thinking, not from a distance, but 'in the presence of' those who may have to bear the consequences of our actions.[90] This calls for a recognition that actions and (good) intentions can only be evaluated through a confrontation with practice, and through the 'rapports' between the diverging, conflicting standpoints.[91] Hence, Stengers's 'ecology of practices', rather than being preoccupied with 'what ought to be', encourages one to think about the world 'through what is happening'.[92] It is a hopeful and transformative undertaking that, rather than describing the probable, 'activates the possible'.[93] By slowing down reasoning, one can 'arouse a slightly different awareness of the problems and situations mobilizing us'.[94] Stengers reminds us that in the pragmatist tradition, the meticulous descriptions of a situation are *transformative* acts because they allow for reliving the choices that have been made. In this way, descriptions of the becoming of practices expose how a state-of-affairs has come into being, and how it could have been composed differently. It implies that alternative routes could have been chosen, and that different choices could have been made.[95]

Criticality-from-within can also be seen as a response to architectural historian Reinhold Martin's call for a 'utopian realism'. Martin posits 'utopian realism' as a critical alternative to the realism of the post-critical theorists, whereby utopia is not defined in terms of an idealised, 'other' world, but in terms of possible worlds that are present within the everyday reality.[96] The transformative potential of criticality-from-within resides not in plans or blueprints for the future, nor in unrealistic utopian dream, but in the understanding and description of the practices of becoming of the present, of the current state-of-affairs or, as Haraway writes: 'in the sense that things might be otherwise'.[97] Offering detailed accounts of such processes of becoming, therefore, *is* the critical and transformative act. I believe that this approach is relevant in response to the central question of this book: How to imagine, for architecture, a critical mode of inquiry that operates through practice?

BECOMING A 'MODEST WITNESS'

> [Care is] everything that we do to maintain, continue and repair 'our world' so that we can live in it as well as possible. That world includes our bodies, our selves, and our environment, all of which we seek to interweave in a complex, life sustaining web.[98]

Criticality-from-within derives its ethical force not just from the descriptive-transformative nature of its accounts. Moreover, these accounts are situated and embodied, and as *embodied* accounts, stress the ethical responsibilities and duty of care that come with networked and relational accounts offered by ANT. Notwithstanding their differences, authors such as Irit Rogoff, Haraway, Stengers, Maria Puig de la Bellacasa, and Rosi Braidotti equally argue for embodied accounts based on ethics and care. A theorist is considered as being affected or 'polluted' by their situatedness, thus bearing the responsibility to care for the effects of their critiques; to be compassionate and empathetic with what they research.[99] Puig de la Bellacasa reminds us that care is, first and foremost, an ontological, rather than moralistic, requirement of being situated; an awareness of the consequences that come with relations. She stresses that, once researchers think from-within they cannot help but *care* for that world, because they are part of it, or, as Braidotti has argued, because they are 'neither detached nor uncaring'.[100] Embodied accounts, particularly so with Braidotti, Haraway and Stengers, push this even further by calling for *re-living* the world. Instead of neutral accounts, theorised from a comfortable distance, to re-live is a matter of what Braidotti calls 'forgetting to forget', or, as Stengers puts it: 'to smell the smoke [of the burned witches] in our nostrils [again].'[101]

Criticality-from-within, with its embodied and situated accounts, is not to be misunderstood as a dismissal of theory; rather, it is sceptical of what Stengers calls the *authority* and *generality* with which theory is associated, and refuses to take conceptual, historical categorisations for granted.[102] Instead, the theorist is invited to deliver situated and *specific* accounts of processes of de-and re-assembling. These specific accounts are not to be used as a basis for generalisation, but are, nevertheless, confronted with an awareness of their entanglement with larger collectives, a wider common good.[103] Following Stengers, the task of the theorist is to be as attentive as possible to the specificity of a situation, whilst balancing this with a more general reasoning:

> What you are responsible for is paying attention as best as you can, to be as discerning, as discriminating as you can about the particular situation. That is, you need to decide in this particular case and to obey the power of some more general reason.[104]

Haraway, therefore, calls the theorist a 'modest witness'; a 'witness' because the critical thinker aims at witnessing, not judging from the outside, through external referents, and 'modest' because witnessing also contains a level of accountability.[105]

Inspired by Haraway, Stengers, and Braidotti, this book puts these new challenges for theory to the test. I will bring a specific account of critical practices in Brussels, and confront the resultant situated knowledge with the wider theoretical and ethical preoccupations of the practice turn in architectural theory. I take calls for *embodied* descriptions seriously, and also to engage with those inherited worlds of theoretical concepts and categories that are, perhaps, too often taken for granted; I am prepared to work towards thick, embodied, and complex descriptions of the world. In order to do so, Brussels does not figure as a case serving as a mere resource or touchstone for theory, but it is taken seriously as a practice.[106] This means becoming sensitive to as many actors as possible. Given the infinite number of actors that are available, I will have to understand which actors and networks are worth following by asking questions about the difference that they make in a *specific* situation. This can be achieved by slowing down reasoning, and by learning to 'wonder' and to become receptive to unexpected, surprising, and disruptive forces.[107] Therefore, if this book is a work of theory, it is a theory that becomes akin to a craft, an embodied practice. Instead of an autonomous and abstract endeavour, theory becomes, what Haraway aptly called, an 'on-the-ground working project'.[108]

UNPACKING BRUSSELS: THE STRUCTURE OF THE BOOK

In addition to the ANT/pragmatist studies focusing on the design and controversies of architecture and cities, cited in previous sections, I study critical architectural operations. Throughout this book, I will unpack various types of critical practices as found in Brussels after 1968. I will not study Brussels through chronology; through thematic lenses limited to architectural themes, tools, and cultures; or through realised buildings alone. This book is not to be considered an anthology. It is also not intended as an overview work about architecture, the practice turn, or Brussels.[109] Instead, it adopts a series of partial views, the selection of which is reflected in the structure of the book, and was informed by key moments of critical transformations (for example 1970s, 1990s); by instructive critical tools (for example counter-projects, interstitial activism, participation); and by relevant actors that deserve being re-inserted into architectural debates (for example a urinal, *architek*). The chapters in this book can be read independently as stand-alone analyses or, taken together, as a contribution to both the Brussels historiography and the conceptual refinement of criticality under the practice turn.

The next chapter in this book, 'Counter-projects', will focus on the first key moment of critical architectural culture, namely the oppositional activism of the 1970s. Historically, Brussels citizens have fallen victim to a legacy of destruction. Whether it is the construction of the Palace of Justice in the late 19th century, or the modernisation fever of the 1960s, vast parts of the historic city were demolished and its inhabitants expelled. In reaction to this situation, and with 1968 as a pivotal moment, numerous action committees were involved in the struggles for the Right to the City. From a unique collaboration between local activists, most notably the Atelier de Recherche et d'Action Urbaines (ARAU), and architects connected to the Archives d'Architecture Moderne (AAM) and architectural education at La Cambre, an activism emerged that attempted to put a halt to urban destructions *and* develop alternative proposals for reconstructing and repairing the historic city. It did so through the use of a specific activist tool, the counter-project; a type of drawing-manifesto that proposed to articulate spatial alternatives but was, nevertheless, not intended to be built. The counter-project deserves scholarly attention: firstly, because it was an important instrument in Brussels' architectural culture of the 1970s with effects lasting into the subsequent decades and, secondly, because it was at the basis of the consolidation of a strong European traditionalist postmodernism. Further, the counter-project is, in itself, a fascinating and instructive critical tool for studying the, at times, ambiguous relationship between politics and aesthetics, and between real-world activism and autonomous, disciplinary critique. I have, therefore, chosen to study 1970s Brussels through counter-projects. Their political embedding allows for re-validating the radical basis of what was to become traditionalist postmodernism in architecture. With its intense production of counter-projects, Brussels offers a fascinating yet little-known setting for refining our understanding of postmodernism's uses of history *beyond* discussions on form and style. Counter-projects are, in this next chapter, studied as complex assemblages mobilising politics, aesthetics, Marxism, craftsmanship, the everyday, production processes, and citizens. The study of counter-projects through the specific situation of Brussels, where they were produced at the intersections of political activism and the intellectual work of Maurice Culot and his students at La Cambre, will allow for studying the emerging theory on the Reconstruction of the City as a political–aesthetic construct. Rather than following the architectural profession and the discipline's irritation with traditionalism, I will re-live, re-claim and digest this troubled past.

The third chapter in this book, 'Interstitial activism', discusses a different form of criticality; namely, that which emerged in Brussels throughout the 1990s. Whilst the large-scale urban destructions of the 1960s and 1970s had, thanks to the actions of the ARAU, been significantly tempered, the Brussels' inner-city was, in the 1990s, in a state of despair. It had been abandoned by policy makers, and inhabitants had, where possible, fled. This had resulted in an uninhabitable city centre, left to decay, with developers baiting for lucrative deals. In response to this situation, and instigated by the epochal squat of a vacant Brussels housing block under threat of demolition, called the *Hôtel Central* action, Brussels saw to an explosion of urban activism. With its focus on urbanity, urban culture, and socio-economics, this activism had an important impact on Brussels' architectural and urban culture, and contributed, whether or not deliberately, to challenging the common urban embellishment solutions. Instead of aestheticised and cosmetic solutions, urban activists and designers sought for solutions in tune with Brussels' everyday reality. Initially manifest through urban–cultural events and public space happenings/installations, actions gradually grew more designerly. This generated a new confidence in contemporary urban design, and triggered also an architectural emancipation that was nevertheless gradual and cautious. It was an emancipation that was optimistic, yet close to Brussels' fragile socio-economic reality. It was, consequently, also careful in embracing the newfound architectural optimism under neoliberal urban regeneration. In this third chapter, I study this cautious emancipation, which will be instructive for further defining the merits of criticality-from-within. I will discuss this type of critical operation in terms of an 'interstitial event', and through the example of the socio-cultural collective Recyclart. Recyclart is particularly instructive because its activism emerged as a form of disruption from *within* the Brussels establishment; its public administrations; and secondly, because of its strong alliances with architectural culture. By confronting the philosophical notion 'interstice' – as developed by Isabelle Stengers and Didier Debaise – with examples of 1990s activism in Brussels, particularly the collective Recyclart, this chapter will demonstrate how a situated criticality-from-within has powers that are potentially as disruptive as the ones offered by the oppositional activism of the 1970s counter-projects.

The fourth chapter of this book, titled 'Participatory Challenges', continues the exploration into the practice turn, this time through a theoretical analysis of participation in architecture, a field wherein the ethical challenges were particularly felt. Under the practice turn, it became evident that neoliberal politics celebrated virtues such as inclusiveness, participation, individual freedom and creativity, values which had previously been part of oppositional activism. With these virtues now incorporated into the politics of consensus, participatory efforts were urged to re-think their political activism. Rather than instigating new forms of activism from-within, this re-imagination was largely reduced to either a radicalisation of practice, and the affirmation of oppositional pairs, or a fatalist relinquishing of any hope for critical practice. This chapter unpacks how, in the discussions of participation in architecture, oppositional pairs prevail; between design and use, top-down and bottom-up, expert and layperson. Moreover, it looks at how some of the longstanding tensions in participatory architecture, such as between democratic decision-making and individual authorship, and between politics and aesthetics, are magnified under the practice turn. Analysing the heightened tensions in participation under the practice turn is particularly important to understand the workings of participation in Brussels, where citizen participation is, since the 1970s, considered a cornerstone of democratic city-making. In the 1990s, participation underwent a further revival, which was felt in the urban activism of the time (as discussed in the third chapter) but also in the creation of Neighbourhood Contracts (NC). As such, this chapter provides an important theoretical contextualisation of the participation which emerged in the 1990s, and resulted in an official instrument for local neighbourhood renewal that includes a participatory component. It will inform an analysis of such participatory practices, not in terms of oppositional pairs, but in terms of the actions around 'participatory artefacts'.

A close study of those Neighbourhood Contracts is the subject of Chapter 5, 'Learning from Things'. This chapter starts from the observation that when studying citizen participation through oppositional pairs one can overlook a lot of the action. Drawing from studies on artefacts and things, I suggest studying the *numerous* actors and networks that are mobilised by 'participatory artefacts'. One such participatory artefact of significance in Brussels is the Neighbourhood Contract. This well-established urban planning tool aims to revitalise deprived neighbourhoods through housing renovation, urban design, and socio-cultural initiatives. It is effectuated as an official contract between the Brussels Capital Region and local municipalities and development takes place through an elaborate participatory process. In this chapter, we will discover that many more actors take part in these participatory processes than one might expect; apart from planners, administrators and citizens, time, perimeter, taxon, experience, finance, language, and even abbreviations can be seen to 'act' in Neighbourhood Contracts. Although sometimes barely visible in participatory meetings, I will give voice to these actors and allow them to enter the discussions on participation. Moreover, we will discover how participatory practices operate on moral, as much as practical, grounds, and that these cannot easily be evaluated in separation. We will discover that what appears during participatory meetings as democratic deficits or political stubbornness may well originate in practical requirements or limitations. This in turn helps us to better understand some of the recurring tensions and frustrations of participation.

The sixth and final chapter of the book, 'Unsung Heroes' will take seriously the call to 'wonder', and expand the actors we include in architectural and urban studies. It follows actors that play an important role in understanding Brussels' architecture, but are rarely included in architectural discourse; these include a public urinal; a 'building' that is too mundane to include in architectural discourse, but is, nevertheless, instrumental in understanding some of the frustrations and tensions in the negotiation of the built environment; and some 'situated icons' (projects for Place Flagey and Place Rogier). Such projects are both mundane and catalytic; they are landmark projects that energised Brussels' architectural culture yet depended for their survival on their situatedness in Brussels. Finally, I will take some of the everyday signs in Brussels' architectural culture seriously, such as the sensation that Brussels' architects for some time have felt trapped in a city suffering from a mild neophobia: I will unpack Brussels' fear of the new through the words *architek* and *Bruxellisation*, and will argue that studying this fear – what it means and how it travels – is not anecdotal or folkloristic, but important for an architectural and urban understanding of the *specific* context of Brussels.

Through studying concrete instances of critical operations, this book aims to contribute to architectural theory's quest for critical modes of engagement and, as such, aims to contribute to the refinement of our understanding of what Martin called postmodernism's 'rules of engagement'.[110] This book shows how pragmatist and relational philosophies can be made relevant for architectural theory; and how such approach can work in the concrete setting of a city. It suggests the possibility to depart from the well-bound situations (or: laboratories) and venture into those 'larger, less well-defined domains', such as cities, that still seem to sit rather uncomfortably within ANT.[111] During this journey, we will discover critical modes of engagement that are realistic, transformative, and hopeful. We will discover how critical manifestations emerge from oppositional actions as much as from-within, and from architectural efforts as much as mundane activities of the everyday; and how they *together* tell us something about different possibilities for criticality. The acknowledgement of criticality-from-within therefore challenges a romanticising, and naïve over-celebration, of the critical merits of everyday practice, for these practices are unavoidably tempered by the lures of appeasement, and informed by their pragmatic inscription in (rather than opposition to) late-capitalist consumer society. At the same time, however, I challenge a fear of appeasement that paralyses any attempt towards critical action from-within. At the end of the book, we will learn how the Brussels situation suggests a fascinating form of criticality from-within; namely a 'cautious pragmatism' that is realistic as much as it is hopeful, optimistic yet cautious. I will argue that this cautious pragmatism forms an optimistic response to timely questions related to the crises of criticality in architecture.

NOTES

1 Official website of the City of Brussels, accessed January 7, 2015, http://www.brussel.be/artdet.cfm/5629.

2 Jonathan Meades, *Further Abroad – Belgium*, 1994, from: *The Jonathan Meades Collection* (DVD, BBC, 2008).

3 The scaffolding installed in 1989 for the restoration of the dome, required renovation two decades later. Replacing the scaffolding was not an option because it had been tailor-made and was fixed at several points. See 'Stellingen rond Brussels Justitiepaleis aan renovatie toe', *De Morgen*, June 4, 2009; 'Il faut rénover les échafaudages', *La Capitale*, June 4, 2009.

4 This book operates more explicitly within architectural, critical, theory and resonates with, for example, Steven A. Moore's explorations of pragmatism at the intersections of theory and practice; Andrew Ballantyne's non-essentialist take in his edited collection *Architectures: Modernism and After* (Oxford: Blackwell, 2004); and with studies of the ethical agency of practice such as Nicholas Ray, ed., *Architecture and its Ethical Dilemmas* (Abingdon: Routledge 2005).

5 Derk-Jan Eppink, *Belgian Adventures*, quoted in Richard Hill, *The Art of Being Belgian: Brussels, Belgium and Beyond* (Brussels: Europublications, 2005), 88.

6 Staf Nimmegeers, *Chagrijn en Charme: verhalen uit Brussel* (Amsterdam/Antwerpen: Meulenhoff/Kritak, 1997), 21.

7 Hill, *The Art of Being Belgian*, 55. On *Belgitude* see also Eric De Kuyper, 'Belgitude', in *Een passie voor Brussel* (Amsterdam: Babylon-De Geus, 1995), 140–141.

8 The exhibition *bMa Man of Thoughts: 5 jaar Brussels bouwmeester – 5 ans maître-architecte à Bruxelles – 5 years Brussels head architect* ran from September 12, 2014 until September 25, 2014 at BNB Paribas Fortis in Brussels. Despite using the word Head

Architect in the English exhibition title, I will use the term Master Architect throughout as it is much closer to *Bouwmeester* and *Maître Architecte*. It is also distinct from the English version of the Flemish *Bouwmeester* which means Government Architect, accessed October 17, 2014, http://english.vlaamsbouwmeester.be/.

9 'bMa – Mission statement,' translated from Dutch and French, accessed October 16, 2014, http://www.bmabru.be/#page/missions-introduction.

10 Municipalities with language facilities are obliged to offer administrative services in another than the first language of that municipality. Located across the country's language borders (such as around the Brussels region), they have been the source of political friction.

11 Important influences from the Walloon region include Charles Vandenhove's design of the royal suite, in collaboration with artists Daniel Buren and Sol Lewitt, as part of the renovation of the *La Monnaie* theatre in 1986; and Lucien Kroll's *La Mémé*, or *Maison Médicale*, a hostel for medical students at the University of Louvain, near Brussels (1970–1972).

12 Others in the new generation of Flemish architects include: Eugeen Liebaut, Paul Robbrecht and Hilde Daem, Henk De Smet and Paul Vermeulen, Marie-José Vanhee, Bob Van Reeth, Christian Kieckens, Frank Delmulle, and Luc Deleu. Flemish (and Belgian) architecture had hitherto received little international attention, allegedly due to commissions limited to single-family houses in suburban contexts.

13 Geert Bekaert, 'Belgische Architectuur als gemeenplaats. De afwezigheid van een architectonische cultuur als uitdaging', *Archis* 9 (1987): 10–11; Geert Bekaert, *Architectuur zonder schaduw* (Rotterdam: 010 Publishers, 1988), see also Marc Dubois, *Belgio Architettura gli ultimi vent'anni* (Milan: Electa, 1993), 43–51.

14 Francis Strauven, *De Rijkdom van de eenvoud: Hedendaagse architectuur in Vlaanderen*, exposition catalogue (Brussels: Fondation pour l'Architecture, 1997). Due to the individuality of these new oeuvres, the declaration of a movement was debated in the architectural press during the 1990s, such as *Archis*. A number of dedicated Belgian 'specials' in international journals such as *Archis*, *Bauwelt*, and *L'Architecture d'Aujourd'hui* were triggered, as well as expositions at De Singel Antwerp, Museum voor Sierkunst Ghent, the Architecture Biennale in Venice, and Arc en Rêve Bordeaux.

15 *Jaarboeken Architectuur Vlaanderen* (since 1994), published by the Ministerie van de Vlaamse Gemeenschap and S/AM co-founder Marc Dubois; since 2002–2003 by the Flemish Architecture Institute. Other important impulses include Geert Bekaert's anthology *Hedendaagse architectuur in België* (Tielt: Lannoo, 1995); and Jacques Aron, Patrick Burniat and Pierre Puttemans's *L'Architecture contemporaine en Belgique: guide* (Brussels: Éditions de l'Octogore, 1996); and the writings of critics and historians including Hilde Heynen, André Loeckx, Pieter Uyttenhove, Mil De Kooning, Jan Bruggemans, Jos Vandenbreeden, and Marc Dubois. The Flemish emancipation has also to be seen in the context of the global promotion of architecture in The Netherlands, triggered by the successes of Rem Koolhaas/OMA, and promoted through the *Nederlands Architectuur Instituut* (NaI) since 1993; and the SuperDutch as accounted by Bart Lootsma, *SuperDutch: New Architecture in the Netherlands* (New York: Princeton Architectural Press, 2000).

16 There were three special issues on public–private investment in the architecture journal *A Plus* 108–110 (1990–1991).

17 This *Stadsvernieuwingsbesluit* was also called the 'public–private act'. See Guido Knops, ed., *Stadsvernieuwing in beweging* (Brussels: Koning Boudewijnstichting, 1992), 129;

Pascal De Decker, Bernard Hubeau, and Stefan Nieuwinckel, eds, *In de ban van stad en wijk* (Berchem: EPO, 1996).

18   Both are included, as a priority, in the policy plan *Beleidsnota Antwerpen 1989–1994*, Pascal De Decker, 'Plangroep Stad aan de Stroom stopt', *Planologisch Nieuws*, no. 1 (1994): 75.

19   Studio Open City and Pieter Uyttenhove, *Taking sides: Antwerp's 19th-Century Belt: Elements for a Culture of the City* (Antwerpen: Open Stad, 1993).

20   Pierre Loze, 'Het Nieuwe HST station van Brussel-Zuid', *A Plus* 132 (1995): 60–65. The uncontrolled and opportunistic planning associated with the Brussels South station was criticised in the journal *Planologisch Nieuws*, and by Brussels activist Gwenaël Breës in *Bruxelles-Midi – l'urbanisme du sacrifice et des bouts de ficelle* (Brussels: Éditions Aden, 2009).

21   Joris Sleebus et al., *Eurotaurus en andere verhalen uit de hedendaagse Brusselse legend* (Brussels: Brukselbinnenstebuiten, 1993); Carola Hein, 'The Polycentric and Opportunistic Capital of Europe: A New Model for the Siting and Reallocation of EU Headquarters and the Design of European Districts in Brussels and other Host Cities', *Brussels Studies* 2 (2006); Carola Hein, ed., *Bruxelles l'Européenne: Capitale de qui? Ville de qui? Cahier de La Cambre Architecture*, no. 5 (Brussels: ISACF-La Cambre, 2006); Annette Kuhk, 'Layered Urban Development: Managing the European Quarter in Brussels', in *Brussels and Europe/Bruxelles et l'Europe*, ed. R. de Groof (Brussels: APS, 2008).

22   The Reconstruction of the European City movement is discussed in greater detail in Chapter 2.

23   CIVA is subsidised by the French community. It includes foundations with a Reconstruction bias, such as the Fondation Philippe Rotthier pour l'Architecture.

24   The 1989 call for young architects to renovate an urban block in central Brussels followed the Reconstruction idiom. See Caroline Mierop and Françoise Deville, eds, *Oproep aan de jonge Europese architecten* (Brussels: Fondation pour l'Architecture, 1995). The 1997 competition for the design of the new CIVA buildings was allegedly dominated by traditionalism.

25   Notably the river Zenne, which crosses the city centre from North to South, was covered and replaced with grand Parisian-style boulevards. These works were in the hands of Jules Anspach, Mayor of Brussels, and King Leopold II who was also known as 'the Urbanist King'.

26   Maurizio Cohen, *Les îles flottantes* (Brussels: La Lettre Volée and Communauté Française de Belgique, 2002), French Community's contribution to the 2002 Venice Architecture Biennale.

27   Maurizio Cohen, *Brussels on our Doorstep: Architecture in Neighbourhood Contracts* (Brussels: Brussels Capital Region, 2007). Flemish architects active in Brussels included Paul Robbrecht, Hilde Daem, Marie-José Van Hee, Poponcini & Lootens and Eugeen Liebaut and those involved in small-scale conversions in the trendy Dansaert Quarter. Key works on the francophone side, include, the library of human sciences (Art & Build), the ULB Medicine Faculty Auditorium (Philippe Samyn), and the apartment building in Rue des Chartreux and Mogador (Pierre Blondel).

28   Prisme Éditions was founded in 1995: notable publications include *Bruxelles Ville Nouvelle: Architectures 1989–1995* (1995) and *Change: Brussels Capital of Europe* (2005); Studio Open City (SOC) originated in the Open City events of Antwerp, founded in 1993, see *A Moving City: Three Years of Architectural Explorations in Brussels' Canal Zone* (Brussels: Centrum voor Architectuur en Design, 1998).

29 The book series A16 has concentrated on young Flemish architects (*Jonge Architecten in Vlaanderen*) since 2003; and, since 2005, on Francophone architects (*Jeunes Architectures*). See also the *(Re)nouveaux plaisirs d'architecture* exhibition (La Cambre/CIVA, 2005 and 2007).

30 *Supernova* showed the work of 44 young Belgian architects. Design workshop: Bruno De Meulder and Karina Van Herck, *Vacant City: Brussels' Mont des Arts Reconsidered* (Rotterdam: NAI Publishers and Leuven: OSA, 2000).

31 Direction de l'Architecture, directed by Chantal Dassonville since 1996, intensified its activities in the 2000s by organising architecture competitions, staging regular exhibitions and lectures at the *Centre Wallonie-Bruxelles de Paris* and publishing the book series *Visions: Architectures Publiques*, dedicated to contemporary, public architecture.

32 Jean-Louis Genard and Pablo Lhoas, eds, *Qui a peur de L'Architecture? Le Livre Blanc de L'Architecture contemporaine en communauté Française en Belgique* (Brussels: La Lettre Volée and I.S.A. La Cambre, 2004); ISACF La Cambre and Philippe Flamme, *Vade-Mecum: Commande d'architecture publique à Bruxelles. Comment choisir un auteur de projet? Exemples et bonnes pratiques* (Brussels: ISACF La Cambre, 2007).

33 Mathieu Van Criekingen called this a 'hard' regeneration replacing a 'soft' one; as discussed in Isabelle Doucet, 'Brussels: The *Soft* Regeneration' in *Houses in Transformation, Interventions in European Gentrification*, ed. J.J. Berg et al. (Rotterdam: NAI Publishers, 2008), 130–143.

34 In 2009, for example, 30,000 households were on the waiting list for social housing, constituting only 7.7 per cent of the total housing stock. 26.2 per cent of the population lives below the poverty risk boundary. See Observatorium voor Gezondheid en Welzijn Brussel, *Welzijnsbarometer: Brussels armoederapport 2009* (Brussels: Gemeenschappelijke Gemeenschapscommissie, 2009), 15; 57. Half of Brussels' population lives in neighbourhoods that are recognised as 'deprived'; see Christian Vandermotten, Christian Kesteloot, Bertrand Ippersiel, *Dynamische Analyse van de Buurten in Moeilijkheden in de Belgische Stadsgewesten* (Brussels: POD Maatschappelijke Integratie/Grootstedenbeleid, 2007), 20. See also Guy Baeten, 'The Europeanization of Brussels and the Urbanization of "Europe": Hybridizing the City. Empowerment and Disempowerment in the EU District', *European Urban and Regional Studies* 8 (2001): 117–130; Linda Boudry et al., eds, *White Paper: The Century of the City: City Republics and Grid Cities* (Brussels: Ministry of the Flemish Community, 2003); and Eric Corijn and Eefje Vloeberghs, *Brussel!* (Brussels: VUB Press, 2009).

35 This strain of thought is notably represented by the journals *Assemblage* (1986–2000) and *Oppositions* (1973–1984). For a detailed analysis see C. Greig Crysler, *Writing Spaces: Discourses of Architecture, Urbanism, and the Built Environment, 1960–2000* (New York and Abingdon: Routledge, 2003), 57–79.

36 Critical theory is inspired by Marxist theory through the Tafurian categories of autonomy and negation, continental philosophy, and the Frankfurt School. On the debates about critical theory in the US around the work of K. Michael Hays, Peter Eisenman, and Frederic Jameson see Louis Martin, 'Fredric Jameson and Critical Architecture', in *The Political Unconscious of Architecture*, ed. Nadir Lahiji (Farnham: Ashgate, 2011), 171–209.

37 George Baird refers to a 'first wave' of radical architecture that was obsessed with political design, technological innovation, and design methodology, being replaced with a 'second wave' thriving on the rather innocent use of history and a growing obsession with the city and its history (known as 'rationalism' in Europe and 'contextualism' in the United States); George Baird, '1968 and its Aftermath:

'The Loss of Moral Confidence in Architectural Practice and Education', *Reflections on Architectural Practices in the Nineties,* ed. William S. Saunders (New York: Princeton Architectural Press, 1996), 64–70. See also Simon Sadler, 'An Avant-Garde Academy', in *Architectures: Modernism* and After, ed. Andrew Ballantyne (Oxford: Blackwell, 2004), 33–56; and Harry Francis Mallgrave and David Goodman, *An Introduction to Architectural Theory: 1968 to the Present* (Chichester: Wiley-Blackwell, 2011), 53–64.

38   K. Michael Hays, *Architecture Theory since 1968* (Cambridge, MA: The MIT Press, 1998); and Kate Nesbitt, *Theorizing a New Agenda for Architecture: An Anthology of Architectural Theory, 1965–1995* (New York: Princeton Architectural Press, 1996).

39   George Baird, '"Criticality" and its Discontents', *Harvard Design Magazine* 21 (2004–2005): 16–21; Robert Somol and Sarah Whiting, 'Notes around the Doppler Effect and Other Moods of Modernism', *The Yale Architectural Journal,* 33 (2002): 72–77; Reinhold Martin's 'Critical of What? Towards a Utopian Realism', *Harvard Design Magazine,* 22 (2005): 104–109; Arie Graafland, 'On Criticality' [2006], in *Constructing a New Agenda: Architectural Theory 1993–2009,* ed. A. Krista Sykes (New York: Princeton Architectural Press, 2010), 394–420.

40   A. Krista Sykes, ed., *Constructing a New Agenda: Architectural Theory 1993–2009* (New York: Princeton Architectural Press, 2010), 16.

41   Ibid., 14–27.

42   Erik Swyngedouw, 'The Post-Political City', in *Urban Politics Now: Re-Imagining Democracy in the Neoliberal City,* ed. BAVO (Rotterdam: NAI Publishers, 2007), 58–76. See also Neil Brenner, and Nik Theodore, 'Cities and the Geographies of "Actually Existing Neoliberalism"', in *Spaces of Neoliberalism,* ed. Neil Brenner and Nik Theodore (Chichester: John Wiley & Sons, 2002), 2–32.

43   Joan Ockman, ed., *The Pragmatist Imagination: Thinking About Things in the Making* (New York: Princeton Architectural Press, 2001); Albena Yaneva, *The Making of a Building: A Pragmatist Approach to Architecture* (Oxford, Berlin and New York: Peter Lang, 2009); William S. Saunders, ed., *The New Architectural Pragmatism* (Minneapolis, MN and London: The University of Minnesota Press, 2007). For a more complete introduction to the post-critical, see Sykes, *Constructing a New Agenda,* 14–29; Mallgrave and Goodman, *An Introduction to Architectural Theory,* 177–193 ('Pragmatism and Post-Criticality'); and Saunders, *The New Architectural Pragmatism.*

44   Examples include geographers such as Edward Soja, Neil Brenner, and Erik Swyngedouw. In architectural scholarship please see Łukasz Stanek, *Henri Lefebvre on Space: Architecture, Urban Research, and the Production of Theory* (Minneapolis, MN: University of Minnesota Press, 2011); Łukasz Stanek, Christian Schmid, and Ákos Moravánszky, eds, *Urban Revolution Now* (Farnham: Ashgate, 2014). In architecture please see, Steven Harris and Deborah Berke, eds, *The Architecture of the Everyday* (New York: Princeton Architectural Press, 1997); Claude Lichtenstein and Thomas Schregenberger, *As Found: The Discovery of the Ordinary* (Baden: Mueller Publishers, 2001); and special journal issues, for example, 'The Everyday and Architecture', *Architectural Design Profile,* 134, ed. Jeremy Till and Sarah Wigglesworth; *Architectural Design* 68, no. 7/8 (1998).

45   Key examples include Margaret Crawford, John Kaliski, and John Chase, eds, 1999. *Everyday Urbanism* (New York: The Monacelli Press, 2008 [1999]); Klaus Overmeyer, ed., *Urban Pioneers, Temporary Use and Urban Development in Berlin* (Berlin: Jovis, 2007); Michael Shamiyeh, ed., *What People Want: Populism in Architecture and Design* (Basel: Birkhauser, 2005); Jeremy Till, *Architecture Depends* (Cambridge, MA: The MIT Press, 2009); Isabelle Doucet and Kenny Cupers, eds, 'Agency in Architecture: Reframing

Criticality in Theory and Practice', *Footprint Journal* 4 (Spring 2009); Nishat Awan, Tatjana Schneider, and Jeremy Till, *Spatial Agency: Other Ways of Doing Architecture* (London: Routledge, 2011).

46 Bryan Bell, ed., *Good Deeds, Good Design: Community Service through Architecture* (New York: Princeton Architectural Press, 2004).

47 Jonathan Hill, *Occupying Architecture – Between the Architect and the User* (London: Routledge, 1998); Iain Borden, Joe Kerr, Jane Rendell, eds, *The Unknown City: Contesting Architecture and Social Space* (Cambridge, MA: The MIT Press, 2000); Jane Rendell, Barbara Penner, Iain Borden, eds, *Gender, Space, Architecture: An Interdisciplinary Introduction* (London and New York: Routledge, 2000); Jane Rendell, Jonathan Hill, Murray Fraser, Mark Dorrian, eds, *Critical Architecture* (Abingdon: Routledge, 2007).

48 Halina Dunin-Woyseth and Fredrik Nilsson, 'Building (Trans)Disciplinary Architectural Research – Introducing Mode 1 and Mode 2 to Design Practitioners', in *Transdisciplinary Knowledge Production in Architecture and Urbanism: Towards Hybrid Modes of Inquiry*, ed. Isabelle Doucet and Nel Janssens (Berlin: Springer, 2011), 79–96.

49 Murray Fraser, 'Introduction', in *Design Research in Architecture: An Overview*, ed. Murray Fraser (Farnham: Ashgate, 2013), 1–14, 1–2.

50 Bruno Latour and Albena Yaneva 'Give me a Gun and I Will Make All Buildings Move: An ANT's View of Architecture', in *Explorations in Architecture: Teaching, Design, Research*, ed. Reto Geiser (Basel, Boston, Berlin: Birkhauser, 2009), 80–89.

51 Stewart Brand, *How Buildings Learn: What Happens After They're Built* (New York: Viking 1994); Thomas F. Gieryn,'What Buildings Do', *Theory and Society* 31, no. 1 (2002): 35–74; Michael Guggenheim, 'From Prototyping to Allotyping. The Invention of Change of Use and the Crisis of Building Types', *Journal of Cultural Economy* 7, no. 4 (2014): 411–433; Sophie Houdart and Chihiro Minato, Kuma Kengo, *Une monographie décalée* (Paris: Les Éditions donner lieu, 2009); Albena Yaneva, *The Making of a Building: Mapping Controversies in Architecture* (Farnham: Ashgate, 2012); Albena Yaneva, *Made by the Office for Metropolitan Architecture: An Ethnography of Design* (Rotterdam: 010 Publishers, 2009); Jane Jacobs and Stephen Cairns, *Buildings Must Die: A Perverse View of Architecture* (Cambridge, MA: The MIT Press); Jane Jacobs, Stephen Cairns and Ignaz Strebel, 'A Tall Storey … but a Fact Just the Same: The Red Road High-rise as a Black Box', *Urban Studies* 44, no. 3 (2007): 609–629; Victor Buchli, *An Anthropology of Architecture* (London and New York: Bloomsbury, 2013); Steven A. Moore and Barbara B. Wilson, *Questioning Architectural Judgment: The Problem of Codes in the United States* (London: Routledge, 2014); Bruno Latour, 'A Cautious Prometheus. A Few Steps Toward a Philosophy of Design (with Special Attention to Peter Sloterdijk)'. Keynote Lecture for the *Networks of Design* meeting, Cornwall, September 3, 2008.

52 The use of pragmatism is particularly marked in urban studies following Nigel Thrift's 'An Urban Impasse?', *Theory, Culture & Society* 10 (1993): 229–238; Ignacio Farias and Thomas Bender, eds, *Urban Assemblages: How Actor-Network Theory Changes Urban Studies* (Abingdon: Routledge, 2011); Colin McFarlane, *Learning the City: Knowledge and Translocal Assemblage* (Chichester: Wiley-Blackwell, 2011); Stephen Graham and Simon Marvin, *Splintering Urbanism: Networked Infrastructures, Technological Mobilities and the Urban Condition* (London: Routledge, 2001); and Benedikte Zitouni, *Agglomérer: Une anatomie de l'extension bruxelloise (1828–1915)* (Brussels: VUB Press, 2010). In cultural studies see Scott Lash and Celia Lurry, *Global Culture Industries* (London: Polity Press, 2007). In philosophy, see Diana Coole and Samantha Frost, eds, *New Materialisms: Ontology, Agency, and Politics* (Durham, NC and London: Duke University Press, 2010); and Jane Bennett, *A Political Ecology of Things* (Durham, NC and London: Duke University Press, 2010).

53 It is telling that *The Sage Handbook of Architectural Theory*, eds, C. Greig Crysler, Hilde Heynen, Stephen Cairns (London: Sage, 2012) includes a section related to STS.

54 Bruno Latour, *Re-assembling the Social: An Introduction to Actor-Network-Theory* (Oxford: Oxford University Press, 2005).

55 Ibid., 71.

56 Ibid., 73.

57 A good overview of this debate can be found in Hilde Heynen, 'Space as Receptor, Instrument or Stage: Notes on the Interaction between Spatial and Social Constellations', *International Planning Studies* 18, nos. 3–4 (2013): 342–357.

58 In terms of designing for crime prevention, Oscar Newman's *Defensible Space, Crime Prevention Through Urban Design* (London: Macmillan, 1973) is particularly influential.

59 Heynen, 'Space as Receptor, Instrument or Stage'; Crawford et al., *Everyday Urbanism*.

60 According to the 'Principle of Irreducibility', nothing is *in itself* reducible or irreducible to anything else. Bruno Latour, *The Pasteurization of France*, trans. John Law and Alan Sheridan (Cambridge, MA: Harvard University Press, 1988 [1984]), 151–236, 159.

61 Latour, *Re-assembling the Social*, 71.

62 The social world is an 'entanglement of interactions' existing out of 'many entanglements of humans and non-humans' (Latour, *Re-assembling the Social*, 65; 84). Instead of constructivism and positivism's respective abandonment of or obsession with truth claims, Latour suggests an engagement with hybrid worlds ('realistic realism'); Bruno Latour, *Pandora's Hope: Essays on the Reality of Science Studies* (Cambridge, MA and London: Harvard University Press, 1999), 1–23.

63 For 'quasi-object' see Michel Serres, 'Theory of the Quasi-object', in *The Parasite* (Baltimore, MD: The Johns Hopkins University Press, 1982); and Bruno Latour, *We Have Never Been Modern* (Cambridge, MA: Harvard University Press, 1993). For 'fluid object', see John Law and Annemarie Mol, 'Regions, Networks and Fluids: Anaemia and Social Topology', *Social Studies of Science* 24 (1994): 641–671; and 'Boundary Variations', *Environment and Planning D: Society and Space* 23 (2005): 637–642; Annemarie Mol and Marianne De Laet, 'The Zimbabwe Bush Pump: Mechanics of a Fluid Technology', *Social Studies of Science* 30, no. 2 (2000): 225–263; For assemblage, see Bruno Latour, *Re-assembling the Social*; Manuel DeLanda, *A New Philosophy of Society: Assemblage Theory And Social Complexity* (London and New York: Continuum 2006). On 'imbroglio', see The Loyalties of Knowledge research project involving amongst others Serge Gutwirth, Isabelle Stengers, and Bruno Latour, dedicated to the study of imbroglios of knowledge, institutions, actants and things (www.imbroglio.be).

64 Bruno Latour, 'Is There a Non-Modern Style?', *Domus* 866 (2004).

65 Latour and Yaneva, 'Give me a Gun and I Will Make All Buildings Move'.

66 Ibid., 88.

67 Yaneva, *Mapping Controversies in Architecture*.

68 Central Pavilion, Venice Architecture Biennale, *Fundamentals*, June 7–November 23, 2014.

69 This was part of the caption of the façade element included as 1:1 scale in the Technologies of the Envelope section curated by Zaera-Polo; for a building in Eschborn, Germany (2010), designed by KSP Juergen Engel Architekten, Manufacturer Permasteelisa Group. Also worth mentioning is the 'balcony' section at the Elements

show. Co-curated by Tom Avermaete, it revisits architectural history through the balcony as a socio-political assemblage.

70   Isabelle Stengers, 'Réinventer la ville, le choix de la complexité', lecture at the *Urbanités, rencontres pour réinventer la ville* colloquium, Département de la Seine Saint-Denis, Fondation 93, part of citésplanète, and in collaboration with ASTS, 2000. Accessed February 6, 2010, http://www.urbain-trop-urbain.fr/wp-content/uploads/2011/04/Isabelle-Stengers_R%C3%A9inventer-la-ville_Le-choix-de-la-complexit%C3%A9.pdf; and see Isabelle Doucet, 'Learning from Brussels. An irreductive approach to architectural and urban problématiques?', *Belgeo* 1–2 (2011): 29–39.

71   Stengers, 'Réinventer la ville'.

72   Ibid. The complex city is a city that *learns*: 'la ville qui apprend'.

73   Bruno Latour and Émile Hermant, *Paris Ville Invisible* (Paris: Institut Synthelabo, 1998).

74   Latour and Yaneva, 'Give me a Gun and I Will Make All Buildings Move', 86.

75   I have shown how *words* make-city, not just through their meaning but as full-blown actors. See Isabelle Doucet, 'Making a City with Words. Understanding Brussels through its Urban Heroes and Villains', *City, Culture, and Society* 3, no. 2 (2012): 105–116. This is further explored in Chapter 6 in this book.

76   This debate was famously triggered by Langdon Winner's 'On Opening the Black Box and Finding it Empty. Social Constructivism and the Philosophy of Technology', *Science, Technology and Human Values* 18, no. 3 (1993): 362–378. see also Wiebe Bijker, 'The Need for Critical Intellectuals: A Space for STS', *History and Technology* 19, no. 1 (2003): 78–82. Discussions on politics and the reinsertion of activism in STS can be found in *Social Studies of Science*, such as Bruno Latour's response to Gerard de Vries's article 'What is Political in Sub-politics? How Aristotle might help STS', *Social Studies of Science* 37, no. 5 (2007): 781–809.

77   The term 'transdiscipline' is taken from Jane Rendell, 'Architectural Research and Disciplinarity', *Architecture Research Quarterly* 8, no. 2 (2004): 141–147; and see Isabelle Doucet and Nel Janssens, eds, *Transdisciplinary Knowledge Production in Architecture and Urbanism: Towards Hybrid Modes of Inquiry* (Dordrecht, Heidelberg, London, New York: Springer, 2011).

78   For example, by providing detailed accounts of how architecture works, researchers may, unwittingly, offer designers the knowledge needed for creating ever more resilient designs and thereby offering more effective mechanisms for control.

79   Isabelle Stengers, 'Introductory Notes on an Ecology of Practices', *Cultural Studies Review* 11, no. 1 (2005): 193. Stengers refers to the 'mattering' in Deleuze: 'an idea always exists as engaged in a matter, that is as "mattering"'.

80   Isabelle Stengers, 'Experimenting with Refrains: Subjectivity and the Challenge of Escaping Modern Dualism', *Subjectivity* 22 (2008): 38–59, 44.

81   Luc Boltanski, *On Critique: A Sociology of Emancipation* (Cambridge and Malden: Polity Press, 2011), 13–15.

82   In contrast to Bruno Latour, Haraway claims to be 'more willing to live with indigestible intellectual and political heritages' (such as critical theory), see Nicholas Gane, 'When We Have Never Been Human, What is to Be Done? Interview with Donna Haraway', *Theory, Culture & Society* 23, nos. 7–8 (2006): 139. Also Rosi Braidotti's 'nomadic activism', is an embodied-political practice; a 'productive form of activism' based on an active working through negative emotions, pain and sufferings (*Transpositions: On Nomadic Ethics* [Cambridge and Malden: Polity, 2006], 88).

83   Donna Haraway, 'Situated Knowledges: The Science Question in Feminism and the Privilege of Partial Perspective', in *Simians, Cyborgs and Women: The Reinvention of Nature* (New York: Routledge, 1991), 188.

84   Boltanski, *On Critique*, 22.

85   Isabelle Stengers, 'Comparison as a Matter of Concern', *Common Knowledge* 17, no. 1 (2011): 48–63, 61. Stengers draws on the American pragmatist thinker William James who contrasts the 'pluriverse in the making' to a 'made' world; 'made' as either universe (celebrating readymade oneness) or multiverse (disconnected, mutually indifferent parts).

86   The distinction between critique and criticality follows that of the visual culture theorist Irit Rogoff, 'What is a Theorist?' [In German.] In *Was ist ein Künstler*, ed. Katharyna Sykora (Berlin: Wilhelm Fink Verlag, 2003). The translation by Rogoff is available online. Accessed April 1, 2011, http://www.kein.org/node/62.

87   Irit Rogoff, '"Smuggling" – An Embodied Criticality'. European Institute for Progressive Cultural Policies (2006), 1. Accessed April 1, 2011, http://eipcp.net/dlfiles/rogoff-smuggling.

88   Haraway, 'Situated Knowledges', 196, my italics. Haraway calls embodied, partial perspectives, 'subjugated viewpoints' (190).

89   Isabelle Stengers, 'William James: An Ethics of Thought?', *Radical Philosophy*, 157 (September/October 2009): 9–19.

90   Isabelle Stengers, 'The Cosmopolitical Proposal', in *Making Things Public – Atmospheres of Democracy*, ed. Bruno Latour and Peter Weibel (Cambridge, MA: ZKM and The MIT Press, 2005), 994–1003, 996.

91   Stengers, 'Comparison as a Matter of Concern', 61–62.

92   Stengers, 'Introductory Notes on an Ecology of Practices', 185.

93   Isabelle Stengers, '"Another science is possible!" A plea for slow science', Inaugural lecture Chair Willy Callewaert 2011–2012 (VUB), December 13, 2011, 1. Thinking through allows one to spend time on 'questions that do not directly contribute to the immediate and evaluable progress of their field' (4–5).

94   Stengers, 'The Cosmopolitical Proposal', 994.

95   Stengers, 'William James: an Ethics of Thought?'; and see Isabelle Stengers, 'Including Nonhumans in Political Theory', *Political Matter: Technoscience, Democracy, and Public Life*, ed. Bruce Braun and Sarah J. Whatmore (Minneapolis, MN: University of Minnesota Press, 2010), 3–34, 26.

96   Reinhold Martin, 'Critical of What? Towards a Utopian Realism', *Harvard Design Magazine* 22 (Spring–Summer 2005): 104–109; in Sykes, *Constructing a New Agenda*, 360.

97   Donna Haraway, 'Cyborgs, Coyotes, and Dogs: A Kinship of Feminist Figurations and there are Always More Things Going on Than You Thought! Methodologies as Thinking Technologies, an Interview with Donna Haraway in two parts conducted by Nina Lykke, Randi Markussen, and Finn Olesen', in *The Haraway Reader*, ed. Donna Haraway (London and New York: Routledge, 2004), 321–342, 326.

98   Joan Tronto and Berenice Fisher, in Joan C. Tronto, *Moral Boundaries: A Political Argument for an Ethic of Care* (London: Routledge: 1993), 103. Cited from Maria Puig de la Bellacasa, '"Nothing Comes Without its World": Thinking with Care', *The Sociological Review* 60, no. 2 (2012): 198.

99 Maria Puig de la Bellacasa, '"Nothing comes without its world"', 206–207. Rosi Braidotti, in reference to Donna Haraway's 'modest witness', argued that only through empathy and affinity can one move from a negative to a positive criticism; Rosi Braidotti, 'Posthuman, All too Human: Towards a New Process Ontology', *Theory, Culture & Society* 23, nos. 7–8 (2006): 197–208, 206.

100 Care is an 'ontological requirement of relational worlds' (Puig de la Bellacasa, '"Nothing comes without its world"', 199–200) and see Rosi Braidotti's notion of the 'nomadic subject' as part of a 'dynamic web of potentialities and intensities in constant move and transformation' ('Nomadism with a Difference: Deleuze's Legacy in a Feminist Perspective', *Man and World* 29 [1996]: 305–314, 307; and see Braidotti, 'Posthuman, All too Human', 206).

101 Isabelle Stengers, 'Reclaiming Animism', *E-flux journal* 36 (July 2012): 6; and 'Experimenting with Refrains', 58, in reference to Starhawk, *Dreaming the Dark: Magic, Sex & Politics* (Boston: Beacon Press, 1982), 219. Braidotti's 'forget to forget' needs to be addressed as one tends to forget inequality, for example, when one is in a privileged location (*Transpositions*, 141).

102 Stengers, 'The Cosmopolitical Proposal', 994.

103 This relates to Braidotti's nomadic subject that 'combines qualitative shifts with a firm rejection of liberal individualism [...] a collectively-oriented externally bound, multiple subject whose singularity is the result of constant re-negotiations with a variety of forces.' Rosi Braidotti, *Metamorphoses: Towards a Materialist Theory of Becoming* (Cambridge: Polity Press, 2002), 260.

104 Stengers, 'Introductory Notes on an Ecology of Practices', 188.

105 Donna Haraway, *Modest_Witness@Second_Millenium.FemaleMan©_Meets_OncoMouse*™ (New York and London: Routledge 1997), 23. Haraway borrows the term 'modest witness' from Steven Shapin and Simon Schaffer, *Leviathan and the Air-Pump: Hobbes, Boyle, and the Experimental Life* (Princeton, NJ: Princeton University Press, 1985). Further discussion of 'modest witness' can be found in Braidotti, 'Posthuman, All too Human', 206–207.

106 I follow Haraway's suggestion to study an object of knowledge as an agent, not a resource or ground, see 'Situated Knowledges', 198.

107 Stengers notes that one should 'learn to wonder about what we take for granted', in 'A Constructivist Reading of *Process and Reality*', *Theory, Culture & Society* 25 no. 4 (2008): 91–110, 101.

108 Haraway contrasts this with characterisations of utopian dreams, 'When We Have Never Been Human, What is to Be Done?', 137. Stengers' conceptualises utopia in a non-transcendental way in Isabelle Stengers, 'A "Cosmo-Politics" – Risk, Hope, Change. A conversation with Isabelle Stengers', in Marie Zournazie, *Hope: New Philosophies for Change* (Annandale: Pluto Press, 2002), 244–272, 245.

109 A partial view comes with regrettable but unavoidable exclusions. For example, I do not discuss the European presence in Brussels, a case so specific and complex better left to specialised scholarship (see note 21). Instead, I discuss numerous material practices, but comparably little actual buildings. Discussions of practices such as OMA/Rem Koolhaas's exhibition in a circus tent on the history of Europe and the European Union; the Berlage Institute's research on Brussels (*A Vision for Brussels*); and architectural experiments such as Vacant City, Disturb, and Studio Open City either fall outside the scope of this book or are addressed elsewhere. See Doucet, 'Learning from Brussels'; Isabelle Doucet, 'A Vision for Brussels: Fuel to the Urban Debate or, at Last, an End to the Brussels Trauma?', *Footprint Journal* 1 (Autumn 2007): 97–105.

110 Reinhold Martin, *Utopia's Ghost: Architecture and Postmodernism, Again* (Minneapolis, MN: University of Minnesota Press, 2010), xxi. Martin revisits a series of concepts that were reworked under architectural postmodernism such as territory, history, language, image, materiality, subjects, and architecture.

111 Thomas Bender, 'Postscript', *Urban Assemblages*, 315.

2

Counter-projects

> *The photographer captured something, but the moment right before and right after it was entirely different. That is of course the case with each photograph, but not with each city.*[1]

Brussels is a traumatised city. The two main historical settings for its trauma are the 19th century 'hygienist' urban restructurings *à la* Haussmann, and the modernisation fever throughout the golden decades of the post-war period, both of which resulted in vast parts of the inner city being demolished and its inhabitants expelled.[2] Notable projects of the first period include Joseph Poelaert's Palace of Justice, a building of baffling proportions, and the culverting of the river Zenne that allowed for the creation of grand Parisian-style boulevards in its place.[3] The second period witnessed the construction of the underground North–South railway junction which, although completed in 1952, had commenced before the First World War. Cutting through Brussels historic centre, it left in its wake an enormous above-ground scar. Another emblematic project of this period was the disclosure of Brussels, in the form of a ring road across tunnels, urban highways and flyovers, and multi-storey car parks, for the World Expo in 1958. Further, in 1965 and despite international protests, Victor Horta's Art Nouveau masterpiece, the Maison du Peuple, was demolished and replaced with a modern office tower; and just two years later, the Manhattan Plan, an American-style Central Business District received planning approval. For its creation, a large residential area underwent expropriation and demolition.[4] The project was emblematic of Brussels' aspiration to become an international business city in keeping with its growing international function. Uncompleted, however, the Manhattan Plan left behind a vast urban no-man's-land and became a symbol of failed modernisation for Brussels' citizens in the battle for their city. This battle was also fought in the historic inner-city neighbourhoods. With the help of slum clearance legislation – in particular the 1953 *Wet inzake Krotopruiming* – reputedly insalubrious areas underwent radical sanitation; in practice, rather than replace those 'insanitary' dwellings with improved housing, this initiative also encouraged widespread economic speculation and the erection of private office developments.[5] Where replacement housing was provided, often modern high-rise blocks, these significantly disrupted the historic urban morphology. In the opening quote to this chapter, Eric De Cuyper aptly depicts the sense that Brussels underwent dramatic transformations perhaps more so than other cities.

By the late-1960s, the destruction of Brussels' historic core was of such a magnitude that a reaction from the citizens was inevitable. Locally, two events of 1969 proved to be the tipping point for turning discontent into revolt: the first was the planned extension of the Palace of Justice, which required the demolition of parts of the popular La Marolle (part of the Les Marolles neighbourhood); the second was the proposed ITT building, an office tower for the International Telephone and Telegraph Company, which was to become part of a wider plan to turn the affluent Avenue Louise into an office district.[6] Whilst the objections to the Palace of Justice extension – known as the Battle of the Marolle (*bataille de la Marolle/slag om de Marol*) – symbolised the working-class struggles for their Right to the City, the resistance to the ITT project showed that the middle-classes had become part of the *luttes urbaines* [urban struggles] too. In his article 'La Longue Marche', architect and historian Maurice Culot emphasised the importance of this combined trigger; the middle-class involvement in the ITT revolts, and the press attention it received, ensured that the struggles in La Marolle could not be dismissed.[7] Internationally, the term *Bruxellisation* was used to depict the destruction of a city by profit-driven developers and architects.

Beyond such struggles, discontent with the functionalist idiom had also entered the wider architectural debate. Robert L. Delevoy, director of the French-speaking architecture school at the École Nationale Supérieure d'Architecture et des Arts Visuels de la Cambre (hereafter La Cambre), encouraged a more socially engaged, urban architecture. Delevoy had been appointed as director in 1965 and, in his opening speech of the academic year 1965–1966, called for a better social and historical embedding of art and architecture.[8] Instead of individual creators making art works for the privileged few, he encouraged collective endeavours.[9] Delevoy was joined by others in his call for a more humane and democratic city; critiques varied from Archigram's techno-utopian experiments which stressed the relationship between city and its inhabitants, to Aldo Rossi's articulation of the collective memory of cities as embedded in urban archetypes.[10]

The year 1968 proved to be pivotal: in May, students at La Cambre called for less hierarchical relationships between students and teachers, for the social engagement of the architect, and for re-politicising architecture; whilst between June and September, graduates organised the *Etats généraux de l'architecture et de l'urbanisme* symposium whereby they too pleaded for involving architects, students *and* the population to be present in the discussion of architecture.[11] These actions resonated with Delevoy's earlier speech, and were merely the start of rivalries to come within the school; notably, between the socio-politically engaged teachers with whom the politicised students allied, and those teachers defending a focus on construction.[12] 1968 also witnessed the creation of the Atelier de Recherche et d'Action Urbaines (ARAU) and, in its wake, an explosion of citizen action committees. According to Culot, this explosion was informed by the continuous destruction of the urban fabric, political changes that made certain parties more receptive to urban movements, and regionalisation processes.[13] No less than one hundred action committees were created in Brussels between 1970 and 1975.

Brussels' activism in the 1970s, in many ways, resonated with the outbreak of urban revolts internationally. In other respects, however, it was unique. This uniqueness was largely due to the development of counter-projects, organised through collaborations between urban activists (the ARAU), architects connected to the Archives d'Architecture Moderne (the AAM), and architecture students (La Cambre). From these collaborations emerged a criticism that combined real-world activism (the ARAU) with a broader theoretical reflection (La Cambre/the AAM). Counter-projects were produced for specific sites to act as a critique of existing proposals by architects, authorities, and developers. Although not intended to be built, they were, nonetheless, realistic projects and, expressed through architectural drawings, were intended to support action committees in their debates and press conferences.

Counter-projects played an important role in the 1970s urban struggles and architectural critique, both in Brussels and beyond. Apart from supporting local actions, counter-projects assisted in the consolidation of an international architectural movement which favoured the reconstruction of the European city.[14] Given their importance for architectural postmodernism, it is somewhat remarkable that counter-projects have received little scholarly attention; this may be due to an association with the traditionalist branch of postmodernism, which has been accused of being reactionary in its use of historical forms stripped of social or political concerns.[15] Brussels' counter-projects are, however, essential in understanding theories concerned with the reconstruction of the city, such as those promoted by Maurice Culot and Léon Krier amongst others. As K. Michael Hays confirms:

> *Even if the theory of Culot and Krier should be understood as a general proposition, the particular situation of Brussels is the best context for an understanding of their position [...] a uniformly bureaucratic and scaleless environment that begged for 'counterprojects', even if only as critiques or only as a heuristic.*[16]

The Brussels counter-projects deserve to be re-inserted into the debates on postmodern traditionalism. They are, in my view, instructive methodological–critical devices which combine disciplinary critique with real-world activism; and the critiquing of an existing situation through alternative proposals. Moreover, they operate through the architectural drawing, rather than through theory. Therefore, counter-projects can be considered a drawing-manifesto which offers the means to study the co-existence of elements often treated in separation: politics and aesthetics, critique and actions, theory and practice.

This chapter gives voice to this fascinating critical–architectural tool that, thus far, has largely been 'spoken' of in a fragmented manner.[17] For example, the anthology *Contreprojets – Controprogetti – Counterprojects*, despite its historical importance, is a selective account.[18] Published as an exhibition catalogue for the

Belgian contribution to the 1980 Venice Architecture Biennial, curated by Paolo Porthoghesi on the theme The Presence of the Past, it offers an account that is not fully representative of the richness and diversity of counter-projects produced in Brussels. Similarly, the press coverage of counter-projects is vast but fragmented, and only occasionally available in English. Through key publications and press coverage of the movement including special issues in architectural magazines, anthologies and other documents published by the movement, the *Bulletin des AAM*, and other selected press, this chapter will revisit the critical discourse of the reconstruction of the city through counter-projects as they emerged in Brussels during the late 1960s and the 1970s.[19]

This chapter focuses on how the Reconstruction of the European City discourse is activated and practised through counter-projects; and shows how counter-projects can be considered to be acting as many things at the same time. They acted as political provocations, but also as concrete alternative projects for the city; and as instruments for radical architectural discourse and test-grounds for formal-aesthetic developments.[20] I will begin by discussing counter-projects as part of the political actions of the ARAU, its merits as an architectural critique, and method of radical architectural education. I will elaborate on how counter-projects operated as drawing-manifestoes (whereby drawings served as resistant practices), and focus upon the search for an appropriate 'style' to reflect their political–ideological ambitions. Although the Reconstruction movement is predominantly associated with Léon Krier and the rationalists, this applies largely to a 'second generation' of counter-projects, which emerged after 1975. My encounter with the 'first generation' counter-projects, 1971–1975, revealed a gradual aesthetic maturation of counter-projects throughout the 1970s. Thus, the 'second generation' of counter-projects came to fruition because of a much longer stylistic search. The analysis will also allow an understanding to emerge of just how this aesthetic maturation did not (yet) announce the de-politicisation with which the Reconstruction movement is widely associated, but was, nevertheless, still part of an important radicalisation.

URBAN STRUGGLES AND THE RIGHT TO THE CITY

> *To the ARAU the city is the instrument to be cherished to strengthen the powerless.*
>
> *The struggle for power = the struggle for the city.*[21]

The activism of 1970s Brussels was instigated by the Atelier de Recherche et d'Action Urbaines (ARAU) and local action committees so great in number that it required the creation of coordinative bodies. In 1969, against the backdrop of the Battle of the Marolle, the ARAU was founded by the sociologist René Schoonbrodt, architect Maurice Culot, and Jacques Van der Biest, a theologian who was at the same time Pastor in Les Marolles. The ARAU was critical of the functionalist city and the damage it had caused to the urban fabric and its population. While sharing this criticism with its activist contemporaries, the French-speaking

Inter-Environnement Bruxelles (IEB) and the Dutch-speaking *Brusselse Raad voor het Leefmilieu* (BRAL) – important coordinative bodies for citizen actions as part of a wider environmental agenda – the ARAU adopted an urban politics that, influenced by Henri Lefebvre's *Le Droit à la Ville* (1968) and Manuel Castells's *Luttes urbaines et pouvoir politique* (1975), was explicitly preoccupied with socio-economic issues more than, for example, cultural heritage.[22] Close to the working-class and immigrant population, the ARAU was concerned with the consequences of Brussels' transformation into a service industry for the employment of the labour working classes.[23] As such, its origins lay as much in the urban activism of the popular Marolles neighbourhood as in the broader actions of unionists, leftists, militants and architects. Its urban–political activism informed bold political statements such as the suggestion that the 19 municipalities of Brussels, accused of developing destructive urban plans, and of ignoring the unpopular electorate of working classes and immigrants, be abolished and replaced with more inclusive and democratic neighbourhood councils.[24] In urban planning terms, the ARAU targeted the Brussels' urbanism of the *fait accompli*, referring to plans being discussed in secret and behind closed doors. It fought for a more democratic decision-making process based on citizen participation.[25] In support of such ambitions, the ARAU combined strategic political negotiations with timely actions around specific problems or sites. In that sense, the ARAU adopted a critical position even within Marxist–leftist circles. Schoonbrodt was, for example, critical of the unions for not being actively involved in the urban struggles, and of Marxism's failure to develop an alternative project for the city.[26] Counter-projects can, in part, be seen in response to such criticism.

The ARAU's strategic work was carried out in the context of Belgium's processes of regionalisation, a process whereby five Agglomerations had been created in 1971, including the Agglomération de Bruxelles. The 'Agglo', as it became known, carried important responsibilities for planning, including the preparation of a *Plan Secteur*; a plan for developing the Brussels' agglomeration. Finding support within the Agglo, the ARAU was in a position to negotiate a *Plan Secteur* that challenged the destruction of the city and enforced more advanced participatory procedures.[27] The final version of the *Plan Secteur*, produced in 1979, was considered so great a victory for the Brussels' activists that it marked a 'turn' in Brussels' urbanism.[28] Firstly, it moved away from functional zoning, and towards a mixed-use, liveable city. Secondly, its procedures for citizen participation had significantly improved. Public consultation was required for any alterations to the agreed plan, and public communication was optimised through on-site posters. Importantly, citizens were given the opportunity to comment on proposals during organised consultation committees.[29]

In addition to strategic negotiations around the *Plan Secteur*, the ARAU is known for its day-to-day urban activism through press conferences, petitions, manifestations, festivities, posters, and counter-projects. Because the urban struggle involved different layers of the population, not all of whom were easily mobilised (working class *and* middle class; permanent residents *and* 'nomads'), actions were diversified. It had become apparent that, despite the fact that all classes were suffering from the destruction of their environment, not all were thought to be equally *victims*.[30] In more affluent areas, where socio-economic problems were less pressing, actions often centred on wider cultural concerns related to public space and cultural heritage. By contrast, in socio-economically vulnerable neighbourhoods, the ARAU adopted a role more akin to a social worker, and developed tools for permanent cultural education such as the École Urbaine and the Boutique Urbaine.[31]

COUNTER-PROJECTS AS POLITICAL *PROVOCATEURS*

Counter-projects were part of the ARAU's actions in relation to the development of specific sites, and were, for example, often used in press conferences. They acted as *provocateurs*; they provoked debate and supported negotiations.[32] Counter-projects challenged the illusion created by developers and authorities that the proposed solution was unavoidable by showing that alternative solutions for a given site were possible. In some cases, these alternative solutions remained vague and schematic, but could, nevertheless, be used in discussions and press conferences organised by the ARAU. Such efforts encouraged the public authorities to reconsider existing proposals for a site, and organise an architectural competition.[33] In other circumstances, formulated alternatives were more precise, investigative, and spatially articulate, and proposed a concrete project for a site. The provocative nature of counter-projects is confirmed by the fact that the ARAU would acknowledge projects it disagreed with, as long as they served as a decent basis for discussion.[34] That the ARAU's activism could be equally political and spatially articulate is demonstrated by the actions around the Museum of Modern Art in Brussels (Musée d'Art Moderne). These actions emerged in response to the 1973 design proposals by the architect Roger Bastin. Bastin's project consisted of an underground museum and a visual landmark in the form of a closed, solid building, which was criticised for being alien to Brussels' everyday life and mocked as a 'concrete bunker'.[35] The ARAU's criticism was, however, not just against the creation of a landmark object, but formed part of a wider critique of the functionalist city and undemocratic decision-making. The ARAU was critical of the creation of a mono-functional cultural island of museums from which all other functions, such as housing and commerce, were removed. The liveable, functionally mixed city defended by the ARAU, was informed by the Right to the City, but it required a fitting urban design. The ARAU's political activism thus coincided with a spatial argumentation in favour of qualitative public space, the recovery of housing, and the repairing of the urban morphology of the site. The importance of this spatial component was manifest in the ARAU's criticism of Bastin's project for not spatially enclosing the Place du Musée where the project was located.[36] The ARAU also argued that Bastin's drawing depicting the integration of the statue of Charles de Lorraine, was deceptive. Pictured out of proportion and from an unusual angle, it was believed to show how the project was conceived from the viewpoint of the car, not the pedestrian.[37] This capacity to offer precise and spatially articulate criticism assisted the ARAU in impressing the authorities. For example, in response to counter-projects developed by fourth year students of La Cambre in 1973–1974 for the wider surrounding area, the City of Brussels developed a special urban development plan or *Plan particulier d'aménagement*.[38] These, and other counter-projects, distinguished the ARAU from other action groups of the time such as advocacy planners, anti-schemes, and the *architecture urbaine* in France, in that, in addition to combining analysis with the proposal of 'seductive' alternatives, the precise and spatially articulate nature of its analyses underlined its authority.[39] This was made possible thanks to its collaboration with architects.

ARCHITECTURAL PROVOCATIONS AT THE INTERSECTIONS OF ACTIVISM, HISTORY, AND EDUCATION

Counter-projects were developed through collaborative actions involving members of the ARAU, architects connected to the AAM, and architecture students at La Cambre. The AAM, co-founded in 1968, amongst others by Culot and Delevoy, were committed to historical research and to the preservation of private archives of architects. In addition, their editorial work – the *Bulletin des AAM* (published between 1975 and 1990) and various book publications – offered a platform for both local and international debate.

La Cambre was a State-led institution for higher education, under the Ministry of French Culture. Apart from architecture, it contained four other schools, specialised in visual arts, cinema and animation, urbanism, and industrial design. Informed by the intellectual impetus of Culot, the support of La Cambre director Delevoy, and the exchanges with the ARAU, a group of students and teachers formed throughout the 1970s dedicating their work to the *luttes urbaines*. The school's production of counter-projects was demonstrative of the recognition of political reflection as part of architectural education.[40] Under Delevoy, as stated in a 1976 advertisement for the school, La Cambre was imagined as 'a school at the service of society'.[41] It aimed to train professionals whilst, at the same time, encouraging its students to question the capitalist basis of their chosen profession. Whereas the AAM and La Cambre assisted the ARAU in refining its spatial analyses and propositions, the ARAU, in turn, formed the 'necessary complement' to the disciplinary reflections at La Cambre.[42] It gave students both the militant force for resisting the pressures from the professional milieu, and a reality-check to their intellectual experiments.

This collaboration of education (La Cambre), cultural history (the AAM), and political activism (the ARAU) informed a new architectural criticism that would become known as the Reconstruction of the European City movement (hereafter called the Reconstruction movement). The involvement of La Cambre and the ARAU was important in that it connected, but also distinguished, Culot's application of Marxist critique from Krier's. Compared to Krier, who operated

COUNTERPROJECTS   1980   COUNTERPROJECTS

RECONSTRUCTION OF INHABITED PARTS OF HISTORIC CITY CENTRES

MODERN URBANISM HAS DESTROYED MORE THAN ALL PRECEDING WARS PUT TOGETHER.

Destruction of the historic part of Brussels began at the end of the XIXth century.

Whole blocks were demolished in the centre of the city to allow for the construction of a railway linking the Nord and Midi stations.

Of 150,000 inhabitants in 1900, less than 40,000 remain today.

The ten viable and complex districts which made up the old part of the city were all destroyed, with the exception of a few blocks.

We are convinced that the city is a place of power and that this power should be given to the inhabitants rather than to the multinationals.

We thus propose the reconstruction of residential areas in the centre of Brussels, such as the area located between the station and the Grand'Place, presently occupied by a huge parking lot.

Project by P. Neirinck, G. Busieau and S. Birkiye.

2.1 Counter-projects combining critique with alternative proposal. Proposal for the Carrefour de l'Europe site, Brussels (Sefik Birkiye, Gilbert Busieau, Patrice Neirinck, La Cambre, 1978) as part of the 'Différents Projets pour la Reconstruction et l'Embellissement de la Partie de Bruxelles éventrée par la Jonction des Gares du Nord et du Midi'. Source: Léon Krier and Maurice Culot, *Contreprojets – Controprogetti – Counterprojects*, Brussels: AAM, 1980, no page numbers. Copyright: Archives d'Architecture Moderne. Used with permission.

primarily through theory, draughtsmanship, and drawings, Culot's criticism was more intertwined with urban activism. Culot called this his 'three façades' of cultural history, education, and political action.⁴³ Originating in the rejection of the functionalist city and the technocratic planning of CIAM, the Reconstruction of the European City movement proposed, instead, a return to and recuperation of the traditional city. It criticised the public authorities and developers who had actively contributed to the destruction of the historic city, and it also criticised the architectural profession for having alienated architects from the 'real world' and working but for their peers.

This criticism was popularised by presenting counter-projects as alternatives to destructive planning examples whose dismissal was emphasised by means of a large red cross drawn onto existing, destructive examples (Figure 2.1). Here, Léon Krier's mockery of architects' refusal to live themselves in their creations is brought to mind; in a photographic series published in the *Bulletin des AAM*, titled '*Virtus privées et vices publics*', Krier compared the architects' creation of modern buildings 'for the people' with their own private residences in historical buildings.⁴⁴ Perhaps even more striking is Krier's 1979 cartoon of the architect as 'the exterminating angel'.⁴⁵ Whilst I will not elaborate further on this more humorous aspect of the counter-projects, it is present, albeit implied, in several of the drawings here discussed.⁴⁶

As an alternative to the functionalist city, whose structure is based upon mobility, economic development, and functional zoning, the Reconstruction of the European City movement suggested the traditional city, which was based upon the form of the historic city; here, working and living happened in proximity, and public spaces were considered the main building components of the city rather than the residue of built-up space. Public space, therefore, should no longer be thought of in terms of neutral large-scale surfaces disconnected from the surrounding buildings, but as enclosed spaces following the logic of streets and squares.

An illustration of this difference in functionalist and historic urban configuration is the 1973–1974 counter-project for the offices of the Communauté Économique Européenne (CEE, now the European Community), by fifth-year students of La Cambre. The project countered the high-rise towers proposed by the official Belgian project with a system of urban blocs which were informed by the streets to create a human-scale residential environment (Figure 2.2).⁴⁷ This proposal, based upon the historic city, had the advantage of being familiar and recognisable to all, rather than decipherable only by architects and experts. As Culot had stated: 'in order to mobilize people for a project on the city, this project must be a familiar one, it must promise all the aspects and sympathy of a common world.'⁴⁸

This was an architectural criticism that was no longer located in the revolutionary powers of the architect's built work, but, instead, in the study of history. The revolutionary architect was to identify and select familiar and qualitative historic forms, and to learn to copy these forms as skilfully as possible.⁴⁹ However, because realisations, no matter how critically informed, always depend on alliances with the capitalist system, such revolutionary projects could not take place through the act of building, but through drawings, that is counter-projects.

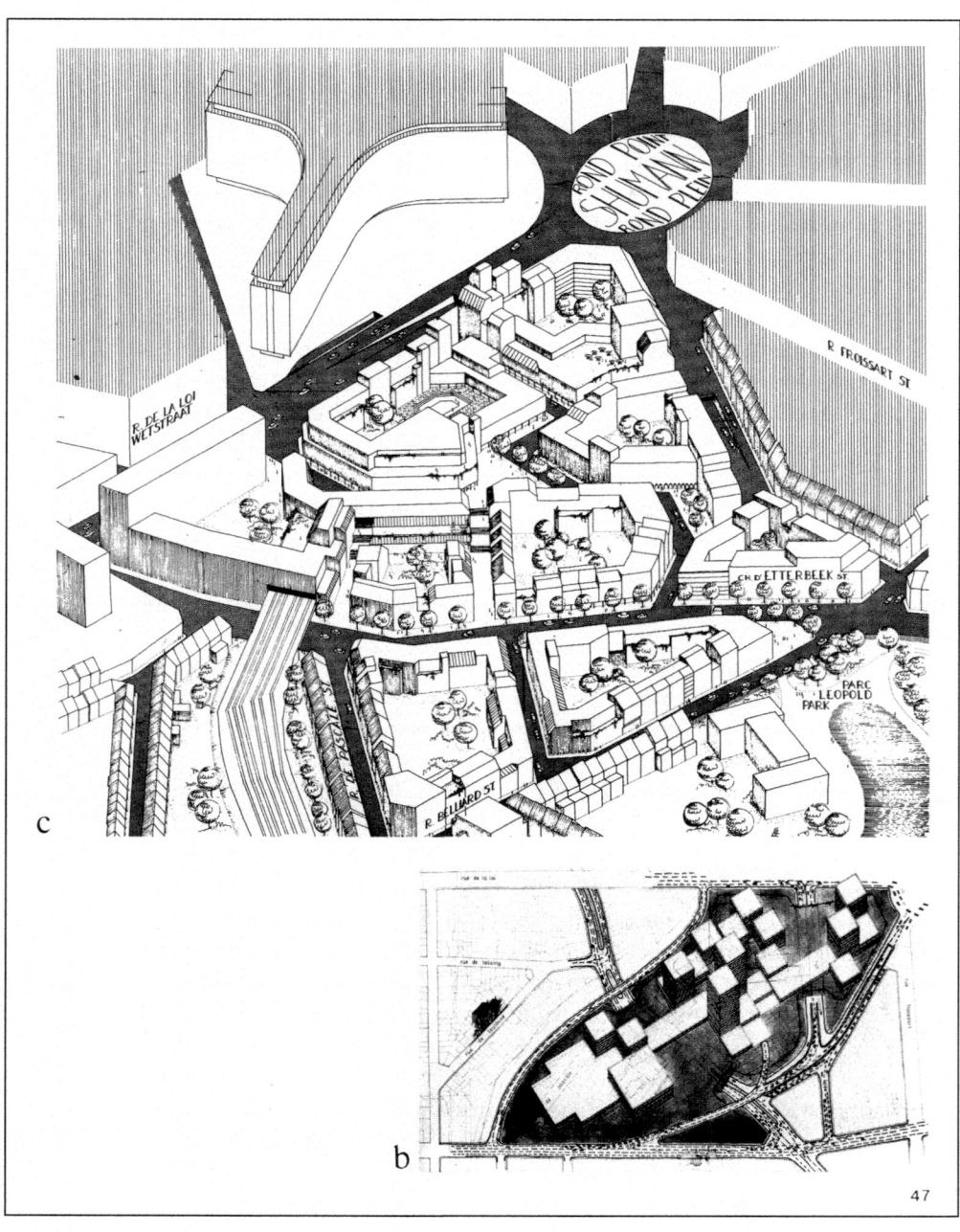

2.2 The counter-project *les extensions des communautés Européennes à Bruxelles* (1973–1974, fifth-year students La Cambre) proposes an urban morphology based on a model of streets and squares, as an alternative to the model of towers in an open landscape as suggested by the original project (bottom page). Source: École nationale supérieure d'architecture et des arts visuels, eds, *Le Bateau d'Élie. Contributions aux luttes urbaines et projets opportunistes, La Cambre 1971–1975* (Brussels: Éditions des AAM, 1975), p. 47. Copyright: Archives d'Architecture Moderne. Used with permission.

For Culot, the task at hand, therefore, was 'less building site, more drawing'.[50] The project, not the building, was 'the only form of resistance'; thus, the counter-projects found political validity in 'the affirmation of its non-realisation'.[51]

This refusal to build can, albeit for different reasons, be found in the ARAU also. In order to safeguard its political credibility, the ARAU refused to realise counter-projects.[52] René Schoonbrodt argued: '[t]here has never been a shortage of offers for realising the ARAU's study-projects. We have *never* taken to it'.[53] This somewhat deflates the 'architectural larceny' that Jencks had in mind for the ARAU if it were to realise its counter-projects.[54]

DRAWING AS RESISTANT PRACTICE

Many, if not all, counter-projects were developed as realistic proposals for actual sites. They were, however, not intended to be built. Rather, they operated as drawing-manifestos blending urban activism with disciplinary critique. But which representational techniques were mobilised in order to make these drawings operate as loci for resistance?

The early counter-projects, developed with students at La Cambre in the early 1970s, appear more explicitly as manifestos than later projects. For example, the *Projet d'aménagement de la vallée du Maelbeek*, a design project for the Maelbeek valley in Brussels developed between 1971 and 1973, tapped into the surreal and absurd as a way to respond to the municipal plans to transform the Rue Gray into a 24-metre-wide express way. By picturing an over-sized naked woman forming a bridge, the project aimed to show citizens that 'the most seductive architectural images do not offer any guarantees as long as the economic and social dimension is missing' (Figure 2.3).[55] Similarly, the *Cinq propositions pour le Square du Bastion* was a series of projects developed in the academic year 1974–1975 by third, fourth, and fifth year students for a residual space around a high-rise construction at *Porte de Namur*, a large traffic junction in central Brussels. Most of these projects were visually suggestive, but slightly surreal. For example, the project called *L'orient est*

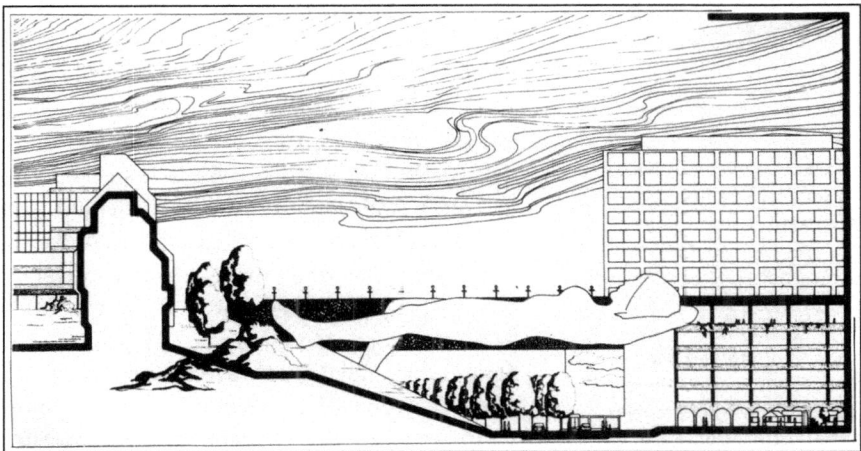

2.3 *Projet d'aménagement de la vallée du Maelbeek* (La Cambre, 1971–1973). In *Wonen TA-BK* (nr. 15–16, 1975, p. 70), the project is credited to Ph. Lefèvre, in the framework of the design by Levy and Mierop. Source: École nationale supérieure d'architecture et des arts visuels. eds, *Le Bateau d'Élie. Contributions aux luttes urbaines et projets opportunistes, La Cambre 1971–1975* (Brussels: Éditions des AAM, 1975), p. 25. Copyright: Archives d'Architecture Moderne. Used with permission.-

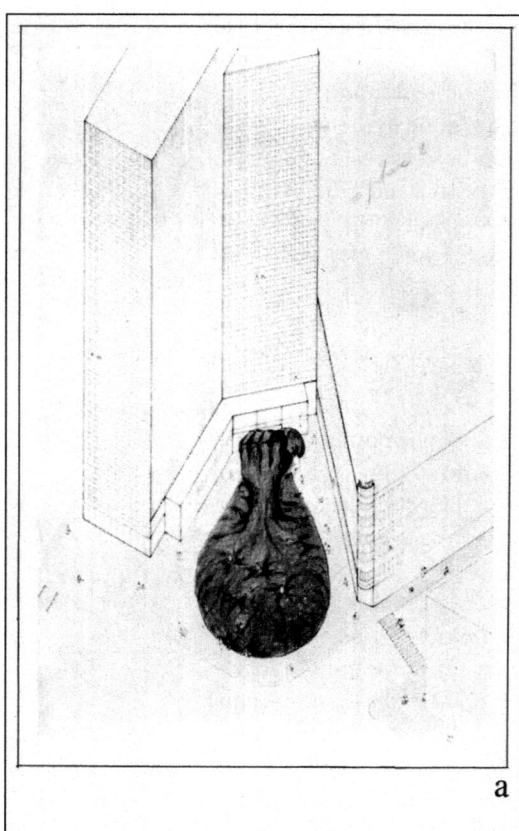

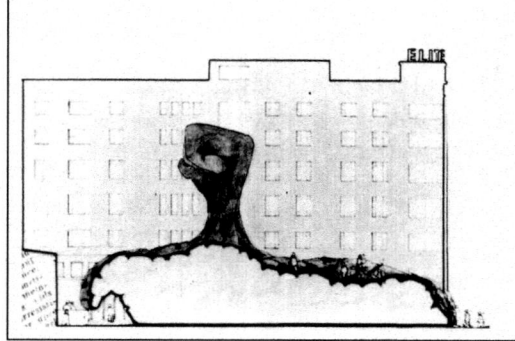

2.4 *L'orient est rouge* (part of the *Cinq propositions pour le Square du Bastion* project, La Cambre, 1974–1975, third-, fourth-, and fifth-year students). In Maurice Culot, 'The right wing in disguise' (*Lotus* 13 (1976): 101) the project is credited to Levy, Lenain, Lefebvre, Mierop, Louis. Source: École nationale supérieure d'architecture et des arts visuels, eds, *Le Bateau d'Élie. Contributions aux luttes urbaines et projets opportunistes, La Cambre 1971–1975* (Brussels: Éditions des AAM, 1975), p. 60. Copyright: Archives d'Architecture Moderne. Used with permission.

rouge (the east is red), proposed an inflatable structure forming a dramatically oversized fist (Figure 2.4).

The drawing techniques of counter-projects were also informed by their role as provocateurs. In order to criticise and expose the architecture community via the general public, counter-projects adopted a graphic language that was accessible to all; namely, the 'ligne claire' technique popularised by Hergé in *The Adventures of Tintin*.[56] Further, axonometric projection was preferred over perspectives, plans, and elevations, because it was capable of communicating a project through one single drawing; a clarity that was welcome in the context of political decision-making. Likewise, the use of 'parallels' allowed for better comparing, with the same scale and graphics, the differences between a functionalist project and a traditionalist alternative.[57] At times, drawings were created, or adjusted, for the sole purpose of turning them into better communicators (Figure 2.5).

The depiction of craftsmanship also formed a key part of the counter-projects in its subtle promotion of the reconstructed city. The city 'acts' through craftsmen being pictured in the everyday streetscape *practising* the work of reconstruction (Figure 2.6). It 'acts' in the image called *'Embellissement de la Place des Radis'*, which suggests a *Maison des artisans* (House of the artisans) and a *Maison de l'expiation* (House of atonement); tellingly, the latter's façade is financed by the City of Brussels as a form of compensation for its 'urban crimes'.[58] Likewise, anti-industrial production processes 'act' through drawings, such as the *'Réorganisation des carrières de soignies'* which unpacked the technical and labour processes behind the extraction of natural stone (Figure 2.7). And they 'act' even better when these drawings travel by being widely published. This was the case with *'le portique des maîtres carriers'* (Figure 2.8, see Plate 1), a drawing of 1978 depicting blocks of stone, donated by Walloon quarries, being sculptured by the artisans of the Marolles

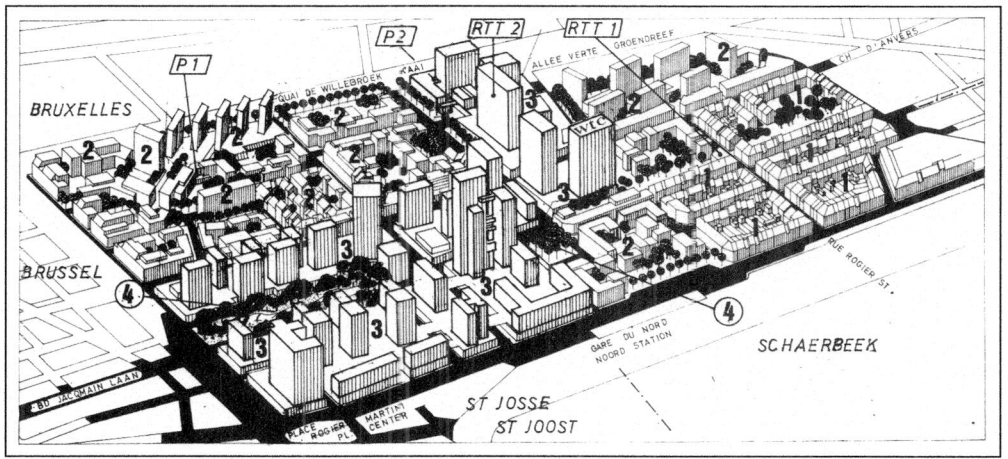

2.5 Interventions of architects were also targetted at optimising and clarifying existing drawings made by action committees. Here shown is a drawing by the ARAU (F. Joachim) as reworked by Maurice Culot: addition of street names and annotations. Source: *Wonen TA-BK*, 15–16 (1975): p. 66. Copyright: Archives d'Architecture Moderne. Used with permission.

2.6 *La Reconstruction des Marolles* (S. Birkiye, G. Busieau, Les AAM, 1978). Source: André Barey, ed. *Déclaration de Bruxelles: propos sur la reconstruction de la ville européenne* (Brussels: Éditions des AAM, 1980), p. 83. Copyright: Archives d'Architecture Moderne. Used with permission.

2.7 *Réorganisation des carrières de soignies* (Dominique Delbrouck and Jean-Pierre Majot, La Cambre, 1979). The caption in the original states 'different stages in the production of natural stone and their *mis en oeuvre* on the building site' (translated from French). Source: André Barey, ed. *Déclaration de Bruxelles: propos sur la reconstruction de la ville européenne* (Brussels: Éditions des AAM, 1980), p. 86. Copyright: Archives d'Architecture Moderne. Used with permission.

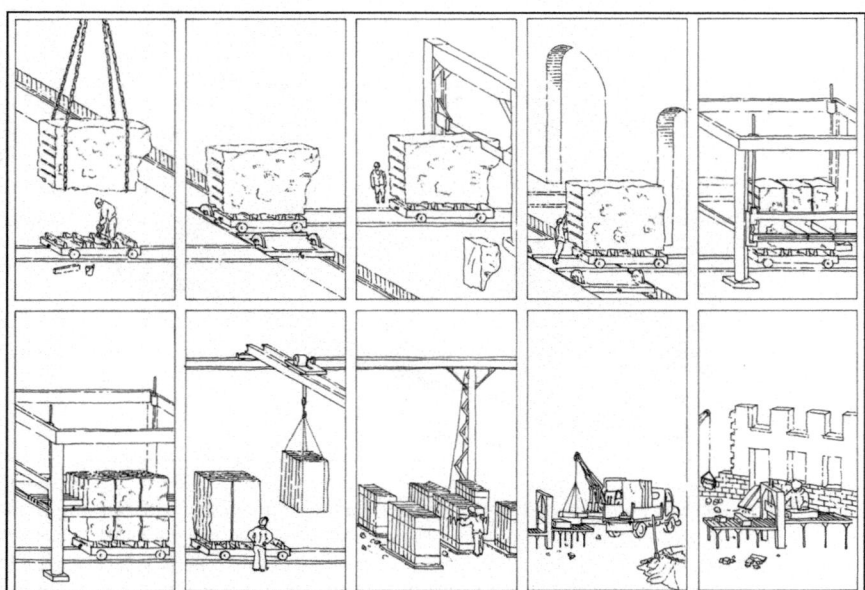

neighbourhood; after sculpting the blocks, they were sent back to Wallonia to be used for ornamental purposes. The image shows the artisans at work whilst onlookers marvel at their activities; one of them is Louis Van Geyt, president of the Belgian communist party, who is explaining to his colleagues why he fully supports the anti-industrial resistance.[59] With its celebratory tone and widespread publication, this drawing was an important promotional image for the Reconstruction of the European City. It was, for example, used as the poster image for the *La Reconstruction de la Ville Européenne* conference held in Brussels in November 1978. The image was also included in Culot and Krier's seminal article, '*L'unique chemin de l'architecture*' and, more recently, Séfik Birkiye chose this image for illustrating his introduction to the 2009 *Vizzion Awards* catalogue.[60]

Apart from the craftsman, the user of the city was also mobilised in counter-projects. Whereas this was often implicit – the 'traumatised user' and 'participating user' were present by default – the user was also pictured strolling, or sitting conversing at a café terrace, to promote the reconstructed city as a social meeting place: in the 1978 drawing '*La rencontre évocatrice*', Culot welcomes Léon Krier at Brussels central station; the image depicts Krier dropping his suitcase and spectacles in amazement with how the centre of Brussels has been reconstructed (Figure 2.8, see Plate 1);[61] in the image '*La visite en ballon*', members of the action committees are pictured giving local politicians a guided air balloon tour of the first reconstruction project; namely, the North Quarter;[62] and in the drawing '*Musée des Formes Urbaines*', Schoonbrodt is shown waiting for the '*Bruxelles vu par ses habitants*' tour to begin, an alternative Brussels coach-tour organised by the ARAU since 1977.[63]

Counter-projects, therefore, did much more than simply showing alternative solutions for specific sites. As sites of resistance they mobilised carefully selected

LA RENCONTRE EVOCATRICE

LE PARVIS SAINT MICHEL

LE PORTIQUE DES MAITRES CARRIERS

2.8 *La rencontre évocatrice* and *Le portique des maîtres carriers*, part of the 'Différents Projets pour la Reconstruction et l'Embellissement de la Partie de Bruxelles éventrée par la Jonction des Gares du Nord et du Midi' (Sefik Birkiye, Gilbert Busieau, Patrice Neirinck, La Cambre, 1978). Image source: A. Brauman, M. Culot, and M. Louis (eds), *La Reconstruction de Bruxelles*, Editions des AAM, 1982, p. 75. Copyright: Archives d'Architecture Moderne. Used with permission.

graphic and representational techniques as well as subject matter that, when combined, helped to promote an anti-industrial attitude, celebrate craftsmanship, mobilise users of the city, and trigger enthusiasm about reconstruction projects.

POLITICS AND/OR AESTHETICS: A 'FIRST GENERATION' OF COUNTER-PROJECTS

What's at stake is not aesthetics.[64]

A significant absentee from this chapter, so far, is the 'style' of counter-projects. Which aesthetics were considered appropriate? The absence of such a question is explained by the opening quote of this section. For the ARAU's Schoonbrodt, counter-projects were, first and foremost, political projects, and not concerned with aesthetics. However, throughout the 1970s, counter-projects did experience an aesthetic maturation: they gradually found an appropriate 'style' for the reconstructed, democratic city.[65]

The 'first generation' of counter-projects was produced by students graduating under Culot in 1975. Since 1972, these students had worked with the ARAU within the design unit of Maxime Wynants, and had subsequently matured as a group under the guidance of Marcel Pesleux, who took over the unit in 1973, and Pesleux's collaborator Culot, who was appointed as Professor of Urbanism in November 1974.[66] These *Bateau d'Élie* graduates later became teaching assistants, and were instrumental in the creation of a strong 'second generation' of students.[67] The first generation's work was widely published, most notably in a 1975 special issue of *Wonen TA/BK* dedicated to the ARAU, and in Culot's seminal article '*La Longue Marche*', published in *Architecture d'Aujourd'hui* in 1975 as part of a special issue on historic city centres undergoing development. The cover of this special issue featured a counter-project for Brussels made at La Cambre.

Adopting a manifesto-like approach reminiscent of Archigram and the Architectural Association, with whom La Cambre had regular contact, these early counter-projects seemed to prioritise political action over stylistic statements.[68] Their architectural écriture was either stylistically aligned with the humanistic modernism of the time or informed by popular techniques such as the *trompe l'oeil*; a technique of optical illusion whereby a three-dimensional space is suggested on a two-dimensional surface. In *Trois projets de crèche dans les marolles* (1972–1973), a *trompe l'oeil* made in ceramic tiles depicts the entry to the historic neighbourhood.[69] Another one is applied to a rooftop that is visible from an adjacent high-rise housing block (Figure 2.9). The use of *trompe l'oeil* demonstrates that it was acceptable for students to use architectural solutions that irritated architects, but were welcomed by citizens.[70] According to Culot, students and architects were not to 'force [their] own architectural tastes on people, but follow the advice of the people involved'.[71] Their talent and imagination, therefore, was at the service of society. It is telling that the

Bateau d'Élie catalogue does not allocate individual credits to the projects, thus refusing to celebrate individual creativity. Instead, the names of contributors are listed as one collective at the end of the book.

The ARAU, therefore, was also flexible on the matter of architectural style. However, it was, for political reasons, keen to find appropriate *urban* forms. As Schoonbrodt states, 'certain spatial organisations induce more liberty than others'.[72] The prioritising of a liveable, functionally mixed city over architectural expression was evoked by the series of counter-projects developed by the ARAU for the Museum of Modern Art. Notwithstanding their architectural differences, these projects shared the privileging of an *urban* form capable of repairing the street morphology and housing configuration. Whereas the counter-project by François Terlinden adopted a contemporaneous, late-modernist aesthetics, the two projects by Daniel Lelubre mark a progression towards reconstruction; Lelubre's 1973 project includes the proposal for a new housing project, but his 1974 project retains all existing buildings.[73] It is telling that, of the different counter-projects developed for the Museum of Modern Art, the ARAU retained the one that pushed the reconstruction ethos still further. This project, also by Lelubre, and dated variably between 1975 and 1978, proposed the reconstruction of the Maison des Pages in an attempt to morphologically repair and enclose the Place du Musée (Figures 2.10, 2.11 and 2.12).[74] A project by La Cambre students, during the academic year 1973–1974, confirmed the reconstruction ethos by stylistically mimicking the Old England Art Nouveau building opposite the project site.[75]

2.9 Third project in the 'Trois projets de crèche dans les marolles'; *trompe l'oeil* applied to a roof visible from an adjacent high-rise housing block. Source: École nationale supérieure d'architecture et des arts visuels. eds, *Le Bateau d'Élie. Contributions aux luttes urbaines et projets opportunistes, La Cambre 1971–1975* (Brussels: Éditions des AAM, 1975), p. 20. Copyright: Archives d'Architecture Moderne. Used with permission.

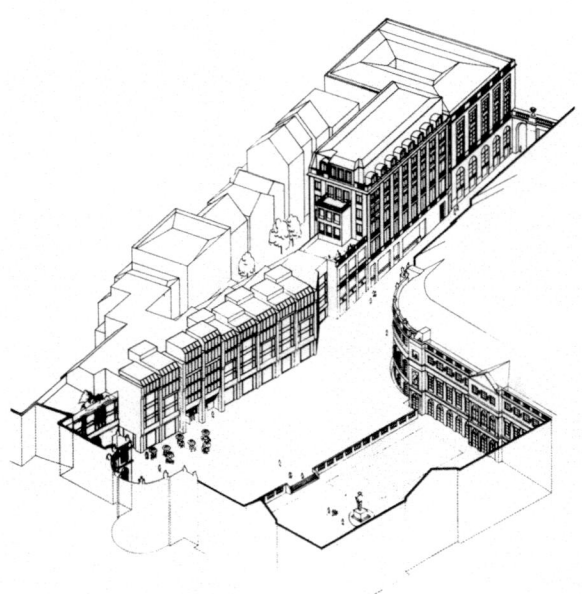

2.10 Project for the Musée d'Art Moderne, Brussels, Daniel Lelubre, 1973.
Source: Maurice Culot, 'La Longue Marche', *Architecture d'Aujourd'hui* 180 (July–August 1975): 18–29, 25. Copyright: Archives d'Architecture Moderne. Used with permission.

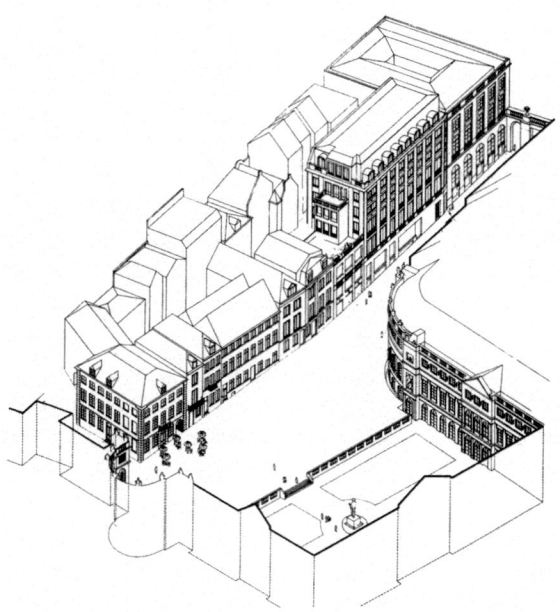

2.11 Project for the Musée d'Art Moderne, Brussels, Daniel Lelubre, 1974.
Source: Maurice Culot, 'La Longue Marche', *Architecture d'Aujourd'hui* 180 (July–August 1975): 18–29, 25. Copyright: Archives d'Architecture Moderne. Used with permission.

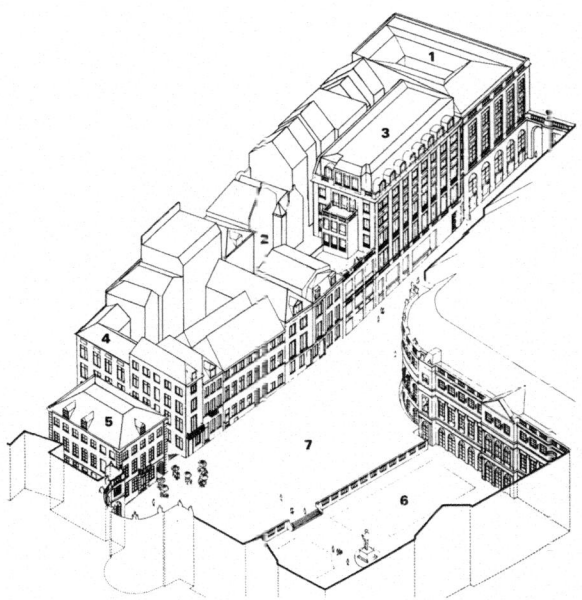

2.12 Project for the Musée d'Art Moderne, Brussels, the ARAU, 1977. Source: ARAU, ed., *Bruxelles Vu par ses Habitants, Quinze années d'action urbaine* (Brussels: Commission Française de la Culture et de l'Agglomération de Bruxelles and ARAU, 1984), 70. Copyright: Archives d'Architecture Moderne. Used with permission.

The ARAU may have been faithful to its political actions aimed at the creation of housing, the fight for a liveable city, and democratic decision-making, but its choices were, nevertheless, in part informed by aesthetic preferences.[76] For example, despite the ARAU settling for a compromise project for the Museum of Modern Art site in 1984, it presented two more counter-projects once it became apparent that the approved plans were being changed at the expense of the residential function. As construction commenced, new plans emerged replacing the buildings destined for housing with a series of gardens.[77] In response, two new counter-projects were developed. At this point, one can detect a sense of nostalgia entering the ARAU's evaluation of these projects. Namely, Schoonbrodt admitted that, of the two counter-projects presented in 1987, he preferred the one by Walloon architect Charles Vandenhove over the one by Raymond Lemaire, an authority in traditional urbanism and the preservation of cultural heritage, who had earlier also suggested the reconstruction of the Maison des Pages on this site. Whereas Lemaire's project followed the rhythm of the existing houses by means of a stepping roof line, Vandenhove proposed one continuous block and roof line. Schoonbrodt favoured the latter for its reminiscence of the original engravings for the Palace for Charles-Quint.[78]

TOWARDS A STYLE FOR THE ANTI-INDUSTRIAL CITY: A 'SECOND GENERATION' OF COUNTER-PROJECTS

Throughout the 1970s, counter-projects gradually found a suitable style for the Reconstruction of the European City. As architectural historian André Loeckx

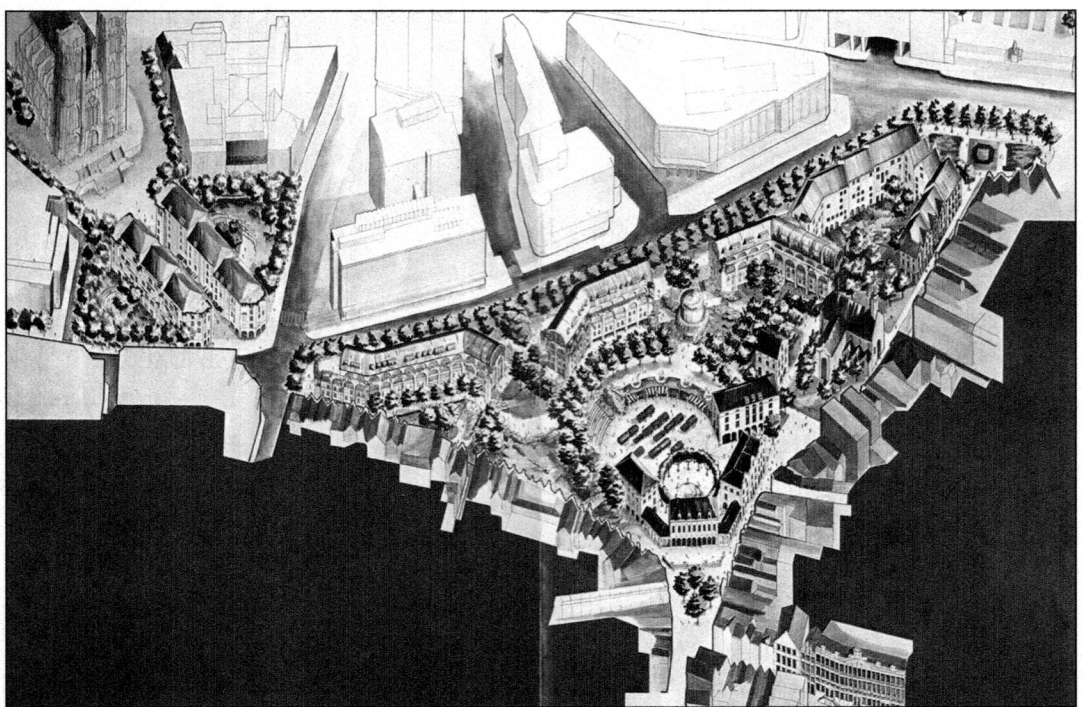

2.13 Proposal for the Carrefour de l'Europe site, by the ARAU, 1976. ARAU, ed., *Bruxelles Vu par ses Habitants, Quinze années d'action urbaine* (Brussels: Commission Française de la Culture et de l'Agglomération de Bruxelles and ARAU, 1984), 65. Copyright: Archives d'Architecture Moderne. Used with permission. Maurice Culot included it also in 'The right wing in disguise', *Lotus International* 13, 94–101, 100; where the caption states: 'the style developed for this project […] unleashed the fury of architects who hold that the use of "pastiche" is an immoral act'.

demonstrated, the different counter-projects for the Carrefour de l'Europe progressed towards greater stylistic confidence in their demonstration of an 'aesthetic alternative' in favour of reconstruction (Figure 2.13, see Plate 2; and see bottom image in Figure 2.1).[79] This style was, via rationalism, found in the neoclassical work of Léon Krier, and in the method of urban embellishment.[80] This combined architectural–urban effort was resonant with *Rational Architecture. The Reconstruction of the European City* (AAM, 1978), which can be seen as a manual for reconstructing the city and, in particular, those parts of the city that were overlooked by the functionalist/modernist architect such as the street, the square, and other public space.[81] It is, however, important to contextualise the aesthetic maturation of counter-projects within the wider transformations of the militancy at La Cambre, where the stylistic refinement of counter-projects coincided with the development of a global, theoretical project for the city.

From 1975 onwards, a 'second generation' of students, working under Culot and his assistants, emerged from La Cambre. Instead of timely interventions in support of local activism, students now focused on a wider reflection on the city. Their projects became larger in scale, and combined the development of counter-projects for specific sites with a wider urban reflection. They were often carried out as stand-alone exercises, and not necessarily commissioned. A more ambitious and comprehensive *'projet global sur la ville'* (global project for the city) was, whilst being developed in constant interaction with local struggles, believed to have overcome the fragmented nature of those struggles.[82] Loyal to Krier's statement that 'one cannot think in the trenches', a rigorous, global reflection on the city was believed to require intellectual autonomy, and was to take place through the architectural drawing.[83] As Culot states:

> *The architectural exercise is not directed at creating an alternative to contemporary production, but participates in the definition of a much wider project that integrates the uncertainties of the time. Only there does it find its historical significance and link with reality.*[84]

From the mid-1970s onwards, counter-projects changed significantly in nature and scale. No longer part of the polemics, and thus in a position to work on fairly neutral ground, students were ever more instrumental. For example, they systematically researched the historic centre of Brussels that had been damaged by speculative development. One project in particular that stands out was *Différents Projets de Reconstruction (et embellissement) du centre de Bruxelles éventré par la réalisation de la Jonction Ferroviaire Nord-Midi* (1978), by Sefik Birkiye, Patrice Neirinck, and Gilbert Busieau. This project was developed for the area of central Brussels that had been disrupted by the tunnelling works for the North–South railway junction. In its entirety, this project delivered a bold theoretical statement of how large parts of a city could be reconstructed. The project was, moreover, divided into individual project sites for which counter-projects were developed in the form of detailed architectural and urban designs (Figure 2.14). This combination of an urban vision along with detailed proposals demonstrated the importance of public space as a 'unifying power'.[85] More importantly, perhaps, these vast urban projects intended to deliver stylistically confident demonstrations of how ambitious visions can be realised. As such, they aimed to provide the authorities with the necessary visual support for promoting and effectuating the reconstruction of the city. Whereas counter-projects had, so far, been developed for specific sites, they were now targetted at the city as a whole.

The shift from timely interventions towards a global project for the city was reflected in the press coverage of counter-projects in the *Bulletin des AAM*. Early editions appeared as pamphlets or newsletters, typically containing short, politically loaded articles which combined architectural criticism with reports from the ARAU and action committees, students' work, and updates on La Cambre. The bulletin issues gradually became longer and, published less frequently, offered in-depth discussions on reconstruction projects in European cities. Published in English and French, and covering international projects and events such as IBA Berlin and the summerschools of HRH Prince Charles, the *Bulletin* became an important international platform for discussion.

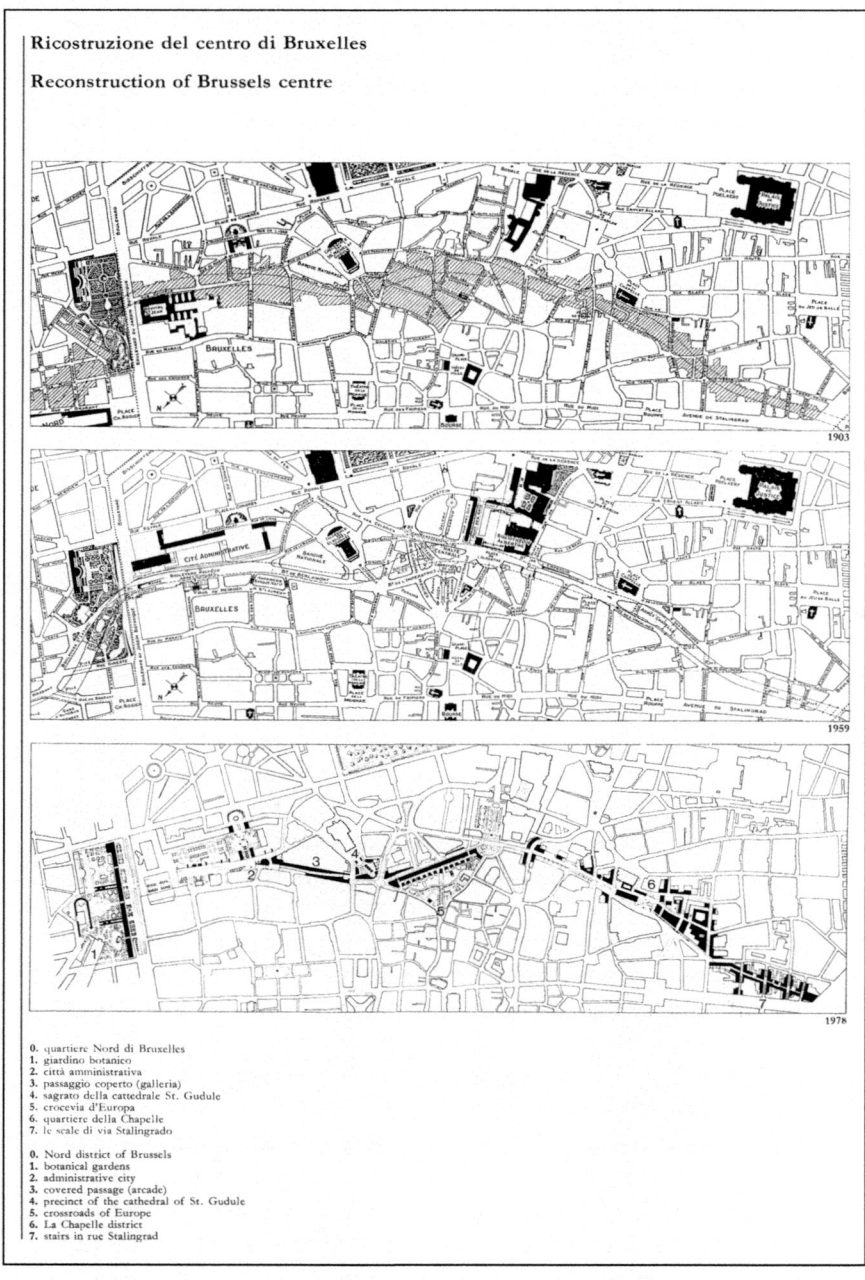

2.14 Overview map of the Reconstruction of Brussels Centre, also called the *Différents Projets pour la Reconstruction et l'Embellissement de la Partie de Bruxelles éventrée par la Jonction des Gares du Nord et du Midi* (Sefik Birkiye, Gilbert Busieau, Patrice Neirinck, La Cambre, 1978). Carrefour de l'Europe is one of seven project-sites. The project was published in its entirety in *Bulletin des AAM* 16 (1979); and in *La Reconstruction de Bruxelles*. Source: Maurice Culot, 'La cambre school of architecture and anti-industrial resistance', *Lotus International*, 21, December 1978, 46–71, 58. Copyright: Archives d'Architecture Moderne. Used with permission.

THE AESTHETIC TURN OF COUNTER-PROJECTS: DE-POLITICISATION OR RADICALISATION?

Given the aesthetic turn of counter-projects and the increased aesthetic ambition of the Reconstruction of the European City project – as expressed through changes in the *Bulletin des AAM* – the question remains as to whether the Brussels' counter-projects represented the de-politicisation with which the Reconstruction movement is often associated. Around the mid-1970s counter-projects underwent an aesthetic turn which coincided with the recognition of two generations of students at La Cambre, whose work was collected in *Le Bateau d'Élie. Contributions aux luttes urbaines et projets opportunistes, La Cambre 1971–1975* (Brussels: Éditions des AAM, 1975) and *La Tour Ferrée. Projets dans la Ville. Projets realizés à La Cambre, Bruxelles de 1975 à 1978* (Brussels: Éditions des AAM, 1978), respectively. The subtitles of these anthologies suggest a shift away from political action; from urban struggles ('*Contributions aux Luttes Urbaines*') to projects ('*Projets dans la Ville*'). Combined with the shift towards a global project for the city, described in the previous section, this turn nevertheless also signalled a significant radicalisation. Increasingly autonomous exercises reinforced the refusal to build and the withdrawal to the architectural project that had always been central to counter-projects. An anti-industrial resistance, which can be considered a further radicalisation of anti-functionalism, is another notable development during this period. Through wider, autonomous reflections on the city and Léon Krier's theoretical work, students and architects at La Cambre gradually gained more comprehensive insights in the city; which informed further radicalisation, rejecting *all* forms of capitalist production processes. For example, Culot had initially been in favour of public transport, which was preferred over private transport. He now rejected also public transport because *any* promotion of mobility was believed to ignore the fact that one should live and work in the same neighbourhood; that the neighbourhood is a key component of the city.[86]

The Reconstruction of the European City's pastiche, traditionalism, and imitation was received with scepticism by the architectural community; but it was also questioned from a political angle. During a round-table discussion organised by the *Cahiers Marxistes* in 1975, for example, one panellist raised a concern about the growing tendency, within the action committees, to defend a return to the past as a solution for the city. Pointing to the limitations of such solution, the pannelist observed that: 'one demolishes high-rise buildings, renovates the 19th century, and believes everything [the city's socio-economic problems] is sorted.'[87] Yet within the wider, international emergence of postmodernism, counter-projects were to invite a study of aesthetics as *part of* political radicalisation. The counter-projects' distinct position was made obvious in the 1980 Venice biennial, entitled 'The Presence of the Past'. Curated by the Italian architect Paolo Porthoghesi, this international exhibition set the tone for the future global theorisation of architectural postmodernism. Drawing from Jencks's definition – 'A postmodern building is [...] one which speaks on at least two levels at once: to other architects and a concerned minority who care about specifically architectural meanings, and to the public at large, or the local inhabitants, who care about other issues concerned with comfort, traditional building and a way of life' – Porthoghesi emphasised the meaning of buildings, through stylistic and formal inspiration from the past, and the concerns of the wider public.[88] The aesthetics of counter-projects was, however, informed by a wider search for the appropriate form for the democratic city. In this respect, it is worth quoting Culot from the exhibition catalogue *Contreprojets – controprogetti – counterprojects*:

> *The problem of urban form cannot be treated separately from urban struggles. […] But to tell the inhabitants that the city is a tool for development (therefore a revolutionary instrument) has no sense unless the sort of city involved is precisely defined. But experience has proven that the city with the greatest sense of conviction, the one most likely to rally a consensus of popular opinion, is the everyday city, the traditional European city, with its districts organised into a complex network of streets and squares. The stakes are therefore a great deal higher than simply aesthetic ones: what is involved is the battle to retain the liberating tool which is the city and to maximize its gains to the profit of the working class, i.e., the victims in an advanced industrial society.*[89]

This long citation gives insights into several key ingredients of the revolutionary roots of the Reconstruction of the European City movement. With the stakes being 'a great deal higher than simply aesthetic ones', Culot linked urban form with urban struggles by viewing the city as a revolutionary tool for the working-class. The appropriate 'style' for this city was, for Culot, a style that was familiar, one that contrasted with the perceived alienating modern styles legible only to architects. These forms were taken from the past, from 'the traditional European city', considered to be cohesive, familiar, and well-functioning. In an editorial of the *Bulletin des AAM* in 1980, Culot emphasised the importance of traditional forms: '[t]he city can only exist under its traditional form; ameliorated, repaired, yes, but not reinvented.'[90] Rather than choosing a style that was fashionable at the time, that 'expresses the time', Culot believed it important that the chosen style resonated with the inhabitants of the city, with what was *familiar* to them: the forms and types of the past.[91] Thus, the reproduction of historical forms was proposed not only on aesthetic but also democratic grounds. The political potential of pastiche was recognised by Robert Maxwell, who believed that if fictitious historicity, such as that found in François Spoerry's Port Grimaud, 'can be used for frivolous commercial purpose, [it] can equally well be used for serious social purpose'.[92] It signalled how counter-projects departed from the more frivolous pick-and-mix attitude towards historical forms by other postmodern architects. This is further demonstrated by the modelling of public spaces, benches, lamps, and fountains on examples from the eighteenth, nineteenth, and early twentieth centuries: 'when they still were, rather than serial products, conceived in their relationship with the city and its architecture'.[93] For example, the Ford T cars often appear in counter-projects as they were considered to be a model that was believed to be less tainted by capitalism than subsequent cars and could thus be recuperated; evoking pleasure rather than 'everyday drudgery'.[94]

The blending of politics and aesthetics in counter-projects was illustrated by their role in the emergence of even more extreme stylistic provocations such as the *fenêtre vertical démocratique* (vertical–democratic window). Making an appearance in the reconstruction project for the Carrefour de l'Europe, the vertical–democratic window was depicted in the images '*La rencontre évocatrice*' and '*la discussion sur la terrasse*'.[95] Such a window was thought to be democratic because of its conventional, straightforward design and use of traditional materials; wood was chosen over aluminium as the metal was considered to be a mere cheap perversion of the original window.[96] One can thus consider the window to be an assemblage of style, materials, production process, familiarity, ecology, and labour; an interpretation that is lent weight by Culot's statement that: 'the vertical window is not only classic, but democratic; the only intelligent response to the energy problem; part of a normal way of life; economic to construct and which makes logical use of natural materials.'[97]

The radicalisation that accompanied the aesthetic turn of counter-projects eventually led to the removal of the group that had gathered under Culot and Delevoy from La Cambre. 1978 was a pivotal year in the radicalisation of the anti-industrial resistance. Culot had become adjunct director and many of the study units, particularly in the Masters years, were concerned with the Reconstruction movement.[98] Additionally, Delevoy, in his capacity of director of La Cambre, had offered continuous intellectual support and, through guest lectures, juries, conferences, and seminars, had opened up the school to a supportive international network including individuals such as Paolo Soleri, Bernard Huet, Léon and Rob Krier, and Massimo Scolari.[99] In 1978, Culot published an article in *Lotus International* titled 'La Cambre school of architecture and anti-industrial resistance', which did not just signal such radicalisation; it was allegedly also received as a provocation in that it implied that the anti-industrial ideas represented the whole of La Cambre; as such heightening the tensions that already divided the school. Whereas tensions had previously arisen regarding what was perceived to be militant education that favoured polemics over technical quality and rigourous, detailed studies, it was believed that the threat to the aesthetic, political, and financial monopoly of the profession also played a role in the demise of the group.[100] Despite student strike action, Culot, Delevoy, and all other staff involved in the *luttes urbaines* were removed from La Cambre in the summer of 1979. After the removal of the so-called *exclus de la cambre*, the project for the reconstruction of the city continued with the creation of a new school, the École d'Architecture pour la Reconstruction de la Ville, with Delevoy as its president and Schoonbrodt as vice-president. Joined by forty former La Cambre students, the new school offered a five-year programme with an explicit European focus; 'forcefully rejecting the American city and become savagely European again'.[101]

COUNTER-PROJECTS IN BRUSSELS: A COMPROMISED LEGACY?

> If such counterprojects are projected onto sites (in Brussels or elsewhere) where an older fabric was never established and where the last vestiges of craft production have long since been displaced, critique and romance are easily converted into ersatz urbanity.[102]

Despite the removal of Culot and his colleagues of La Cambre, counter-projects had an important impact on Brussels and the achievements of the ARAU and the AAM in Brussels are manifold. While their actions significantly reduced the destruction of the historic city, the legacy of counter-projects is not unanimously considered a success. As the opening quote of this section suggests, counter-projects and, more generally, the de-politicised neoclassicism of Krier, have also been accused of 'ersatz urbanity' where the recuperation of the past is purely formalistic; stripped of its political and social origins.[103]

The ARAU and the AAM triggered awareness around the protection of cultural patrimony, and formalised citizen participation in urban planning through the approval of the *Plan Secteur* in 1979. Their activities resonated with a growing awareness around the need to protect cultural heritage as evidenced by the declaration of 1975 as the European Year of Architectural Heritage. In Brussels, several foundations emerged with a specific interest in urban–cultural heritage. Notably, the Fondation Roi Baudouin – Koning Boudewijn Stichting, a think-tank addressing social themes including patrimony, public space, and urban renewal was established in 1976. In 1979, a patrimony 'urgency-inventory' was published, and two issues of the Belgian architecture journal *A Plus* were dedicated to the rehabilitation of the built environment.[104] In addition, the Brussels counter-projects proved important in the consolidation of an emerging *international* Reconstruction movement for whom they provided a test-ground.[105] Through formative events, such as the *La Reconstruction de la Ville Européenne* conference, and the editorial work of the AAM, Brussels formed a nucleus for intellectual exchange.[106] This sensitising work was continued by former students and teachers of La Cambre who, having pursued careers in those cultural foundations dedicated to the promotion of architecture and the city, assisted in the dissemination of the Reconstruction project.[107] A case in point is the European Award for the Reconstruction of the City (*Prix Européenne de la reconstruction de la ville*), awarded since 1982 by the Fondation Philippe Rotthier pour l'Architecture. First awarded to Quinlan Terry, this award honoured those traditionalist architects who, despite the evidence of a growing Reconstruction movement in Europe, were mocked by the architectural press. Perhaps the most controversial legacy of the movement that refused to build is its record of realisations. Culot, however, has defended the realisations of the anti-industrial resistance because the refusal to build was, initially, simply a provocation in order to 'draw attention' and, now that the reconstruction position was more widely supported by clients compared to the 1970s, building was believed to be justified.[108] In contrast to the Anglo-Saxon context, where traditionalism found support amongst the postmodernists and conservationists

2.15 Lakense Straat, Brussels. Photograph by the author, 2015.

in the UK, and with New Urbanism in the US, not one single counter-project was realised in Brussels. One explicitly traditionalist project can, however, be found in the Lakense Straat. This project was the outcome of the design competition *Oproep aan jonge Europese architecten*, which was organised in 1989 by the Fondation pour l'Architecture, and entailed the renovation of an entire urban block. Seven teams of architects were commissioned to work within a given set of design guidelines based upon neoclassical references (Figure 2.15, see Plate 3).[109] Completed in 1995, and inaugurated by HRH Prince Charles, the project was celebrated by the international traditionalist movement.[110] Although traditionalism found only one realisation, the Reconstruction legacy, nonetheless, travelled well through the Brussels architectural production. This can be attributed to several reasons.

Firstly, several graduates of the anti-industrial resistance founded architectural firms which, in time, became influential. For example, in 1983, Brigitte d'Helft and Michel Verliefden created A2RC Architecture et Construction entre Rêve et Réalité; and Sefik Birkiye and Dominique Delbrouck founded the Atelier d'Art Urbain – now re-named Vizzion. Their postmodernism was usually one of 'contemporary historicism'; less about meaning and sign, and more about the revisiting of historical styles and urban morphologies.[111] Offices such as Atelier d'Art Urbain have accepted, despite their anti-industrial origins, commissions for large-scale projects for proto-typical capitalist customers including shopping malls, banks, insurance companies, office buildings.[112] These architects have often promoted the reconstruction ideals, whilst these ideas got also integrated with the rhetoric of the developer. It is, in that sense, surprising to learn that Sefik

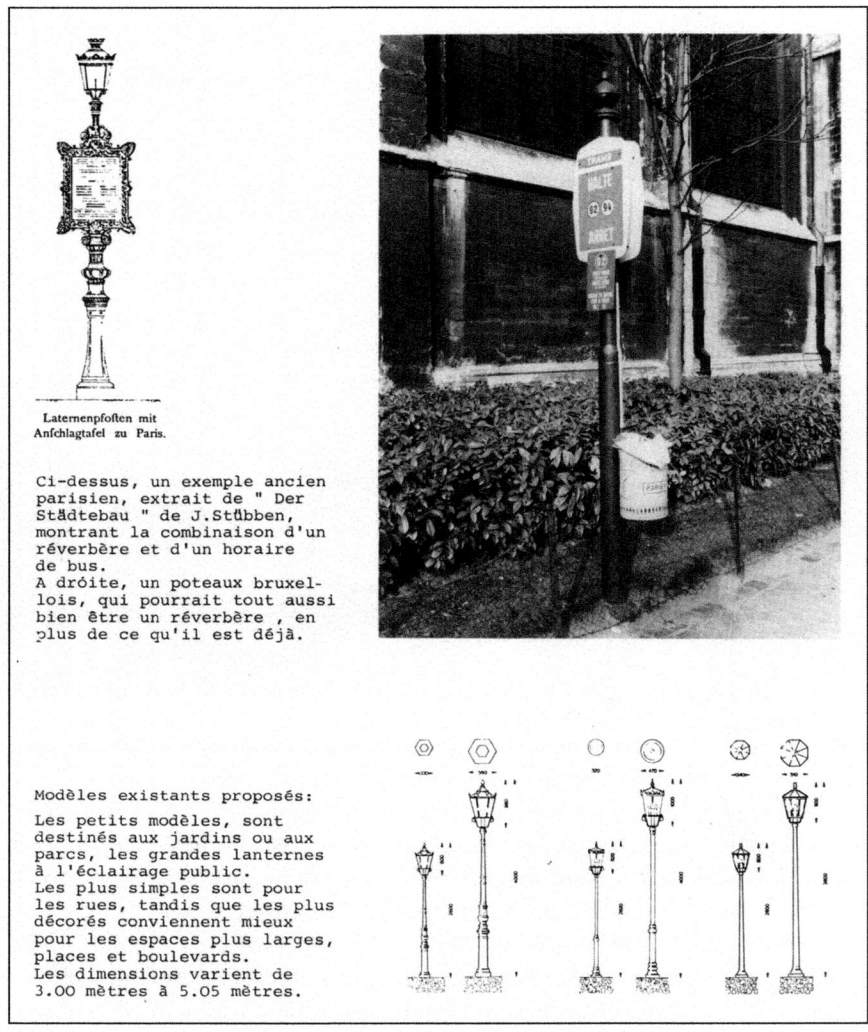

2.16 Maurice Culot and René Schoonbrodt, eds, *Les Espaces Publics Bruxellois: analyse et projets* (Brussels: Fondation Roi Baudoin: 1980; an initiative of IEB and the AAM), 415. Copyright: Archives d'Architecture Moderne. Used with permission.

Birkiye was allegedly involved in a secretive bid commissioned by Calik Holding, for developing the master plan for the Haydarpasa area in Istanbul. Here, he proposed a 'New Manhattan', in the shape of seven skyscrapers. Allegedly, after the project was rejected, owing to the outrage resulting from a report leaked to the press, the design was re-imagined as a 'New Venice'.[113]

Secondly, as tangible advocates of the possibility to repair and reconstruct the city, counter-projects informed the Brussels spatial production through the promotion of urban embellishment. This was reinforced through the publication of urban design 'manuals'. For example, *Les Espaces Publics Bruxellois: analyse et projets* (1981) proposed street furniture should be based on historical examples, 'when they still were, rather than serial products, conceived in their relationship with the city and its architecture'.[114] The *Manuel des Espaces Publics Bruxellois* or *Handboek van de Brusselse Openbare Ruimten* (1995), likewise, offered a detailed study of public space and street furniture (Figures 2.16 and 2.17).[115] The urban embellishment mind-set was further reinforced by political initiatives such as *Chemins de la Ville* by Charles Picqué, Minister-President of the Brussels Capital Region between 1989–1999 and 2004–2013. Started in 1990, *Chemins de la Ville* aimed at reconciling downtown and upper-town Brussels through pedestrian itineraries – the creation of a 'slow city' designed through a 'coherent urban vocabulary'.[116] It was an important instrument for the reconstruction of the Brussels Quartier des Arts, but also a tool for the wider promotion of the pastiche reconstruction of the city. For example, the 2006 winner of the Prix du Quartier des Arts, organised as part of the *Chemins de la Ville* initiative, was commended for acting with 'refinement and delicacy, without giving in to the temptation to propose an original gesture, signature of one's inventiveness'.[117] Meanwhile, Culot has continued to promote façadism, for it offers a valuable solution in cases where the interior of a building is of no historical value, whilst pastiche can help to create coherent wholes by constructing 'in the manner of'.[118]

Thirdly, ever since the 1970s counter-projects, many of the neighbourhoods that were targeted by the action committees were successfully embellished. However, as an unfortunate side-effect, certain neighbourhoods, particularly socially fragile ones, have become easy targets for 'soft' regeneration and, having undergone a process of gentrification, lost their working-class character.[119]

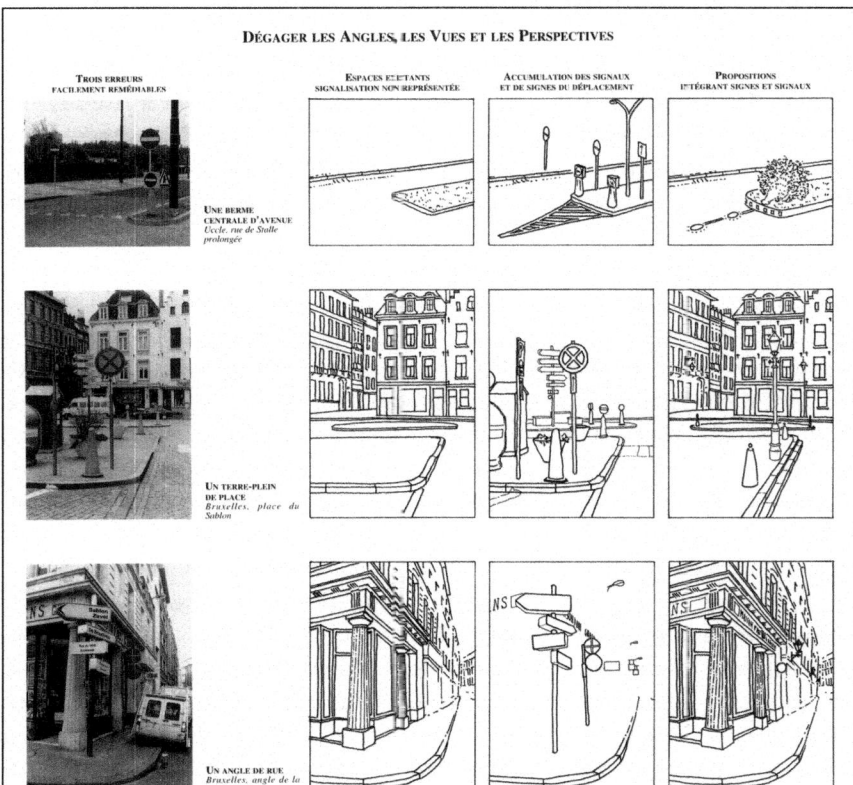

2.17 Marie Demanet and Jean-Pierre Majot, eds, *Handboek van de Brusselse Openbare Ruimten* (Brussels: Iris, 1995; in collaboration with the Brussels Capital Region and the AAM), 35. Copyright: Archives d'Architecture Moderne. Used with permission.

Finally, as *visual* advocates, counter-projects often endured through strong mental images, and thus influenced the future development of certain sites. One of the most well-known cases is the Carrefour de l'Europe site. Whilst the entries for the 1983 Bonduelle competition included both proposals *à la* Reconstruction and more metropolitan statements, the former was favoured.[120] The eventually realised *'faux-flamand'* architecture demonstrated how the Reconstruction movement had been reduced to a superficial and opportunistic reproduction of the past. Likewise, from the numerous counter-projects developed for the Museum of Modern Art in Brussels, one image in particular has been widely published; namely, the one suggesting the reconstruction of the Maison des Pages. The realised project replaced the original landmark building with a glass well, as such resulting in an underground museum.[121]

The actions of the activists and architects of the 1970s have triggered a greater respect for the historic city as much as they have popularised a Reconstruction mindset. Because this mindset does, however, not offer any guarantee for better architecture and urban design, nor a weapon strong enough to resist the speculative powers of developers, the legacy of the ARAU and the AAM is multiple and not uncompromised.

LEARNING FROM COUNTER-PROJECTS

The unpacking of counter-projects enables a refinement and expansion of the theoretical and historical understanding of an important episode in Brussels' recent architectural past. In addition, it allows for recovering a critical–methodological device that is instructive for studying the tense, complex, and often contradicting relationships between the architect and the user, and between political radicalism and aesthetics.

From studying counter-projects as political–aesthetic assemblages, it becomes apparent that the association of counter-projects with de-politicised, merely formal recuperations of the past, in fact applies only to a 'second generation' of projects. The so-called 'aesthetic turn' of the mid-1970s indicates the existence of an earlier generation of counter-projects with more explicit political roots. These counter-projects can be seen as having operated simultaneously as political provocateurs and test-grounds for aesthetic articulation and refinement. Whether in the shape of site-specific, on-the-ground provocations or, later, as theoretical, autonomous, reflections, counter-projects proved, in the Brussels context, *simultaneously* politically informed and spatially articulate. The co-existence of politics and aesthetics was further informed by counter-projects being the product of exchanges between urban activists, who prioritised political action over debates on aesthetics, and architects, who were preoccupied with finding an appropriate form for the anti-industrial city.[122] The Brussels counter-projects, in particular the first generation ones, show a different path than the theoretical, de-politicised route towards Reconstruction as advocated by Léon Krier.

By considering counter-projects as assemblages, it becomes apparent that what appears as oppositional activism also operates from-within. This is not only because of counter-projects insertion in real-world activism, but also because the drawings were entangled with both the Belgian and Brussels situation. Amongst others the use of the popular graphics, which drew inspiration from the popular Belgian cartoon character Tintin, allowed for architects to be addressed *via* the population. Moreover, the many actors that are at work in counter-projects – local craftsmanship, stone extracted from Walloon quarries, labour workers of the Marolles, local politicians – show that the counter-projects are situated within a national and local context. To a certain degree one could argue that even the mockery used in counter-projects and in the AAM's press, was reminiscent of the Brussels' *zwanze*, which is a form of resistance through surrealist mockery.

Studying counter-projects as political–aesthetic statements forms an important departure from the theorisation of architectural postmodernism in terms of formal experimentations, style wars, and the superficial recycling of historical forms alone. As test-grounds for resistant practice, counter-projects operated as assemblages of militancy, urban struggles, aesthetics, craftsmanship, anti-capitalist materials, axonometric projection, citizens, production processes, working-class culture, critical theory, and architectural education. As *drawings*, counter-projects moreover proved to be actors in their own right, powerful enough to perform within local politics, architectural discourse, and the future imaginations for a site; to even perform in an entire city. As such, counter-projects, whether or not compromised, contributed to the dissemination of the Reconstruction idiom, thus demonstrating the importance of studying the complete inner-workings of any architectural movement, rather than appraising it on the basis of its construction output only.

In Brussels, the opportunistic embracement of façadism and pastiche by developers, triggered suspicion as to whether the actions of the 1970s had more impact on the appearances of architecture than on the mechanisms behind it. Façadism became used by Brussels' developers as a speculative strategy that allows them to be non-offensive whilst still being able to proceed with their lucrative developments.[123] And, because counter-projects were not just architectural statements but above all *urban* projects, their impact was felt particularly in terms of urban design. With the help of urban design 'manuals' and Reconstruction-inspired cultural foundations and architectural firms, Brussels saw to the dissemination of an urban embellishment mindset that was believed influential in its thinking-city. It is, therefore, perhaps not surprising that the 1990s 'second turn' in Brussels architecture was not just triggered by architectural culture, but also urban activism. This will be the subject of the next chapter.

NOTES

1. Eric De Kuyper, *Een passie voor Brussel* (Amsterdam: Babylon-De Geus, 1995), 28 [translated from Dutch].
2. Many books dedicated to Brussels' architecture and urban development testify to this legacy of destruction, including Gustave Abeels, *Straten en Stenen: Brussel: Stadsgroei*

1780-1980 (Brussels: Weissenbruch, 1982), catalogue of exhibition organised by Generale Bankmaatschappij and Sint-Lukasarchief, 18/11/82–21/01/83; Jan Apers, Alfons Hoppenbrouwers, and Jos Vanden Breeden, *Bouwen door de Eeuwen heen, Brussel-hoofdstad, urgentie-inventaris* (Brussels: Sint-Lukasarchief, 1979); Joël Claisse, Pierre Loze, and Liliane Knopes, eds, *Change: Brussels Capital of Europe* (Brussels: Prisme Éditions, 2005); Thierry Demey, *Bruxelles Cronique d'Une Capitale en Chantier*, two vols. (Brussels: Legrain, 1990–1992); Yves Jacqmin, ed., *Een eeuw architectuur en stedebouw: Brussels Hoofdstedelijk Gewest* (Brussels: Mardaga, 2000); Marc Lacour, ed., *50 jaar architectuur Brussel* (Brussels: CERAA, 1989); Sint-Lukasarchief, *Brussel, breken, bouwen: architectuur en stadsverfraaiing 1780–1914* (Brussels: Gemeentekrediet van België, 1979), catalogue of exhibition organised by Gemeentekrediet van België, 12/9 – 28/10/1979.

3 Such works were part of the large-scale urban restructuring of Brussels under Jules Anspach, Mayor of Brussels, and King Leopold II, who was popularly christened as the 'King Urbanist'.

4 Mil De Kooning and Iwan Strauven, 'Brussel 1945–1970: Verwachtingen en illusies', in *Een eeuw architectuur en stedebouw: Brussels Hoofdstedelijk Gewest*, ed. Yves Jacqmin (Brussels: Mardaga, 2000), 119–135. On the struggles of citizens to reverse the trends, please see: Nicole Brasseur, Jozef Lievens, Albert Martens, *De grote stad: een geplande chaos? De noordwijk van krot tot Manhattan* (Leuven: Davidsfonds, 1975); and Albert Martens, Myriam Vanden Eede, *De Noordwijk: slopen en wonen* (Berchem: EPO, 1994).

5 Maureen Heyns, 'De krotwoning als "Sociaal Probleem nr. 1". De Wet inzake Krotopruiming van 1953 en de sanering van de oude stadswijken', in *Wonen in Welvaart. Woningbouw en wooncultuur in Vlaanderen 1948–1973*, ed. Karine Van Herck and Tom Avermaete (Rotterdam: 010 Publishers, 2006), 147–164, 153.

6 With its translucency, the building was promoted as 'non-intrusive' (Maurice Culot, '1980-1990: La Décade du n'importe quoi', *Bulletin des AAM* 17 (1980), 1–3, 2.

7 Maurice Culot, 'La Longue Marche', *Architecture d'Aujourd'hui* 180 (July–August 1975): 18–29.

8 Robert L. Delevoy, *Lignes de positions*, Presses de la Cambre, Brussels, July 1, 1966, based on a talk on October 7, 1965. Robert L. Delevoy, 'Adresse prononcée le 4 mai 1965 pour recueillir les pouvoirs', École Nationale Supérieure d'Architecture et des Arts Visuels à Bruxelles, Abbaye de La Cambre, December 15, 1965. Consulted at the Koninklijke Bibliotheek van België (FS XXIV 152 and IV 65.409 B).

9 Delevoy, *Lignes de positions*. For more details on La Cambre, please see Jacques Aron, *La Cambre et l'Architecture: Un regard sur le Bauhaus Belge* (Liege: Mardaga, 1982), 133–144.

10 Aldo Rossi, *The Architecture of the City*, English translation by Oppositions Books, Institute of Architecture and Urban Studies (Cambridge, MA: The MIT Press, 1982 [1966]).

11 Aron, *La Cambre et l'Architecture*, 156.

12 Ibid., 151–162.

13 Culot, 'La Longue Marche'.

14 The movement is variably called traditionalist, reconstruction, neoclassicist, neorationalist, and historicist. I will use 'reconstruction' for the 1970s (their own term) and 'traditionalist' for more recent discourse (in reference to, for example, Charles Jencks and Karl Kropf's (eds) classification in *Theories and Manifestoes of Contemporary Architecture*, John Wiley Academy editions, 1997).

15 Critical voices include Alan Colquhoun, 'Three kinds of historicism', first published in *Architectural Design* 53, no. 9/10 (1983); and *Oppositions* 26 (Spring 1984); and Joan Ockman, 'The Most Interesting Form of a Lie', in *Oppositions Reader: Selected Readings from a Journal for Ideas and Criticism in Architecture 1973–1984*, ed. K. Michael Hays (New York: Princeton Architectural Press, 1998), 412–421; originally published in 1981.

16 See K. Michael Hays introduction to Maurice Culot and Léon Krier's 'The Only Path for Architecture', in *Architecture Theory since 1968*, ed. K. Michael Hays (Cambridge, MA: The MIT Press, 2000), 348–355, 349 (originally published in English in *Oppositions*, Fall 1978). 'The Only Path for Architecture' is a translation of Maurice Culot and Léon Krier, 'L'unique chemin de l'architecture', *Bulletin des AAM*, 14 (1978), 1–5.

17 For example, only one of four counter-projects that featured in Culot and Krier, 'L'unique chemin' were included in Hays, *Architecture Theory since 1968*.

18 Léon Krier and Maurice Culot, *Contreprojets – Controprogetti – Counterprojects* (Brussels: AAM, 1980).

19 The author would like to thank Maurice Culot for making time for a conversation with the author on July 9, 2012, at the AAM in Brussels, and for his comments on an earlier version of this chapter, which were invaluable for clarifying and refining certain observations. I take responsibility for any misinterpretations or inconsistencies that may nevertheless have occurred. The author also would like to thank Mr. Culot for facilitating the consultation of the Archives d'Architecture Moderne in Brussels; in particular the uncatalogued sections. An important source on the French scene, which had connections with Brussels, is Jean-Louis Violeau, *Les Architectes et Mai 68* (Paris: Éditions Recherches, 2005).

20 The term counter-project is used both hyphenated and non-hyphenated. In the anthology, the title is non-hyphenated (*Counterprojects*), while the introduction of the book uses a hyphen in French and English ('contre-projets' and 'the counter-projects') but not in Italian ('controprogetti'). For the sake of consistency, I hyphenate 'counter-project' throughout.

21 Francis Strauven, 'Editorial', in *Wonen TA-BK* 15–16 (August 1975), special issue on the ARAU, 3.

22 For example, in contrast to the ARAU the Quartier des Arts association was preoccupied with the *cultural* threats of the functionalist city, and was closer to the middle-classes. See Maurice Culot, *Brussels Architectures from 1950 to the Present* (Brussels: AAM, 2012), 57–59; 61–62.

23 Brussels underwent an important out-migration of Belgian citizens and influx of immigrants; See Jacques Aron, *Le tournant de l'urbanisme bruxellois: 1958–1978* (Brussels: Fondation Joseph Jacquemotte, 1978), 71–75; 77.

24 The proposals suggested one hundred *conseils de quartier* involving politicians, the users of the city, and both '*belges*' and '*étrangers*'. See the diagram in René Schoonbrodt, 'Bruxelles: pour la Fusion de 19 communes Reactionnaires', *Bulletin des AAM*, 6 (March 1976): 16.

25 Citizen consultation had been introduced within the context of the 1962 Law of Urbanism, but was considered to have been poorly applied; municipalities allegedly organised consultation during the summer holidays or by advertising in non-frequented areas; see editorial in *Bulletin des AAM* 5 (February 1976): 1.

26 René Schoonbrodt, 'Table ronde. Luttes urbaines et lutte politique', *Cahiers Marxistes* 12, no. 32 (March 1975): 15–33, 18. Both Schoonbrodt and Jacques Aron (an important figure in the architectural debates of the 1970s and teaching at La Cambre),

contributed to the Belgian journal *Cahiers Marxistes* which was first published in 1969 by Fondation Joseph Jacquemotte.

27 The ARAU particularly stressed the participation of the public in decision-making; see its 1970 Charte Urbaine, and see ARAU, 'Position d'Inter-Environnement-Bruxelles et des comités d'habitants sur le Projet de Plan de Secteur de l'Agglomération Bruxelloise, résolutions du Congrès du 15 Janvier 1977, Inter-Environnement Bruxelles', 2–3. On the *Plan Secteur*, please see Aron, *Le tournant de l'urbanisme Bruxellois* (from page 70); Alex Ghuys, 'Le plan secteur, la plus grande victoire des comités d'habitants', in *Bruxelles Vu par ses Habitants, Quinze années d'action urbaine*, ed. ARAU (Brussels: Commission Française de la Culture et de l'Agglomération de Bruxelles and ARAU, 1984), 55–60; special issue of *Cahiers Marxistes* 26, no. 45 (1976); and Patrick Burniat, 'Les Enjeux du plan de secteur', *Cahiers Marxistes*, no. 80 (1980): 50–54.

28 'Turn' is translated from the French word 'tournant'. See Aron, *Le tournant de l'urbanisme Bruxellois*.

29 'Consultation committees' is translated from the French expression 'Commission de concertation'. See Ghuys, 'Le plan secteur', 55.

30 Jacques Verbiest, 'Table ronde. Luttes urbaines et lutte politique', 17.

31 Hervé Cnudde and Paul Vermeylen, 'L'École d'action urbaine de l' ARAU', *Cahiers JEB Jeunesse, Education populaire, Bibliothèques publiques* 3, no. 80 (1980): 13–14. The École Urbaine has, since 1970, hosted a series of annual meetings between the public and politicians. The Boutique Urbaine provides for animation, events, and information sessions in vulnerable neighbourhoods, often involving social workers. Further information can also be found in IEB, AAM, *Les Espaces Publics Bruxellois: analyse et projets* (Brussels: Fondation Roi Baudouin, 1981), 97.

32 Pesleux 'pour lire les projets', in École nationale supérieure d'architecture et des arts visuels, eds, *La Tour Ferrée: Projets dans la Ville: Projets realizés à La Cambre, Bruxelles de 1975 à 1978* (Brussels: Éditions des AAM, 1978), 16–17; Maurice Culot, 'ARAU Brussels', *Architectural Association Quarterly* 7, no. 4 (1975) 22–25; Maurice Culot, 'La Droite Masquée', in *Le Bateau d'Élie: Contributions aux luttes urbaines et projets opportunistes, La Cambre 1971–1975*, ed. École nationale supérieure d'architecture et des arts visuels (Brussels: Éditions des AAM, 1975): 11–13.

33 The ARAU agitated for such an action in response to the 1969 proposal for the Carrefour de l'Europe site. See *Wonen TA-BK*, nos. 15–16 (1975): 28; and 'Aménagement du Carrefour de l'Europe à Bruxelles'. Special issue, *Environnement* 11 (November 1970): 2.

34 This was the case with the ARAU's acceptance of the 1970 competition entry for Carrefour de l'Europe by Team Planning as a basis for discussion (*Wonen TA-BK*, nos. 15–16 [1975]: 28).

35 René Schoonbrodt, *Vouloir et dire la ville* (Brussels: AAM Éditions, 2007), 306 and ARAU, 'Le musée qui n'aimait pas la ville', in *Bruxelles Vu par ses Habitants: Quinze années d'action urbaine*, ed. ARAU (Brussels: Commission Française de la Culture et de l'Agglomération de Bruxelles and ARAU, 1984), 68–72. For an image of the project and its urban implementation, see *Wonen TA-BK*, nos. 15–16 (1975): 41–42.

36 Now called Rue du Musée. See 'Remarques de l'ARAU sur les croquis de l'architecte Bastin concernant l'aménagement de la place du musée', as part of ARAU 'Conference de presse du mardi 3 mars 1981. Pourqoui ne pas reconstruire la maison des pages?', consulted at the Archives d'Architecture Moderne: private archives Maurice Culot (uncatalogued).

37 Ibid., 8 (critique of the drawing). Whereas the ARAU had suggested reconstructing the Maison de Pages (dating back to Charles de Lorraine) as a way of closing the square, Bastin had, instead, suggested a statue of Charles de Lorraine; which the ARAU considered an impudent response to the building permit's request to 'reconstruct' on this site (ARAU, 'Le musée qui n'aimait pas la ville', 71).

38 *Bateau d'Élie*, 40–43; and Culot, 'La Longue Marche'.

39 Charles Jencks, 'The Rise of Postmodern Architecture', *Architectural Association Quarterly* 7, no. 4 (1975), 7. The counter-projects' combination of critique and formulating alternatives made Jencks distinguish the ARAU from others in the category 'advocacy planning and the anti-scheme'. On the distinction between counter-projects and Architecture Urbaine, see Marcel Cornu, 'L'Architecture Urbaine en question: II. A Bruxelles avec les "Nouveaux Rationalistes"', *Revue L'Urbanisme* 170 (1979), 65–67.

40 Key publications from La Cambre in the 1970s include Robert Delevoy, Maurice Culot, and Anne Van Loo, *La Cambre 1928–1978* (Brussels: Éditions AAM, 1979); Aron, *La Cambre et l'Architecture*; École nationale supérieure d'architecture et des arts visuels, *Le Bateau d'Élie*; École nationale supérieure d'architecture et des arts visuels, *La Tour Ferrée*; André Barey, ed., *Déclaration de Bruxelles: propos sur la reconstruction de la ville européenne* (Brussels: Éditions des AAM, 1980); Krier and Culot, *Contreprojets*; A. Brauman, M. Culot, and M. Louis, eds, *La Reconstruction de Bruxelles* (Brussels: Éditions des AAM, 1982); ARAU, *Bruxelles Vu par ses Habitants*; and special journal issues in *Lotus International* 21 (December 1978); *Architecture d'Aujourd'hui* 180 (July–August 1975); *Wonen TA-BK* 15–16 (1975), and regular publications of student work in the *Bulletin des AAM*.

41 Translated from French, *Bulletin des AAM* 6 (March 1976): 2.

42 '*le complément nécessaire*', Culot, 'La Droite Masquée', 11.

43 Grahame Shane, 'Culot/Contextualism and Conscience' in *Architectural Design* 47, no. 3 (1977): 189. Culot, Krier, and Tafuri were considered to be connected as the 'three European Marxist architects'; see Robert Maxwell, 'Tafuri/Culot/Krier: The Role of Ideology', *Architectural Design* 47, no. 3 (1977): 187–188. One reason for this is in their sharing of 'operative critique' as an approach; see Colin Davies, 'Leon Krier talks to Colin Davies', in *Léon Krier Drawings 1967–1980* (Brussels: Éditions AAM, 1981), xvii–xxiv, xxi.

44 Léon Krier, 'Virtus privées et vices publics', *Bulletin des AAM* 18 (1980): 7–12 (the London scene); 19 (1980): 83–87 (the Berlin scene); 20 (1981): 41–50 (the Luxemburg scene).

45 Published in Léon Krier, *Drawings 1967–1980* (Brussels: Éditions AAM, 1981), 95; and republished by Culot elsewhere, for example, *Bulletin des AAM* 2 (1984): 2 and in ARAU, *Bruxelles Vu par ses Habitants*, 27.

46 As part of his comments on an earlier draft of this chapter, Culot articulated this simultaneously serious yet humorous and playful aspect of counter-projects, rooted in the revolutionary mood of May '68. Also, the influence of the Archigram-operas could be felt in, for example, the musical night organised during the La Reconstruction de la Ville Européenne conference, held in Brussels in November 1978, whereby La Cambre performed 'anti-industrial songs'.

47 École nationale supérieure d'architecture et des arts visuels, *Bateau d'Élie*, 46–47 (also published in *Wonen TA-BK* 15–16 [1975]: 3). The counter-project was used by IEB to convince the CEE that Belgian citizens did not agree with this Belgian proposal.

48 Maurice Culot, 'We will no longer build', in: *Drawings 1967–1980*, by Léon Krier (Brussels: Éditions AAM, 1981), vii–x, ix.

49 Maurice Culot, 'Le Monoplan de Papier', *Bulletin des AAM* 13 (1978): 1–3, 3. Culot did not view his role at the ARAU as 'the architect' who supposedly creates new forms for the political actions; see Robert Maxwell, 'Architecture, Language and Process', *Architectural Design* 47, no. 3 (1977): 191.

50 Culot, 'Le Monoplan de Papier', 3. Translated from French.

51 Léon Krier, 'Les misères de la confusion', *Bulletin des AAM* 18 (1980): 4–6, 5; Barey, *Déclaration de Bruxelles*, 13.

52 Culot in Maxwell, 'Architecture, Language and Process', 191.

53 René Schoonbrodt, in *Wonen TA/BK* 15–16 (1975): 25. Translated from Dutch, original emphasis.

54 Charles Jencks, *The Language of Post-Modern Architecture*, fifth edition (London: Academy Editions, 1987 [1977]), 106.

55 École nationale supérieure d'architecture et des arts visuels, *Le Bateau d'Élie*, 24, translated from French.

56 Maurice Culot, 'L'invité. Maurice Culot. Interview by Thierry Paquot 3 June 2008', *Revue Urbanisme* 361 (2008): 77–86. Accessed, May 13, 2009, http://www.urbanisme.fr.

57 Culot discusses 'la méthode des parallèles' in reference to Léon Krier's project for Luxemburg. Maurice Culot, 'L'Arau et les architects: la pratique du contre-projet; l'architecture moderne, outil de domination', in *Bruxelles Vu par ses Habitants, Quinze années d'action urbaine*, ed. ARAU (Brussels: Commission Française de la Culture et de l'Agglomération de Bruxelles and ARAU, 1984), 30.

58 'La Cambre 1928–1978', special issue, *Bulletin des AAM* 16 (1979): 56, translated from French; in the context of the discussion of the reconstruction project for the Quartier des Radis (D. Ange, R. De Gernier, A. Lambrichs, La Cambre, 1978).

59 'La Cambre 1928–1978', special issue, *Bulletin des AAM* 16 (1979): 32.

60 Culot and Krier, 'L'unique chemin de l'architecture'; Sefik Birkiye, *Vizzion Awards 2009: European Architecture Competition* (Brussels: AAM, 2009), 2.

61 The image is widely published, amongst others in *Déclaration de Bruxelles*, 25 and *La Reconstruction de Bruxelles*, 75; and more than once in the *Bulletin des AAM*. For more details on the mobilisation of the user in counter-projects, see Isabelle Doucet, 'Counter-projects and the postmodern user', in *Use Matters: An Alternative History of Architecture*, ed. Kenny Cupers (London and New York: Routledge, 2013), 233–247.

62 ARAU, *Bruxelles Vu par ses Habitants*, 113; Culot et al., *La Reconstruction de Bruxelles*, 79.

63 Krier and Culot, 'L'Unique Chemin de l'Architecture'.

64 René Schoonbrodt, 'Tradition et luttes urbaines', in *La Tour Ferrée*, ed. École nationale supérieure d'architecture et des arts visuels, 12.

65 Aesthetic maturation was identified in the designs for the Carrefour de l'Europe. See André Loeckx, '20 jaar ontwerpen voor het Europakruispunt te Brussel, overzicht en kritiek', *Monumenten & Landschappen* 8, no. 2 (1989): 29–48; and Christophe Van Gerrewey, 'Amnesty for the city. The Hoogpoort design for the Carrefour de l'Europe in Brussels (1983)', *The Journal of Architecture* 19, no. 3 (2014): 435–453.

66 Culot was appointed to the role by the Minister of Culture Henri-François Van Aal, who endorsed the actions of the ARAU. See Aron, 'le retour de l'utopie', in *La Cambre et l'Architecture*, 163–178.

67 This second generation included Élie Levy, Caroline Mierop, Philippe Lefebvre, and Anne Van Loo who all appeared in a photograph taken in 1977, published in Delevoy et al., *La Cambre 1928–1978*, 390.

68 Léon Krier, Peter Cook, Nigel Coates, Denis Sharp, and Bernard Tschumi were involved in seminars and juries at La Cambre. The *Bulletin des AAM* regularly reported on AA activities and several AAM exhibitions were shown at the AA.

69 *Bateau d'Élie*, 19; this project served as the cover image for the above mentioned special issue of *Architecture d'Aujourd'hui* 180 (July–August 1975).

70 Culot testifies to this in an interview undertaken by Irmeline Lebeer in *L'art vivant*, no. 56 (1975): 6–9, 7.

71 Culot quoted in Maxwell, 'Architecture, Language and Process', 191.

72 Schoonbrodt, 'tradition et luttes urbaines', 12; translated from French.

73 The project by Terlinden is published in, for example, *Wonen TA-BK*, 42. The Lelubre projects are published in *Wonen TA-BK*, 43 and Culot, 'La Longue Marche', 25.

74 Lelubre was following the advice of Prof. Raymond Lemaire, an authority in traditional urbanism and the preservation of cultural heritage. The Maison des Pages, demolished around 1950, dates back to the time of nineteenth-century ruler Charles de Lorraine, whose palace is located on the site. See ARAU, 'Conference de presse du mardi 3 mars 1981: Pourqoui ne pas reconstruire la maison des pages?' and ARAU, Le musée qui n'aimait pas la ville', 71.

75 See *Bateau d'Élie*, 40–43; and *Wonen TA-BK*, 43 (where the echoing of the Old England is credited to Anne Van Loo).

76 The ARAU's articulation and monumentalising of the entrance to the underground museum was recognised by Culot as a desire for 'architectural grandeur' (Culot, 'Le Monoplan de Papier', 3).

77 Schoonbrodt, *Vouloir et dire la ville*, 316–318.

78 Ibid., 319.

79 Loeckx, '20 jaar ontwerpen voor het Europakruispunt', 34–35; and see Robert Courtois 'Stadsanalyse, het europakruipunt. De grote wonde of de weerstaanbare wederopbouw van het brusselse stadscentrum', *A Plus* 127, no. 2 (1994): 44–54; and Van Gerrewey, 'Amnesty for the City'.

80 The influence of Archigram was, according to Van Loo, only short-lived (*Repertorium*, 86).

81 The Brussels' *architecture rationelle* encompassed the choice for classical and vernacular architecture, the promotion of craftsmanship, and the construction and decoration of public space, that is urban embellishment (*Bulletin des AAM* 24 [1982]: 8). It shared its 'realism' with the French Architecture Urbaine and the Urbanistica Alternativa in Bologne, but the Belgian and Italian scene was considered more political and more focused on the historic city centre. On 'realism', please see Bernard Huet, 'Formalisme – Realisme', *Architecture d'aujourd'hui* 190 (1977): 35–38. See also Anthony Vidler, 'The Third Typology', *Oppositions* 7 (1977): reprinted in *Rational Architecture: The Reconstruction of the European City* (Brussels: AAM, 1978).

82 Maurice Culot, interviewed by Marc Lecomte 'AAM, ARAU, La Cambre et c'est comme ça que tout a commencé', *Bulletin d'Information Pédagogique*, June 1, 1980, 13–14. Consulted at the Archives d'Architecture Moderne: private archives Maurice Culot (uncatalogued).

83 Léon Krier, 'The Age of Reconstruction' in *Drawings 1967–1980* (Brussels: Éditions AAM, 1981), xiii–xv, xv. Krier claimed the refusal to build and the urgency for the reconstruction of a global theory came from Culot (xiv).

84 Maurice Culot, 'Galateo in Citta', *Bulletin des AAM* 17 (1980): 81.

85 *La Tour Ferrée*, ed. École nationale supérieure d'architecture et des arts visuels, 100, translated from French. The projects developed for the reconstruction of the Quartier du Nord, and in particular the *Le Grand Boulevard du Nord* project by Sefik Birkiye and Patrick Kelly (101–109), was, with its grand boulevards lined with trees and linear parks, seen as a case in point. See also Maurice Culot, 'La Cambre School of Architecture and Anti-industrial Resistance. Tradition as the Pedagogy of Action, Bruxelles 1978', *Lotus International* 21 (1978).

86 Culot, 'La Cambre School of Architecture and Anti-industrial Resistance', 46. Culot credits Léon Krier for this insight (Culot, *Counterprojects*); and see René Schoonbrodt, 'L'attitude anti-industrielle', *Bulletin des AAM* 15 (1978): 1–3.

87 Albert Martens, 'Table ronde. Luttes urbaines et lutte politique', 24; translated from French.

88 Jencks quoted in Paolo Porthoghesi, *Postmodern: The Architecture of the Postindustrial Society* (Milan: Electa, 1982): 10.

89 Culot, 'The counter-projects', in Krier and Culot, *Contreprojets*.

90 Culot, '1980–1990: La Décade du n'importe quoi', 3.

91 Davies, 'Leon Krier talks to Colin Davies', xxiii.

92 Maxwell, 'Architecture, Language and Process', 192.

93 Culot, 'L'Arau et les architects', 30.

94 Ibid., 29–30; and see Barey, *Déclaration de Bruxelles*, 12.

95 Barey, *Déclaration de Bruxelles*, 25; 36. The 'original' of the vertical window was said to be found in the nearby Rue de Montagne: in the project 'les maisons devant la gare', part of 'Différents Projets de Reconstruction (et embellissement) du centre de Bruxelles éventré par la réalisation de la Jonction Ferroviaire Nord-Midi' by Sefik Birkiye, Patrice Neirinck, Gilbert Busieau, La Cambre, 1978 (*Bulletin des AAM* 16 [1979], 35).

96 Barey, *Déclaration de Bruxelles*, 12; Culot, 'L'Arau et les architects', 29.

97 Culot, 'Introduction' in Krier and Culot, *Contreprojets*.

98 Several units involved tutors who were affiliated with the Reconstruction movement; see *Bulletin des AAM* 13, 1978.

99 Others included Peter Cook and Archigram, Jean Castex, Philippe Panerai, Jacques Gubler, Françoise Choay, G.C. Argan, Bruno Zevi, and Jean Prouvé (see Van Loo, *Repertorium*, 248).

100 Culot, *Brussels architectures*, 62; Aron, *La Cambre et l'Architecture*, 167–168; Culot, 'la droite masquée'; Robert L. Delevoy, 'Discours d'Inauguration', *Bulletin des AAM* 18 (1980) 88–91.

101 Quoted from Maurice Culot and Léon Krier, 'The Only Path for Architecture', in *Architecture Theory since 1968*, ed. K. Michael Hays (Cambridge, MA: The MIT Press, 2000), 354; and see Culot, quoted in Frederique de Gravelaine, 'Architecture: les amants de la ville', *L'Unité, hebdomadaire du parti socialiste* 361 (1979): 11 (consulted at the Archives d'Architecture Moderne: private archives Maurice Culot (uncatalogued).

Students had to appear for state exams where they at times met hostility; many of them eventually returned to official education (Aron, *La Cambre et l'Architecture*, 186–187).

102 Hays, introduction to 'The Only Path', 349.

103 Notably, Ockman, 'The Most Interesting Form of a Lie'.

104 Apers et al., *Bouwen door de Eeuwen heen*; Sint-Lukasarchief, *Brussel, breken, bouwen* (1979) and *Straten en Stenen* (1982).

105 Hans Ibelings, *Unmodern Architecture: Contemporary Traditionalism in the Netherlands* (Rotterdam: Nai Publishers, 2004), 63. Examples include Critical Reconstruction/IBA Berlin, the Council for European Urbanism CEU, and New Urbanism in the US.

106 Hosted, in Brussels, by André Barey and involving international guests, including Jean Castex, Antoine Grumbach, Léon Krier, Pierluigi Nicolin, and Bernard Huet. The AAM was responsible for key publications of the movement; and its Bulletin enjoyed greater intellectual freedom than some other magazines.

107 Such as the Fondation pour l'Architecture, which was co-founded in 1986 by Culot and, since 1999, became integrated with CIVA; and the Fondation Philippe Rotthier pour l'Architecture.

108 Culot, 'Elegio del "pastiche": intervista a Maurice Culot' by Allessandro Vicari, *Costruire In Laterizio* 10, no. 55 (1997): 26–31, 28, translated from Italian. See Culot in 'da fornovo, Maurice culot e I principi che isperanc I suoi progetti architettonici', in *Cultura e Società, Gazzetta di Parma* 13, June 25, 1993.

109 Caroline Mierop and Françoise Deville, eds, *Oproep aan de jonge Europese architecten* (Brussels: Fondation pour l'Architecture, 1995).

110 Culot, *Brussels architectures*, 120; 142–143.

111 Van Loo, *Repertorium*, 99–101.

112 In *Brussels architectures* (121–122) Culot includes, for example, the Radisson SAS Royal Hotel (1987–1990), a project designed by Vizzion, formerly Atelier d'Art Urbain, with Jaspers Eyers Architects.

113 'View' section in *The Architectural Review* 8, no. 1302 (2005), 22; Omer Cavusoglu, 'Summary on [sic] the Haydarpasa Case Study Site', March 2010. Accessed, August 18, 2014, http://www.lse.ac.uk/LSECities/citiesProgramme/pdf/Haydarpasa%20Summary.pdf. Images of the project can be found on Vizzion's company website. Accessed August 18, 2014, http://www.atelier-art-urbain.com/en/achievements/urbanization/haydarpasa/index.php.

114 IEB, AAM, *Les Espaces Publics Bruxellois: analyse et projets* (Brussels: Fondation Roi Baudouin, 1981). The work was directed by Culot and Schoonbrodt, and carried out by ex-students including Sefik Birkiye, Gilbert Busieau, Michel de Beule, Brigitte d'Helft, Jean François Lejeune, Patrice Neirinck, and Michel Verliefden. It was presented as a 'tool for action', finding further justification in its participatory approach (91).

115 Marie Demanet, Jean-Pierre Majot, eds, *Handboek van de Brusselse Openbare Ruimten* (Brussels: Iris, 1995). It was published in collaboration with the Brussels Capital Region and the AAM (in French: *Manuel des Espaces Public Bruxellois*).

116 Pierre Loze, 'Hofberg, het einde van een lang verhaal', *A Plus* 115, no. 2 (1992): 36–39. Picqué influenced spatial planning through, for example, 1990s Structure Planning and the 2007 Plan de Développement International de Bruxelles, as well as urban renewal through Neighbourhood Contracts, and cultural patrimony.

117 Translated from French. The winner was Christophe Gillis of Bureau d'architecture OZON.

118 Culot, *Brussels architectures*, 134–135. Port Grimaud, François Spoerry's instantly-old holiday resort was believed to give people what they want – Culot in Grahame Shane, 'Culot/Contextualism and Conscience', *Architectural Design* 47, no. 3 (1977): 189.

119 Isabelle Doucet, 'Brussels: The Soft Regeneration', in *Houses in Transformation, Interventions in European Gentrification*, ed. J.J. Berg et al. (Rotterdam: NAI Publishers, 2008), 130–143. See also the overview map of counter-projects developed by the ARAU, included in ARAU, *Bruxelles Vu par ses Habitants*: 52–53.

120 Loeckx, '20 jaar ontwerpen voor het Europakruispunt', 40–41; Van Gerrewey, 'Amnesty for the city'. The counter-project by Birkiye et al. (La Cambre, 1978), as part of the 'Différents Projets de Reconstruction (et embellissement) du centre de Bruxelles', was widely published and therefore formed a strong mental image for the site.

121 Bastin had been forced to make a study for a *puits de lumière* (in 1979); see Paul Emile Vincent, *La Cambre a 60 ans, Les Cahiers de La Cambre Architecture*, no. 4 (Brussels: ISAE – La Cambre, 1978), 54–55.

122 Culot endorsed the ARAU's prioritising of democratic action and conflict over aesthetic concerns. See Culot, 'Bruxelles un terrain du combat anti-capitaliste', *Revue Urbanisme* 153–154 (1976): 122–123; 'La Cambre School of Architecture and Anti-industrial Resistance', 47.

123 As argued by Van Loo (*Repertorium*, 94–96). Van Loo adds that a large part of the building production is in the hands of larger architecture associations, such as Atelier de Genval, Montois, and Jaspers-Eyers.

3

Interstitial Activism

In 1995, a group of activists from the Stichting Open Deur/Fondation Pied de Biche held an epochal campaign in the heart of Brussels by squatting in a vacant housing block threatened by demolition. This action, lasting for ten days, became known as *Hôtel Central*, and involved artists, activists, intellectuals, local organisations, and civil society groups from both the French- and Dutch-speaking communities; taking part were both the new and more established activist groups such as Freetown Brussels (VrijstadBXLVilleLibre), the Beursschouwburg Theatre, the Brusselse Raad voor het Leefmilieu (BRAL), Inter-Environnement Bruxelles (IEB), and the Atelier de Recherche et d'Action Urbaines (ARAU). The protest was against both the condition of Brussels' inner city – blighted by uninhabitable and abandoned sites – and the authorities' apathetic attitude towards this condition.[1] Instigating a widespread urban activism, *Hôtel Central* demonstrated that Brussels was ill 'but its heart was still beating'.[2] For example, in 1996, Kino-Trotter and the Beursschouwburg Theatre improvised an open-air cinema on a vacant lot in Brussels called *Cinema Légumen*. Meanwhile, the urban activist collective City Mine(d), created in the wake of *Hôtel Central*, concentrated on the reclaiming of other public space: one intervention, called *Barake*, involved the erection of a tree house by the Belgian artist Benjamin Verdonck. The tree house, which Verdonck lived in for one week during the summer of 2000, was craned into position and sat 10 metres above the Place Bara (Figure 3.1, see Plate 4).[3] Highly visible from the nearby international high-speed railway hub of Brussels South Station, it was intended as a critique of the recent redevelopment of the square which had ignored its qualities as an inhabitable urban space. Such interventions aimed to draw attention to the condition and policy regarding Brussels' public spaces.

Another activist group that emerged in the wake of *Hôtel Central*, was Cinema Nova. Formerly an organiser of open-air film screening across various vacant sites within Brussels' historic city centre, Cinema Nova gained momentum in 1996 with the legal squatting, and reopening, of the Arenberg Cinema which had been vacant since 1987.[4] Having agreed an initial two-year contract, the cinema is still open today. In 1997, both City Mine(d) and Cinema Nova joined forces for organising a series of open-air cinema screenings under the banner of *PleinOPENair* (Figure 3.2). Taking place each summer, the choice of location for each event is intended

3.1 Benjamin Verdonck, *Barake* project near the Brussels Gare du Midi.
Copyright: City Mine(d). Used with permission.

3.2 *PleinOPENair*. Copyright: City Mine(d).
Used with permission.

to generate critical public awareness around urban problems such as buildings threatened by demolition, public spaces facing privatisation, and *terrains vagues*.

The actions of *Hôtel Central* were pivotal in changing Brussels' attitude vis-à-vis public space with regard to patrimony, urbanity and liveability. The immediate outcome of the squat may not have been entirely successful – the site now contains a corporate hotel – but its actions, nevertheless, had a long-lasting effect on Brussels. This impact was informed by the event's significant media attention and a manifesto signed by more than 100 organisations.[5] But it was also informed by the urban activism that was triggered in the wake of *Hôtel Central*, an activism that, over time, gained scale and momentum. In 2000, Brussels chose, in its capacity of Cultural Capital of Europe, 'the city and the urban challenge(s)' as its central theme, a clear acknowledgement of the importance of urban culture; in 2002, Luxemburg Station, which sits directly underneath the European Parliament, was occupied taking Brussels activism into the heart of the European project;[6] and in August 2004, a further upscaling occurred through the MAPRAC events, a three-day mapping workshop (MAP) on the site of the Rijks Administratief Centrum (RAC). The RAC, a large state-owned, office complex that was home to the Belgian Federal Administration, was questionably sold to private investors. Through workshops and various other public activities, including *PleinOPENair* film screenings, alternative proposals for the site were made. The organisers, City Mine(d) and the collective DistUrb, a multidisciplinary collective preoccupied with triggering architectural-urban debates and actions in Brussels, were particularly preoccupied with how RAC's vast public space could be rescued from privatisation and reclaimed by the citizens.[7] Through mobilising local residents, action committees, and also professional, political and institutional stakeholders, the MAPRAC event operated as an activism from-within, and demonstrates how several of the activists involved in the occupation of *Hôtel Central* have come to occupy strong positions in the Brussels urban debate.[8]

This chapter unpacks the emergence and transformation of the Brussels activism, in terms of an activism from-within, and its impact on the Brussels architectural culture. Because of this impact it deserves greater attention in architectural debates. I will argue that this activism was resistant in an interstitial manner, and that this interstitial activism is instructive for exploring the credentials of critical and resistant operations from-within. The discussion is organised around the activities of Recyclart, a collective that settled in an abandoned railway station in Brussels. Although activist collectives were numerous in Brussels during the 1990s, Recyclart's institutional roots and its ambiguous and somewhat compromised position in the contemporaneous activist climate make it particularly useful for addressing questions of activism from-within. The collective's actions in public space design are also informative; and here Recyclart was not alone. Activists in the 1990s generally used public space as the locus for countering the perceived inhospitable situation of the Brussels city-centre. Being left to the mercy of developers and speculation, the city was interlaced with abandoned houses, vacant lots, and urban cancers; and these formed the locus for action. Compared to those actions, Recyclart had an additional impact on architectural and urban culture, which was effectuated not through one-off actions in specific locations, but through a continuous series of actions; each one different in nature and stretching over an extended period of time.[9]

A NEW 'TURN' IN BRUSSELS' ARCHITECTURE AND URBANISM

Urban activisms in the wake of *Hôtel Central*, had a shared articulation and imagining for re-claiming the city as a lived space. However, rather than through the design or 'embellishment' of space, activists mobilised a combination of actions. In the spirit of the Reclaim the City movement,[10] they highlighted the overlooked qualities of abandoned spaces, vacant lots, and urban fringes, and encouraged the re-appropriation and re-programming of these spaces through temporary events and impromptu actions, and strengthened connections with local culture. Rather than involving users through consultation procedures, activists promoted the co-production of the city, and emphasised use and activities over aesthetics and embellishment as key features for shaping the city. I recognise therein a significant departure from the 'Reconstruction of the European City' activism of the 1970s which engaged the ARAU and the AAM. Whilst both generations hoped to ameliorate the worst excesses of urban renewal in the 1960s and 1970s, their strategies differed. The Reconstruction movement of the 1970s advocated the formal, aesthetic, and morphological repairing of the city. However, in a city that did not just struggle to repair its urban wounds but also required structural interventions in the social and economic fabric of the city, questions emerged over whether physical reconstructions alone would suffice. Moreover, the careful reconstruction of historic neighbourhoods proved ideal for effectuating a gradual, but efficient, 'soft' regeneration of the city centre.[11] Reconstruction strategies lent themselves to a middle-class gentrification of vulnerable inner-city neighbourhoods and their militant actions of the 1970s gradually became reduced to a mere stylistic urbanism, thriving on pastiche and façadism. This nourished a conservative stronghold and urban embellishment mindset within mainstream architectural production that some believed to be exerting a paralysing effect on Brussels' architectural and urban culture.[12]

I believe that the 1990s urban activism offered a novel and refreshing outlook onto urban design. With its impact on urban culture, it also influenced the architectural and urban design culture of Brussels. Signs of change were, amongst others, evinced by the MAPRAC workshop, and by the architectural and urban design workshops and debates organised by urban think-tank Studio Open City.[13] Also, the activities of Brussels 2000 Capital of Culture signalled a change in that they included an international architecture workshop organised for the Brussels' Mont des Art site, and an exhibition, called *Supernova*, dedicated to the work of 44 young Belgian architects.[14] Another indication that things were changing can be found in the creation of the Brussels Architecture Institute which, since 2005, has hosted architectural and urban debates. In November 2009, the first Brussels Master Architect was appointed, and commissioned to guarantee architectural and spatial quality of public design projects in the Brussels Capital Region.[15] In December 2012, the Brussels Master Architect launched an ambitious debate on the future of the Brussels North–South Junction, a 60-year-old urban scar which had resulted from the tunnelling of the inner-city railway connection. The event was called *Jonction* and included the exhibition of four 4 x 4 m tapestries, each created by a selected architecture office.

The *Jonction* event, the Brussels Architecture Institute, the Brussels Master Architect, and, more generally, the Brussels' architectural and urban design emancipation of the 2000s, were, arguably, indebted to the urban activism of the 1990s. This activism challenged both the urban politics of neglect and the embellishment approach to the city, two forces that were considered to have left the city's future at the mercy of private developers, and is, therefore, believed to represent a 'turn' in Brussels' architecture and urbanism. This followed an earlier turn, as identified by Jacques Aron, associated with the 1970s activism of the ARAU and the AAM.[16] Elements associated with the 'second turn' include: the replacement of embellishment, and historical referencing, with more experimental, contemporary design; an emphasis on use rather than the design of space; and a shift from citizen consultation to co-production. It also signalled an architectural and urban critique that operated from-within the Brussels' real. Compared to the drawings of the counter-projects of the 1970s the activism in the 1990s operated through real-life interventions such as urban installations, squats, and public space occupations. Changes in architectural and urban design thinking were no longer informed by radical ideological revolutions, as had been the case with the anti-industrial resistance of the 1970s (see Chapter 2). Under the second turn, change occurred through piecemeal, small, and fragmented revolutions within architectural and urban culture. For example, a white paper, with the telling title *Who is afraid of Architecture?*, emphasised the importance of architecture 'as a cultural discipline that has a role to play in democratic life', and called for a shared responsibility of making-city and a more pro-active role by public authorities.[17] Another example is the publication of a handbook for organising architecture competitions, which provided policy makers with guidelines and procedures for good practice.[18] In a city where architects felt public architecture and urban design competitions were lacking, such modest steps can be considered milestones.

These efforts coincided with the opportunities created by official urban renewal programmes such as Neighbourhood Contracts, a publicly funded programme for neighbourhood renewal in deprived areas focussed upon housing and public space (see Chapter 5). Architectural critics and theorists recognised important opportunities for young architects in the modest projects produced within the context of Neighbourhood Contracts.[19] Maurice Culot, for example, saw in Neighbourhood Contracts a 'field of expression for a new contemporary architecture' and, together with the wider strengthening of instruments for urban renewal, the most important instigator for the new generation of architects in the period 1995–2000.[20] It is important, however, to also emphasise the influence of the 1990s activism in the architectural and urban design emancipation of the 1990s and 2000s.[21] Let us now turn to Recyclart whose activism can be studied as an 'interstitial event'.

AN INTERSTITIAL READING OF ACTIVISM?

> *There are no oppositions in the real but only differences, productive differences [...].*[22]

International debates on activism and urban theory have recognised the emergence of a new type of urban activism in the 1990s, a period that is also associated with a 'roll-out neoliberalisation'.[23] This period was characterised by a fragmented activist milieu, and an intensification of neighbourhood revitalisation strategies; a period which utilised urban regeneration as a tool for economic growth, as exemplified by the Neighbourhood Contracts in Brussels. Activists and civil society actors were active in this context, contributing to the socio-cultural activities within Neighbourhood Contracts. But at the same time, they were involved in anti-gentrification and anti-globalisation movements such as 'reclaim the streets'.[24] In other words, activists operated both in support of urban regeneration and against it.

In this chapter, I have chosen to study the activism of this period through the lens of 'interstice', drawing from Isabelle Stengers's 'Cosmopolitical Proposal' and 'Ecology of Practices', and Didier Debaise's work on the interstitial. Stengers' 'Ecology of Practices' forms 'a tool for thinking through what is happening.'[25] Thinking through what is happening invites one to grasp (and give voice to) what is residing in the interstices, namely that which 'escapes description because our words refer to stabilised identities and functioning'.[26] Interstices are those instances where activities that were previously illegible, and thus unnoticed, become articulated. Stengers' interstice is 'other' and 'minor' not because it is small, or because it is deliberately oppressed or excluded, but because in the light of dominant norms and visions it goes unnoticed. Despite their minority position, interstices are not too influenced by the 'majoritarian norm, which includes not defining itself as its opposite'.[27] Instead, interstices denote a resistance from-within; a resistance that relies on a capacity to 'not to be too easily impressed'.[28]

Studying the 1990s activism through the lens of the interstice may be instructive for several reasons. Firstly, in the context of advanced neoliberalisation, interstices open up novel ways of reading margins, peripheries, the informal, and excluded, and of analysing their relationship with the centre. Interstices emphasise the emancipatory powers of such places and are, therefore, spaces of hope and resistance where other futures become possible. bell hooks conceptualises the margin in such lines:[29]

> *Survival depends on their [the occupants of the margin] ability to invent alternatives and to find spaces of resistance and radical openness – to invent margins. Understanding marginality as a state and place of creativity is crucial. Those groups staying in the margin develop a special way of observing reality – by focusing on both centre and margin – which results in the awareness that boundary communities are, despite the clear distinction between centre and margin, a vital part of the whole.*

Secondly, in architecture and urban design, peripheries are typically studied as space which is 'other' than that which is organised, structured, and planned. This depiction of what are ubiquitous and transient spaces of the city, serves to magnify the transformative, informal, and self-organised nature of cities.[30] The articulation of the margin as a distinct spatial entity has triggered all sorts of experimental mapping techniques and analytical tactics (for example through walking, strolling, or drifting) for reading peripheries and the city at large.[31] However, by relying on spatial metaphors such as edge, periphery, no-man's land, *terrain vague*, urban fringe, or non-place, the margin is often still depicted as the negative of something else rather than an entity in its own right. The promotion of small-scale, modest, and catalyst interventions for margins, leaves questions regarding the wider, structural impact, unresolved. The interstice, by contrast, locates otherness in cracks *within* the centre as much as in peripheral locations. This allows for a novel imagining of resistance which, according to Margit Mayer, is urgent. Neoliberalisation operates through enclosure, through the privatisation of public space, and the clustering of displaced poverty by, for example, relocating the poor to targeted neighbourhoods or urban peripheries.[32] As a result, *all* gaps and margins are eventually absorbed into neoliberalism's cause of growth. In such a context, as shown by recent debates on the Right to the City, activism becomes fragmented and of varied critical colouring. In the neoliberalised city, one finds activism in the shape of radical actions, emergent calls from precarious urban groups, along with middle-class and artistic calls.[33] It is, therefore, important to re-imagine resistance amidst the 'new metropolitan mainstream',[34] and recognise that resistance resides also in places that are central. The interstice is, consequently, instructive for imagining resistance within the neoliberalised city, and for becoming more receptive to overlooked places of dissent such as, for example, institutional settings.

Thirdly, the interstice helps to cut across polarising distinctions for reading activism including: between centre and periphery, radicalism and appeasement, critical and mainstream, and emancipation and normalisation. Interstices, therefore, radicalise our reading not only of peripheries but centres too. They form a warning against reading peripheries as 'other' spaces whereby, paraphrasing AbdouMaliq Simone, the 'real' city (that is chaotic, self-organising, 'lived') is unleashed whilst the rest of the city (the centre) is treated as stable and normalised.[35] The interstice instead reminds us that destabilising and disruptive forces operate *across* the urban fabric, and breaks with what David Harvey called the 'legitimation crisis' – an acceptance that 'there is no alternative' to the neoliberalised free market world.[36] The potential of radical readings of the centre are demonstrated by the Brussels activist practices. As Lieven De Cauter observed, examples such as *Hôtel Central* and *Picnic the Streets* – an improvised picnic at the traffic-laden Place de La Bourse – are acts of civil disobedience that occurred in plain sight, in the very centre of Brussels.[37]

Finally, interstices manifest temporally, as well as spatially. A temporal reading of the interstice invites a study of the transformations of activism over time. This is particularly relevant in the context of 'compromised' activism, because it allows for studying processes of radicalisation and maturation, along with upscaling, institutionalisation, and mainstreaming.

In what follows, I highlight this temporal dimension of the interstice. Through the example of Recyclart, I will focus not just on the manifestations but also the trajectories of activism; and analyse how activist practices safeguard their ethical integrity throughout processes of transformation.

RECYCLART'S INTERSTITIAL ACTIVISM

In 1997, the collective Recyclart settled in the abandoned premises of the Chapelle-Kapellekerk station, occupying its ticket hall, corridors and underpass (Figure 3.3, see Plate 5).[38] Chapelle-Kapellekerk is a small commuter station located on the North–South Railway Junction, central Brussels, and close to the popular neighbourhood Les Marolles. The North–South Railway Junction is an infrastructural tour de force. At nearly 3 kilometres in length, and mostly tunnelled, it provides a link between the North and South Stations, stations that were previously disconnected. As such, it allows trains to pass through Brussels uninterrupted from the different corners of the country. When inaugurated in 1952, its disruptive effect on the historical urban fabric was evident. The over-dimensioned functionalist urbanism that came in its place could not, despite its architectural grandeur, compensate for the lost urbanity of the demolished popular neighbourhoods. Recyclart's choice to settle in this spatial interstice was, therefore, an act of reclaiming some of that urbanity.

Apart from its location, Recyclart is, institutionally and programmatically, an interstitial event. When the City of Brussels applied for the European funding for Urban Pilot Project (UPP), it opted to do so through its Delegation of the Pentagon, a sub-administration focusing on the development of the city centre.[39] This choice came down to the Alderman for Urbanism, who felt affinity with some individuals within the Delegation of the Pentagon who had also been involved in the actions

3.3 Location of Recyclart, Brussels, January 2015. Photograph by the author.

around *Hôtel Central*. Upon approval of the funding, the City of Brussels created the non-profit organisation Recyclart. Thus, from the outset, Recyclart adopted an activism from-within, and was presided over by an Administrative Board which originally consisted solely of political and administrative actors. Over time, Recyclart gradually down-scaled the Board's political representation, thus following a contrarious activist trajectory of *de*-institutionalisation.[40]

Combining artistic activities, socio-professional training, and urban design projects, Recyclart operates programmatically as an interstice. Whilst Recyclart's artistic production is anchored in international arts scenes, it also involves inhabitants of local neighbourhoods, and runs socio-professional activities aimed at re-inserting the long-term unemployed back into the job market. It does so through two sub-organisations – Bar Recyclart and Fabrik. Bar Recyclart runs the foyer bar of Recyclart, and operates a training programme for cooks and bartenders. Fabrik trains apprentices in its metal and timber workshops to produce street furniture for public clients and for projects initiated by Recyclart[41] (Figure 3.4). As such, it acts as a contractor as well as a designer, reinforcing Recyclart's urban activist mission through skill training activities. The weight of Recyclart's urban design activism resides in this blending of architectural–urban with political–economic operations.

3.4 The Fabrik workshop, Recyclart. Copyright: Recyclart. Used with permission.

Additionally, Recyclart shows how institutional embedding can facilitate, rather than hamper, activism. Its institutional origins have helped in innovating public space design mind-sets from-within the Brussels planning administrations. Further, the financial stability that comes with an institutional affiliation allows for a certain level of freedom and experimentation that would be difficult to obtain in more insecure, fragmented funding landscapes.[42] Institutional affiliation, moreover, triggers mainstream media-attention which, ultimately, acts at the service of activism. This was the case with the public space project called *Arabesk-Palaverboom* by Jozef Legrand and Recyclart, completed in 2005. The project was initiated by Recyclart as a social project created in collaboration with local citizens and artists, and through debates, local festivities and workshops. The street furniture was realised by Fabrik. The project was envisaged as an 'urban salon', epitomising Recyclart's belief in the (design of the) city in terms of 'active pluralism'.[43] Moreover, the 'urban salon' is a public space that is not designed through embellishing techniques based on historic references, rather it emerges from the articulation of spaces that *already* serve as an informal meeting place. In the *Arabesk-Palaverboom* project, an urban salon was created by means of an arabesque-shaped bench,

3.5 Arabesk-Palaverboom project, Brussels. Photograph by the author, 2015.

located under a palaver tree (Figure 3.5, see Plate 6). The palaver tree is reminiscent of the West-African tradition of palaver, a prolonged dialogue and discussion with a strong community component. If not under a palaver tree, palaver typically takes place in public space or as part of negotiations at, for example, local markets.[44] The bench's meandering shape is intended to encourage such palaver. Also, by working with the topography of the square, one can sit on the bench in some areas, whilst one is invited to 'hang' onto it in others. The design encourages people to linger, whilst the engraved texts onto the benches are intended to evoke memories of youngsters who would once leave their mark on paint-exfoliated benches.[45]

The project's activism resides precisely in the choice of the palaver tree, the particular shape of the bench, the invitation to loiter, and the inclusion of the engravings which serve as an invitation to youths who are typically overlooked by gentrification projects. In sharp contrast to the consumer environments of brasseries and terraces, as typically envisaged by developers, *Arabesk-Palaverboom* was more faithful to the socially and culturally mixed population of the area. Further, as part of a larger refurbishment project for the Breughel Square, coordinated by federal and regional authorities, when the refurbished square was inaugurated in the presence of Brussels authorities, also the *Arabesk-Palaverboom* enjoyed significant media attention:

> *There was a time when, in Brussels, benches were removed from public space because they attracted loitering youths. Anno 2005, public benches are inaugurated in the presence of federal ministers.*[46]

3.6 *De Roze Verspreiding* project, design by Les Saprophytes. Copyright: Les Saprophytes. Used with permission.

The project's activism was, as such, *reinforced* by its operating from-within. Another project that demonstrates the benefits of Recyclart's activism from-within is the *De Roze Verspreiding* project (The Pink Dissemination). This project was created within the institutional context of a Neighbourhood Contract. Conceived as an 'urban salon', *De Roze Verspreiding* turned 24 ordinary traffic poles into seats simply by painting them fuchsia. The location of the posts was co-determined by the youngsters who already informally used the space (Figure 3.6, see Plate 7). Rather than designing a new public space, the project simply articulated existing usages and capitalised upon existing public infrastructure such as nearby parks.[47] I recognise in this type of project an alternative to the urban embellishment tradition, formulated from-within the official context of Neighbourhood Contracts.

Another particularly influential urban design project is Ursulines Skate Park which, completed in 2007, is illustrative of the collaborative nature of Recyclart projects (Figure 3.7, see Plate 8; and Figure 3.8, see Plate 9). The project was instigated in 2003 by Brusk, a collective of Brussels skateboarders, who approached Recyclart for advice in creating a skate park. Acting as project coordinator, Recyclart joined with the Brussels Institute for Management of the Environment[48] who, by coincidence, wanted to create public spaces with an active component attached to it. Together, they developed a project for the site which is located at the intersection of the Les Marolles neighbourhood and the gentrified neighbourhoods of Place de Sablon, and overlooks the North–South railway junction at the point where it disappears underground. It is surrounded by housing, offices, a youth hostel, a school, an elderly home, and the premises

3.7   Ursulines Square / Skate Park, Brussels. Photograph by Filip Dujardin.
Copyright: L'Escaut. Used with permission.

3.8   Ursulines Square / Skate Park, Brussels.
Photograph by the author, 2015.

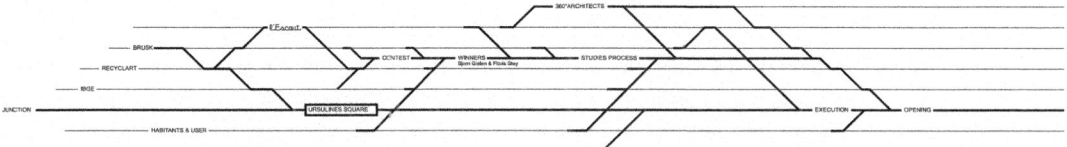

3.9 Ursulines Square / Skate Park. Design timeline. Copyright: L'Escaut. Used with permission.

of Recyclart itself. Recyclart organised a student design competition which was subsequently won by Bjorn Gielen and Floris Steyaert. The final design was the product of intense collaborations between the student-laureates, the architectural office L'Escaut that was appointed in support of the students, Brusk, Recyclart, Fabrik, and the Brussels Institute for Management of the Environment. By actively involving institutional stakeholders, this internationally acclaimed project was also taken seriously *locally*. In addition, through an intensive participatory process, involving users as far apart as pensioners and skaters, the design team developed a careful understanding of existing user patterns. To mobilise as many of these users as possible, Recyclart organised workshops with neighbours and prospective users, skate classes, and a mini-festival. This allowed for developing design scenarios that encouraged the co-existence, rather than separation, of conflicting uses and needs.[49] This collaborative approach informed the innovative design of the square: rather than design a public space that includes a skate park, the entire site can be used as a skate park but, at the same time, accommodates multiple uses. This is made possible by designing the project not just in space, but also in time (Figure 3.9); and by allowing the street furniture to become *part of* the design. As such, a public landscape emerges where skating, sitting, strolling, and playing subtly co-exist, and where the topography welcomes larger public events. This approach offers a very different kind of public space than the one created through the simple embellishment of public squares by means of benches, trees, and street lanterns.

Recyclart has also collaborated with the Brussels Institute for Management of the Environment on the Parckdesign competition which, since its inception in 2006, has focused on the design of public spaces in the city. By focusing on the innovation of street furniture for parks, these competitions 'questioned the approach of design through urban furniture in the city's parks and gardens'.[50] By collaborating with the public administration, Recyclart ensured that its innovative proposals would not go unnoticed as valuable alternatives to established public design traditions. However, by handling the manufacturing of the street furniture in the Fabrik workshop, Recyclart also guaranteed the socio-economic component of the project. In the wake of these pioneering editions, Parckdesign grew from a focus on street furniture innovation into more comprehensive design interventions. For example, whereas Parckdesign 2012 focused on the 'reinterpretation of undeveloped grounds, residual spaces and interstices in Brussels', the 2014 edition centred on the co-production of a Parckfarm involving local and regional actors. Parckdesign, as such, gradually underwent upscaling, established closer ties with architectural and urban design firms, and reinforced its international focus.[51]

EMPOWERING FROM-WITHIN

As the above examples demonstrate, Recyclart's public space activism is driven by a gradual, cautious emancipation of interstices. It operates through concrete urban interventions (for example Arabesk, Ursulines, Parckdesign), and through collaborations with, rather than opposition to, urban policy makers. This piecemeal emancipation is also evidenced by Recyclart's instigation and gradual maturation of an architectural and urban debate culture. In this respect, Recyclart adopts an interstitial position in the Brussels architectural debate. On the one hand it is distinct from the institutionalised French-speaking debate culture as represented by the Centre International pour la Ville, l'Architecture et le Paysage (CIVA),[52] whilst on the other it seeks closer ties with the debate culture of the Dutch-speaking Vlaams Architectuur Instituut, the Flemish Architecture Institute.[53]

Confronted by such titans, Recyclart proposed a different kind of platform for discussing architecture, and created the Brussels Architecture Institute or IBAI: a French–Dutch acronym for Institut Bruxellois d'Architecture / Brussels Architectuur Instituut. The IBAI is modelled on the Flemish Architecture Institute, but rather than focus on the promotion of contemporary architectural culture, the IBAI aims at discussing architecture as part of a larger urban, social, and cultural discourse. By transgressing the boundaries of design culture, the IBAI remains close to urban culture and activism appealing to philosophers, theorists, and anthropologists, as well as architects, planners, and graphic designers. Despite its international character, the IBAI remains closely entangled with Brussels' activist legacy. As a platform, it is more informal than the Flemish Architecture Institute, which is based in De Singel, an important cultural foundation in Antwerp. The IBAI operates instead from under the railway tracks of the Gare de Chapelle, where architecture and urban design are discussed under the rattling noise of bypassing trains, and debates meander, *à la Bruxelles*, between French, Dutch, and English.

INTERSTITIAL ACTIVISM AS RESISTANCE FROM-WITHIN

Earlier in this chapter, I introduced the MAPRAC workshop, an activist event that, in 2004, revolted against the privatisation of the city. This event did not have an immediate impact on the development of the site itself, but it did, nonetheless, influence the direction of future Brussels urban policies. In 2006, the site was the first to be allocated as a Director Scheme, a new participatory planning instrument for developing Sites of Regional Importance.[54] Participatory planning which had, thus far, been limited to local neighbourhood regeneration was now applied to more ambitious, regional sites. MAPRAC is, therefore, demonstrative of the slow and gradual impact of interstitial events, and highlights the importance of considering the phases of activism through time.

This phasing of activism may, in fact, be a *deliberate* choice. Rather than an undesired side-effect, the temporal frictions and resistances of activism may well be an effort to keep interstices open, and avoid premature closure. Activists may

COLOUR PLATES

LA RENCONTRE EVOCATRICE

LE PARVIS SAINT MICHEL

LE PORTIQUE DES MAITRES CARRIERS

1   *La rencontre évocatrice* and *Le portique des maîtres carriers*, part of the 'Différents Projets pour la Reconstruction et l'Embellissement de la Partie de Bruxelles éventrée par la Jonction des Gares du Nord et du Midi' (Sefik Birkiye, Gilbert Busieau, Patrice Neirinck, La Cambre, 1978). Image source: A. Brauman, M. Culot, and M. Louis (eds), *La Reconstruction de Bruxelles*, Editions des AAM, 1982, p. 75. Copyright: Archives d'Architecture Moderne. Used with permission.

2   Proposal for the Carrefour de l'Europe site, by the ARAU, 1976. ARAU, ed., *Bruxelles Vu par ses Habitants, Quinze années d'action urbaine* (Brussels: Commission Française de la Culture et de l'Agglomération de Bruxelles and ARAU, 1984), 65. Copyright: Archives d'Architecture Moderne. Used with permission. Maurice Culot included it also in 'The right wing in disguise', *Lotus International* 13, 94–101, 100; where the caption states: 'the style developed for this project […] unleashed the fury of architects who hold that the use of "pastiche" is an immoral act'.

3   Lakense Straat, Brussels. Photograph by the author, 2015.

4   Benjamin Verdonck, *Barake* project near the Brussels Gare du Midi.
Copyright: City Mine(d). Used with permission.

5   Location of Recyclart, Brussels, January 2015.
Photograph by the author.

6 *Arabesk-Palaverboom* project, Brussels.
Photograph by the author, 2015.

7 *De Roze Verspreiding* project, design by Les Saprophytes.
Copyright: Les Saprophytes. Used with permission.

8 Ursulines Square/Skate Park, Brussels. Photograph by Filip Dujardin. Copyright: L'Escaut. Used with permission.

9 Ursulines Square/Skate Park, Brussels. Photograph by the author, 2015.

10   Théâtre National, Brussels, by SCA Architectes Associés, Atelier Gigogne, and L'Escaut. Photograph by the author, 2015.

11   Théâtre National, Brussels, by SCA Architectes Associés, Atelier Gigogne, and L'Escaut. Entrance foyer: used also as an informal semi-public space. Photograph by the author, 2015.

12 Wall tapestry designed for the *Jonction 4 x 4* exhibition. Photograph by Kevin Laloux and Maxime Delvaux. Copyright: Bouwmeester Maître Architecte bMa, asbl Recyclart, and asbl Congrès. Used with permission.

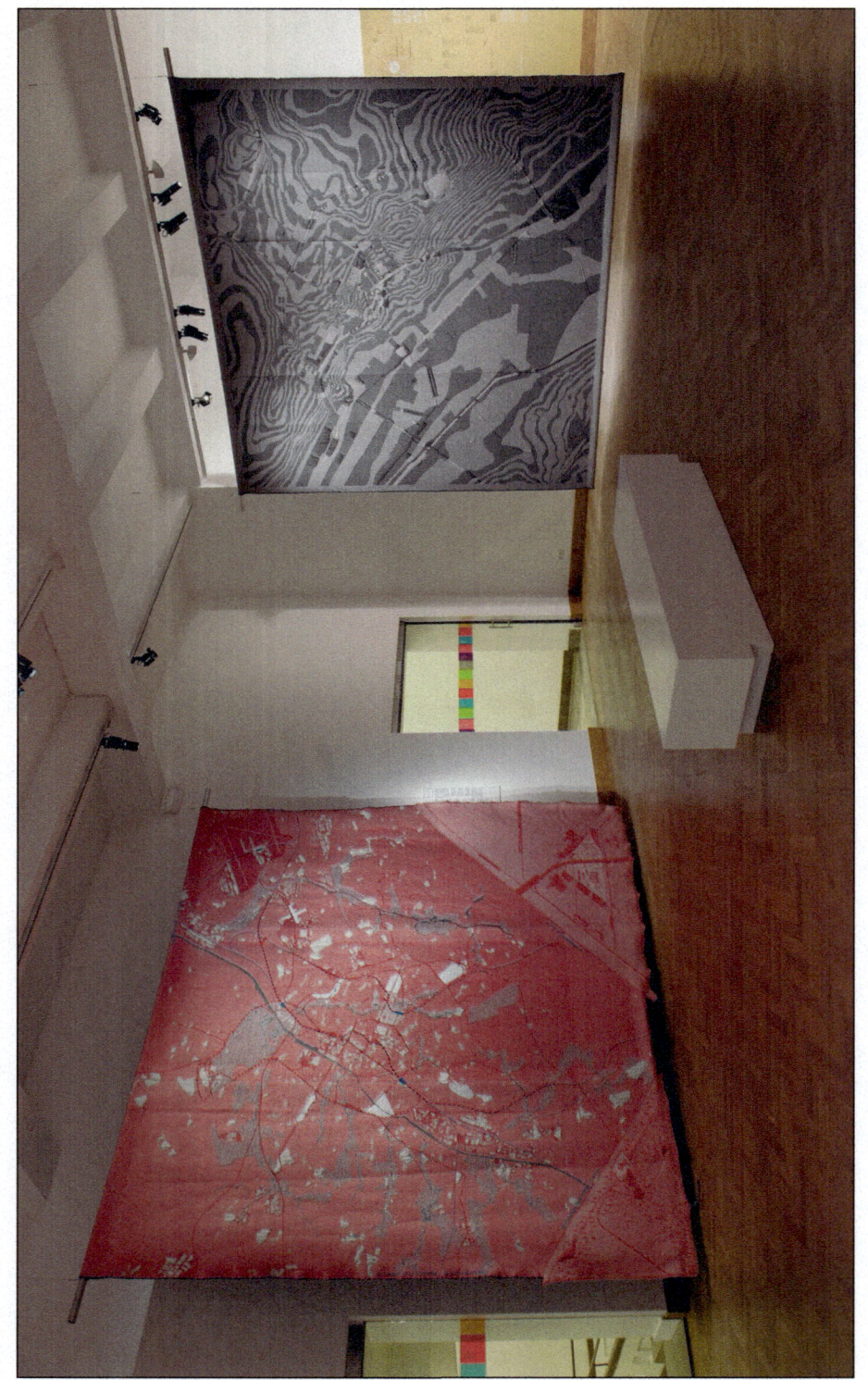

13 Wall tapestry designed for the *Jonction 4 x 4* exhibition. Photograph by Kevin Laloux and Maxime Delvaux. Copyright: Bouwmeester Maître Architecte bMa, asbl Recyclart, and asbl Congrès. Used with permission.

14 Les Vignes Blanches, Cergy-Pontoise, France. 1976–1979. Copyright: Lucien Kroll. Used with permission.

15 *Maison des Citoyens* by Atelier d'Architecture Pierre Hebbelinck. Photograph by Marie-Françoise Plissart. Copyright: Pierre Hebbelinck. Used with permission.

16 Signs indicating that this location is not a place for urination ('ceci n'est pas un urinoir') whilst directing towards nearby public urinals. Photograph by the author, 2015.

17 Example of a new urinal. Eight of those were installed from late 2013 onwards, replacing the original brick ones. Photograph by the author, 2015.

18 Place Flagey, Latz & Partners / D+A International. Copyright and photograph by Serge Brison. Used with permission.

19 Place Flagey, Latz & Partners / D+A International. Copyright and photograph by Bernard Capelle. Used with permission.

20 Rogier Project, Xaveer De Geyter Architects.
Copyright XDGA Architects. Used with permission.

choose to operate slowly and gradually rather than formulate immediate responses to a situation. They may, therefore, choose to operate from-within. In specific circumstances, as was shown by some of the Recyclart projects, it can be more effective to operate patiently from-within rather than through radical opposition. Indeed, certain forms of resistance depend on their capacity to operate discretely from-within. For example, in the context of urban informality, resistance from-within challenges the reading of peripheries, margins, and the informal as bound categories of otherness that, inadvertently, reaffirm the presumed homogeneity and stability of the centre. What can be learned from such interstitial activism from-within?

Firstly, we have learnt that slow, steady resistance may have longer-lasting effects than immediate, oppositional action. Recyclart's gradual and steady urban design emancipation serves as an example. The fact that Recyclart operated from-within helped in disseminating activism where it was most needed: within the mind-set of the Brussels' authorities. Recyclart created an interstice that formed, what Isabelle Stengers called, a 'space for hesitation' where 'slowing down' creates an opportunity 'for a slightly different awareness of the problems and situations mobilizing us'.[55] Nevertheless, resistance from-within does not come without side-effects. Recyclart, for example, insists on operating across language borders, and collaborates with funding bodies from both the Flemish- and French-language communities, which requires accepting the administrative burden that comes unavoidably with complex funding structures.

Secondly, despite operating from-within, interstitial activism can be resistant and disruptive, not affirmative. The *Arabesk* and *De Roze Verspreiding* projects operated within institutionalised contexts yet disrupted traditional, normalised ideas on urban design by articulating existing urban activities that are often perceived to be unwanted (that is loitering youths). Such disruption from-within is not unlike that of Stengers' 'idiot', an interstitial figure of disruption. The idiot *produces* interstices by 'resisting the consensual ways in which the situation is presented', and by demanding others to slow down.[56] The idiot is, therefore, 'within', and disrupts situations by asking unexpected questions, and creating the kind of instances that disturb and confuse.[57] The idiot, so Stengers argues, 'nags' us by forcing us to ask ourselves 'what am I busy doing?' *whilst* we are doing it; namely 'in the presence of' the consequences of our actions, and in the presence of the possible victims or beneficiaries of these actions.[58]

Thirdly, we learn that activism from-within may be more, not less, resistant to the derailments, appeasements, and compromises that often accompany processes of upscaling and maturation. Activists operating from-within are acquainted with negotiating their critical integrity on a continuous basis. For such practices, scrutinising one's critical integrity under change is somewhat second nature. Consequently, during periods of important transformations, such as upscaling or maturation, they are already in the habit of critical self-reflection. In the development of the IBAI, for example, Recyclart shows a gradual and steady emancipation which remained close to its activist roots. They seem to have resisted the temptation to flourish prematurely, and to turn into a powerful institute such as CIVA or the Flemish Architecture Institute. Instead, the IBAI balances the *sérieux* of cultural foundations with the more spontaneous and informal culture of urban activism. Whilst seeking a balance between opposition and appeasement, the issues of institutionalisation, professionalisation, and growth remain open to negotiation. At each change, whether through financial support, participation in official planning instruments, or upscaling, working formats, frameworks and outputs are re-negotiated. Such continuous negotiation of autonomy and integration has been aptly referred to as 'quiet encroachment' by Asef Bayat: a 'quiet and gradual grassroots activism' that implies that 'quiet non-compliance' may, at times, help the cause better than collective resistance.[59] Bayat gives the example of mobile street vendors in Cairo and Istanbul, and argues that these street vendors will turn to collective, oppositional action, as happened with the riots of the 1980s, when need to fight for their gains and rights is felt. At the same time, when it comes to going about their daily business, the street vendors will adjust compliantly in order to retain already achieved gains and rights. Instead of collectively standing by their businesses, vendors retreat into the back streets when police officers arrive, and resume work when they have left.[60] Quiet encroachment therefore 'describes the silent, protracted but pervasive advancement of the ordinary people on the propertied and powerful in order to survive and improve their lives'.[61]

Fourthly, in order to safeguard its critical integrity, activism from-within also depends on a careful set-up and monitoring of collaborations between like-minded, loyal individuals across its activist–institutional alliances. Doina Petrescu referred to such collaboration as 'convivial practice'.[62] Founded by like-minded activists and politicians, all employed within the same institution, such 'convivial practice' can be found in Recyclart. As was the case with Ursulines Skate Park, convivial practice occurred in the project for the Place de Liverpool. The surrounding area is known for informal car trading, an activity that had a disruptive effect on the pedestrian's use of the space. The proposal for the square was anchored in this local *problématique*, and sought to reclaim the space for pedestrians and other public activities. For example, the street furniture is designed and located in such a way that it determines the lay-out of the space, and is robust enough to shield the square from the car-trading and traffic. Such integrated design was made possible by the 'convivial' efforts of urban design (by office Suède 36), locally sourced recycled materials (mobilised by Rotor), a public budget (through a Neighbourhood Contract), and socio-professional insertion (Recyclart's Fabrik).[63]

INTERSTITIAL ACTIVISM AS A SPACE OF ENCOUNTER

Nothing comes without its world.[64]

The interstice, operating from-within yet resistant, suggests a relational and situated understanding of reality, and is resonant with Gilles Deleuze's 'thinking par le milieu'.[65] 'Thinking par le milieu' refers to both thinking *through the middle* (without grounding definitions) and through a practice's environment (it is always entangled and situated).[66] It is a call for understanding things through their relations. The interstice, as we have seen with Brussels' activism, offers such a relational reading, not just in spatial terms but also temporally. Philosophically, this spatial–temporal relationality derives from the particular relationship between interstices and 'life', as is made explicit in Stengers' work on Alfred North Whitehead:

> *If life lurks in the interstices of each living cell, one may say just as well that the singularity of living societies, what justifies them as such, should be called a 'culture of interstices'.*[67]

Stengers studies such 'culture of interstices' in the context of scientific practices where the interstice is defined as moments of refusal of the dominant orders.[68] Didier Debaise, also a reader of Whitehead, emphasises the spatial *and* temporal dimension of interstices. Debaise starts from the observation that the interstice refers to 'empty, intermediary spaces, fissures inside a body, all those in-between zones that contrast with the apparently "full" body parts'.[69] Life has no reality as such; 'life is rather the non-occupied space between bodies or body parts'.[70] For Whitehead, so Debaise argues, 'life has no positive quality whatsoever, no reality as such […] life presupposes the existence of "occupied spaces" and has no positive reality apart from the effect that it can have on them'. Debaise continues:

> *Everything happens in the zones in between bodies and their environment, in what we have described as 'interstices'. Bodies and environments are infected in their non-occupied spaces.*[71]

> *The living can neither be explained by its environment nor by its own components. Everything happens in the encounter.*[72]

In other words, life emerges from interstices; that space of encounter between body and environment, thing and milieu. That the interstice is a condition, or relationship (of encounter), implies that it is 'the smallest possible unit of analysis'.[73] The interstice can no longer be read in merely spatial terms, as a bound entity such as a margin, edge, or crack. The interstice is a relationship; not a place or location that can be claimed. Hence, there is no such thing as an event happening 'in' the margin. Instead, the interstice is relational both spatially and temporally, and can only be understood in terms of their historical trajectory.[74] As Debaise writes: 'Being part of a society produces specific constraints – a weight of the past – that orient the becoming of its new entities. These new entities take up the society's heritage, giving it new life, but they do so in their own way that is not entirely determined by the heritage. The novelty that they embody nevertheless only exists on the grounds of what they inherit.'[75] As Steven Shaviro also argues: once an event has taken place, it 'adds itself to the past that weighs upon all subsequent events'.[76]

This 'weight of the past' is important in the analysis of the transformations of activist practices. Namely, interstitial processes of becoming always occur as practices that work their way through the 'weight of the past', digest it, and, at the same time, direct it towards something new. The interstice is, therefore, a temporal space of encounter (between past, present, and future); a space of working one's way through 'temporal thickness'.[77] The difference between interstices does not reside in their essence, but in their differing trajectories.

INTERSTITIAL ACTIVISM AS A DIGESTIVE PRACTICE

A consequence of 'temporal thickness' is that the effects of actions are multiple and relational. Moreover, these effects may be rendered invisible over time. For example, the activism of Brussels in the 1990s had, in my view, a significant impact on architectural and urban design culture, but this impact was slow and implicit, and risks going unnoticed. In order to not overlook such agencies, it is important to unpack architecture's spatial and temporal thickness. One way to do this is through *reclaiming*. Reclaiming should not be understood as the recuperation of a lost past, but the re-integration of those parts of the past that were either previously excluded or have, over time, become indecipherable.

In Brussels, an example of temporal thickness can be found in the new building for the Théâtre National, one of two national theatres located in Brussels.[78] The building opened in November 2004, and was realised by SCA Architectes Associés, Atelier Gigogne, and L'Escaut. It is an unmistakeably contemporary work of architecture; a far cry from the pastiche and embellishment of the Reconstruction legacy. Nevertheless, the building is strongly entangled with Brussels' history. Firstly, the building emerged from a contractual agreement that is unusual for cultural buildings, but commonly used in Brussels' office development. The building was the result of a private–public 'marriage of reason' whereby public authorities delegate construction of their buildings to the private sector who, in exchange for co-financing and constructing, receive building permissions elsewhere.[79] The resultant 'tertiary reasoning' was argued to have influenced the building's aesthetic realism, its functionality, and its adoption of an architecture that is neither autonomous nor is it a visual–symbolic landmark.[80] It was believed to demonstrate that, in a complex and multi-stakeholder context such as Brussels, 'productive consensus' is not only possible, but it can also generate qualitative architecture.[81] This is expressed in the façade of the building which, fully glazed, is reminiscent of the office buildings of the neighbouring Quartier du Nord, but still manages to stand out. Instead of the usual mirror-effect, this façade is textured and, at least in part, transparent; showing the offices behind it[82] (Figure 3.10, see Plate 10; and Figure 3.11). Secondly, the Théâtre National is connected to Brussels' urban activism, albeit in an implied way only. The most obvious connection is one of its architects, L'Escaut, who was involved in the Ursulines Skate Park, and whose work is intellectually close to the urban culture of the 1990s. Further, the theatre is located at a formerly derelict site which, almost a decade earlier, had been occupied by urban activists protesting against the negative effects of real-estate speculation.[83] Its activist connection was also implicitly present in the theatre's relocation from its original home, the Centre International Rogier – Internationaal Rogiercentrum, a mixed-use high-rise building. Better known in Brussels as the Martini Tower, this

3.10 Théâtre National, Brussels, by SCA Architectes Associés, Atelier Gigogne, and L'Escaut. Photograph by the author, 2015.

3.11 Théâtre National, Brussels, by SCA Architectes Associés, Atelier Gigogne, and L'Escaut. Photograph by the author, 2015.

3.12 Théâtre National, Brussels, by SCA Architectes Associés, Atelier Gigogne, and L'Escaut. Entrance foyer: used also as an informal semi-public space. Photograph by the author, 2015.

1958 architectural landmark by Jacques Cuisinier was famous for its architectural and formal qualities, and for its mixed-use programme. Amid protests by, amongst others, City Mine(d) and Cinema Nova, who organised a *PleinOPENair* film screening on the site, the building was demolished. The new Théâtre National building was not conceived as a freestanding landmark, but instead as an accessible and explicitly urban theatre (Figure 3.12, see Plate 11). Its urbanness was intended in terms of the building's programming rather than through formal, historical, or morphological integration. Parts of the building, such as the restaurant, were conceived as being accessible to the general public outside of the theatre's programming times, and the free movement of staff and stage actors throughout the building between rehearsals, for example, is to a certain degree visible from the outside. Philippe van Kessel, a former director, stated: 'From the boulevard, something suggests there is a theatre here … There is a quick change booth on the ground floor: the actors move around there in the corridor and only a thin, transparent partition separates them from the streets and passers-by. During the rehearsals of *Tartuffe*, we could see the actors in costume coming and going, discussing the rehearsal. I found this very beautiful.'[84] The theatre's aesthetic and urban performance can, therefore, be considered an outcome of a temporal thickness which mobilised not just the desire for a prestigious, as much as popular theatre, but also the quest for consensus in a contractually challenging setting.

Reclaiming suggests learning from the past, and re-situating and re-embedding contemporary questions in the complexity and messiness of the world. It implies 'the exploration of the often messy web of other and new questions that matter in the new environment'.[85] Stengers beautifully confesses, for example, that she 'received' the term reclaiming 'as a gift from witches and other activists'.[86] As such she reminds us also that unusual knowledge (such as from witches) forms an essential part of thinking.

Reclaiming, and unpacking the 'temporal thickness', is also instructive for understanding processes of upscaling and maturation in activist practices. This was the case with the *Jonction* event, a series of cultural activities organised between September 2011 and December 2012 as part of the celebration of 60 years of the Brussels North–South railway junction.[87] The *Jonction* event had an interesting organisational set-up. It was initiated by cultural partners with an activist past, such as Recyclart, and sought the support of institutional partners, namely the Urban Development Agency of the Brussels Capital Region and the Brussels Master Architect (bMa).[88] Whilst this institutional alliance promised wider impact and scope, potentially it threatened the critical integrity of activist agendas. In this instance, however, the activists' institutional embedding was moderated by the presence of individuals in these administrations who had roots in, or at least affinity with, the 1990s activism, and by the ideological alliances between individuals across the different partners.[89] The creation of the Urban Development Agency as a regional urban think-tank, and of the Brussels Master Architect as a 'gatekeeper' of spatial quality, was moreover demonstrative of how Brussels was becoming more receptive to the importance of contemporary, qualitative architecture and urban design.

Amongst the wealth of events organised within the *Jonction* event, one stands out as an act of *digesting*; namely, the architecture exhibition and symposium *4 x 4 Four Visions on the North–South Junction*[90] (Figure 3.13). In using the phrase 'digesting', I refer to what Donna Haraway called her willingness to 'live with indigestible intellectual and political heritages'.[91] 'To digest' is closely connected to reclaiming as it invites one to recuperate, relive, and learn from such undigested pasts.[92] The *4 x 4* exhibition was the result of an architecture competition organised by the bMa whereby four architectural firms were commissioned to develop proposals for the North–South scar, one of Brussels' most notorious modernisation traumas. It was financially supported by the Belgian architecture journal *A Plus* and hosted by the Brussels Centre for Fine Arts (Bozar). *4 x 4* forms an act of digesting because, in promoting positive urban imaginaries, it challenged Brussels' scepticism vis-à-vis innovative and ambitious designs. However, in doing so it remained loyal to the Brussels urban culture. This was achieved by mobilising numerous stakeholders more or less equally: political representatives *and* 'the people'; and those in power *and* activist groups. For example, the *4 x 4* symposium involved architects, officials of the National Railway Company (NMBS/SNCB), and political representatives, but it was also open to the general public.[93]

3.13 Poster of the *Jonction 4 x 4* event. Copyright: Bouwmeester Maître Architecte bMa, asbl Recyclart, and asbl Congrès. Used with permission.

3.14 (*top*) & 3.15 (*bottom*) Wall tapestries designed for the *Jonction 4 x 4* exhibition. Photographs by Kevin Laloux and Maxime Delvaux. Copyright: Bouwmeester Maître Architecte bMa, asbl Recyclart, and asbl Congrès. Used with permission.

The architectural competition itself may also be read as an act of digesting. Whilst it was symptomatic of Brussels' growing confidence in the importance of architectural and urban design competitions, this was no ordinary competition. Rather than seek iconic projects designed by star-architects, the competition encouraged architectural innovations that were bold, but also in tune with Brussels' complex architectural and political legacy. The commissioned architects – Studio 012 Secchi-Vigano / Karbon, V+, XDGA, and 51N4E – were not just renowned architectural firms, they also had a thorough knowledge of the Brussels *problématique*. The architects were not asked to present their proposals through sections, plans, models, elevations. Instead, they were invited to 'tickle' the imagination for this site through the design and creation of a 4 x 4 m wall tapestry (Figures 3.14 and 3.15, see Plates 12 and 13). The choice of wall tapestry, historically a means for rulers to communicate with their people and a way of avoiding technocratic jargon, was demonstrative of an ambition to communicate with the wider public. Such ideals of public outreach did not, however, prevent the tapestries from acting as artistic works in their own right. Each tapestry was carefully designed and crafted, and transmitted a bold, imaginative message that hoped to stay close to 'the people'. By equally mobilising Brussels' activist legacy, the traumatisation and empowerment of its population, institutional scope, and artistic prestige, *4 x 4* formed an act of digesting that operated through the 'temporal thickness' of Brussels.

INTERSTITIAL ACTIVISM: CHOOSING ATTACHMENTS OVER AUTONOMY

The interstice is a useful vehicle for studying urban activism beyond the categories of margin, edge, or residual space. As a *spatial* event, the interstice allows for recognising activism in peripheries as much as in centres or, in other words, the cracks 'within'. This invites for cutting across the polarising distinctions of centre and periphery, radicalism and appeasement, critical and mainstream, and emancipation and normalisation. As a *temporal* event, the interstice invites one to study activism over time; as temporal trajectories. These trajectories reveal forms of resistance that operate as much from-within as through radical opposition. As a spatial–temporal event, the interstice suggests the possibility of forms of resistance from-within, and tells us something about the workings of criticality from-within.

Firstly, we learn that the effects of activism can be slow and gradual. Further, activism may, due to its multiple entanglements and discrete manoeuvring from-within, go unnoticed. We also learn that urban activism can have a significant impact on architecture and urban design; that it can contribute to architectural emancipation processes. The activities of the collective Recyclart were vital in the innovation of architectural and urban design cultures. Likewise, City Mine(d) and other activist collectives of the 1990s have had an important impact on urban design thinking in Brussels. These actors operate largely in the peripheries of architectural culture, but prove central to it. It is important to reclaim these agencies by disentangling architectural culture as broadly as possible both spatially and temporally. The challenge is, therefore, to give voice to as many actors as possible, but also to access architecture's *temporal* thickness. This requires becoming receptive to, and recovering, those histories one has become separated from – even if these histories are uncomfortable.[94] The unpacking of Brussels' activism of the 1990s contributes to this ambition to 'thicken' the descriptions of architectural emancipation under the practice turn, and understand its complex and entangled history.

Secondly we learn from interstitial activism that operations from-within are not necessarily compromised or compliant, but can be resistant. Because of its within-ness, interstitial activism, such as Recyclart, helps to refine the understanding of some of the challenges of activism including how to maintain critical integrity alongside processes of upscaling, mainstreaming, and institutionalising. The temporal trajectories of Recyclart demonstrate that rather than choosing between oppositional or interstitial forms of activism, or between autonomy and involvement, they can co-exist. Autonomy and involvement may well be different *stages* of activism, but not necessarily different types. At different moments of an activist trajectory, opposition and integration may serve as equally appropriate activist strategies. Recyclart's institutional embedding showed how a partial, and cautious, integration can serve as an efficient vehicle for action.

Recyclart's activism can be likened to what Whitehead calls a 'living society': in contrast to 'physical societies', who are indifferent towards how their environment affects them, 'living societies' are prepared to transform and allow themselves to be affected by their environment.[95] The differences between societies, such as Recyclart, is not determined by their essence, but by their trajectories and approach to 'maintaining stability in changing environments'.[96] Societies respond to changing encounters either through indifference or through metamorphosis. If a society is prepared to transform, this is, in fact, a sign of *interest* in that environment and an attachment to it.[97] For activist practices this implies that their ability to act critically from-within depends less on their capacity to safeguard autonomy and detachment than on their willingness to be affected by their environment – or to be 'stained' by it.[98] It requires a willingness 'to negotiate its endurance throughout internal as well as external variations'.[99]

I recognise such critical encounter in Recyclart's interstitial activism. Its actions may have emerged from an encounter with institutions, but they avoided compromising the content of their activism. The consequence for activism more generally is that, whilst immediate radical action has its obvious merits, there are other valuable forms of resistance that operate from-within. However, in order to safeguard critical integrity whilst operating from-within, such activism relies on the continuous negotiation of its positioning vis-à-vis its environment; this includes its degree of engagement, and the extent to which it retains its autonomy or seeks integration. This negotiation can only occur through deliberately *seeking* rather than avoiding encounters, including difficult ones.[100] The guarantor for criticality then is not autonomy, but attachment.

NOTES

1. For more details, see Johan Moyersoen, 'Autonomy and inclusive urban governance. A case of glocal action: *City Mine(d)* in Brussels', in *Can Neighbourhoods Save the City? Community Development and Social Innovation*, ed. Frank Moelaert et al. (Routledge: London and New York, 2012): 153–167, 155.

2. In reference to Michel Michiels, *Bruxelles est malade … mais son coeur bats: chronique de la bruxelloise, affection capitale* (Brussels: Le Livre, 1996).

3. For more information, please see the website: www.citymined.org/projects/barake.php [last accessed April 24, 2014].

4. *Cinema Légumen* in 1996 by Kino-Trotter/Beursschouwburg and, in 1997, the *Cinéma de La Gare*.

5. Moyersoen, 'Autonomy and inclusive urban governance', 155; See also Lieven De Cauter, 'Van Hôtel Central tot Picnic the Streets: klein panorama van het stadsactivisme in Brussels', *Dewereldmorgen.be*, March 25, 2014 http://community.dewereldmorgen.be/blog/lievendecauter/2014/03/25/van-hotel-central-tot-picnic-the-streets-klein-panorama-van-het-stadsactivisme-in-brussel [last accessed June 2, 2014].

6. The occupation took place between October 2001 and January 2002; accompanied by numerous protests by citizen associations, who contested the negative effect of this isolated, mono-functional project on the local neighbourhood. See BruXXel, Gwenaël Breës, *Façadisme, choucroute et démocratie* (Brussels VOX, 2002).

7. A six-hectare modernist complex in the heart of Brussels, including a large public esplanade. For more details on the MAPRAC event: Isabelle Doucet, 'Planning in Search of *Ground*: Committed *Muddling Through* or a Critical View from Above?', in *The Territorial Future of the City*, ed. Giovanni Maciocco (Berlin and Heidelberg: Springer, 2008): 47–70.

8. For example, Gwenaël Breës, co-founder of Cinema Nova and *PleinOPENair*, became a key figure in the activism against Brussels' on-going demolition strategies and profit-based urbanism (notably the European Quarter and the international Gare du Midi); and became in 2009 the new President of Inter-Environnement Bruxelles (an important civil society partner founded in the 1970s).

9. The actions of other groups, such as City Mine(d) and important social architectural projects, such as the Limiet/Limite Tower, have been studied elsewhere. See, for example, Moyersoen, 'Autonomy and inclusive urban governance'; Doucet, 'Planning in Search of *Ground*'; and Johan Moyersoen and Erik Swyngedouw, 'LimiteLimite: Cracks in the City, Brokering Scales, and Pioneering a New Urbanity', in *Spaces of Contention: Spatialities and Social Movements*, ed. Walter Nichols, Byron Miller and Justin Beaumont (Farnham: Ashgate 2013), 141–162.

10. See, amongst others, Margit Mayer, 'Social movements in European Cities: transitions from the 1970s to the 1990s', in *Cities in Contemporary Europe*, ed. Arnaldo Bagnasco and Patrick Le Galès (Cambridge: Cambridge University Press, 2000): 131–152; Eric Corijn and Jacqueline Groth, 'Reclaiming Urbanity: Indeterminate spaces, informal actors and urban agenda setting. A case study in Helsinki, Brussels and Berlin', *Urban Studies* 42, no. 3 (2005): 511–534; and the International Network for Urban Research and Action (INURA; www.inura.org).

11. As opposed to 'hard' regeneration through large-scale development projects. Mathieu Van Criekingen, 'Moving In/Out of Brussels' Historical Core in the Early 2000s: Migration and the Effects of Gentrification', *Urban Studies*, 46, no. 4 (April 2009): 825–848;

and Isabelle Doucet, 'Brussels: The *Soft* Regeneration', in *Houses in Transformation, Interventions in European Gentrification*, ed. by J.J. Berg et al. (Rotterdam: NAi Publishers, 2008), 130–143.

12 On the legacy of the 1970s' counter-projects, see Chapter 2.

13 Originating in the activities around Antwerp's Capital of Culture in 1993, Studio Open City organised, in Brussels, for example, design research workshops on the post-industrial landscape of the Brussels Canal Zone. See Studio Open City, *A Moving City: Three Years of Architectural Explorations in Brussels' Canal Zone* (Brussels: Centrum voor Architectuur en Design, 1998); Hilde Heynen and André Loeckx, 'Studio Open City. In search of a multicultural urbanity', *Archis* 4 (1996): 38–49.

14 Bruno De Meulder and Karina Van Herck, *Vacant City: Brussels' Mont des Arts Reconsidered* (Rotterdam: NAI Publishers and Leuven: OSA, 2000). The *Supernova Jonge Belgische Architectuur – Jeune Architecture Belge* exhibition: held at Centrum Brussel 2000; the catalogue is a collection of thin booklets and foldouts, each dedicated to an architectural practice, and a collection of essays (Vincent Brunetta et al., *Supernova TXT – Jonge Belgische Architectuur – Jeune Architecture Belge*, Brussels, 2000); see also Vincent Brunetta and Véronique Patteeuw, 'Jonge Architecten in België: op zoek naar erkenning', *Archis* 5 (2001): 87–88.

15 Olivier Bastin; the Master Architect's administration is called bMa, which stands for the Dutch-French combo *Bouwmeester Maître Architecte*, accessed October 16, 2014, http://www.bmabru.be/#page/missions-introduction.

16 The 'second' turn was coined by Benoît Moritz who emphasised the role of public space as a trigger for change. See Moritz, 'Du "premier tournant" au "deuxième tournant"', lecture at the Brussels Architecture Institute lecture series on the theme 'le deuxième tournant', May 8, 2008, Recyclart, Brussels; and Moritz, 'Designing and developing public spaces in Brussels', *Brussels Studies*, 50 (June 21, 2011). The first turn was coined by Jacques Aron, *Le tournant de l'urbanisme bruxellois: 1958–1978* (Brussels: Fondation Joseph Jacquemotte, 1978).

17 Jean-Louis Genard and Pablo Lhoas, eds, *Qui a peur de L'Architecture? Le Livre Blanc de L'Architecture contemporaine en communauté Française en Belgique* (Brussels: La Lettre Volée and I.S.A. La Cambre, 2004): 18 (see 21 also); posited by some as the 'Bible' of the architectural emancipation within the French-speaking community.

18 ISACF La Cambre and Philippe Flamme, *Vade-Mecum: Commande d'architecture publique à Bruxelles. Comment choisir un auteur de projet? Exemples et bonnes pratiques* (Brussels: ISACF La Cambre, 2007); it was commissioned by Minister Françoise Dupuis, accessed June 17, 2014, http://urbanisme.irisnet.be/pdf/CAM003_VadeMecum_FR.pdf/view.

19 Maurice Culot, *Brussels Architectures from 1950 to the present day* (Brussels: AAM Éditions, 2013), 146; Maurizio Cohen, *Brussels On Our Doorstep: Architecture in Neighbourhood Contracts* (Brussels: Brussels Capital Region, 2007).

20 Culot, *Brussels Architectures*, 146.

21 Culot instead interprets this new generation in terms of 'artisans of reconstruction' (Ibid., 14). For example, in mentioning, he ignores Recyclart's artistic and urban activist production (Ibid., 149).

22 Elisabeth Grosz in '"Ontogenesis and the Ethics of Becoming." An interview with Elisabeth Grosz by Kathryn Yusoff', *Society and Space*, accessed June 3, 2014, http://societyandspace.com/material/interviews/ontogenesis-and-the-ethics-of-becoming-an-interview-with-elizabeth-grosz-by-kathryn-yusoff/.

23 Margit Mayer, 'First world urban activism. Beyond austerity urbanism and creative city politics', *City* 17, no. 1 (2013): 5–19.

24 Ibid., 8.

25 Isabelle Stengers, 'Introductory notes on an ecology of practices', *Cultural Studies Review* 11, 1 (March 2005): 183–196, 185. Stengers and Debaise both follow the philosophers Alfred North Whitehead and Gilles Deleuze. Other relevant references include: Isabelle Stengers, 'A "Cosmo-Politics" – Risk, Hope, Change. A conversation with Isabelle Stengers', in Marie Zournazie, *Hope: New Philosophies for Change* (Annandale: Pluto Press, 2002), 244–272; Isabelle Stengers, 'The Cosmopolitical Proposal', in *Making Things Public – Atmospheres of Democracy*, ed. Bruno Latour and Peter Weibel (Karlsruhe and Cambridge: ZKM and The MIT Press, 2005), 994–1003; Didier Debaise, 'The Living and its Environments', *Process Studies* 37, no. 2 (2008); and Didier Debaise, 'A philosophy of interstices: Thinking subjects and societies from Whitehead's philosophy', *Subjectivity* 6, no. 1 (2013): 101–111.

26 Stengers, 'A "Cosmo-Politics" – Risk, Hope, Change', 245.

27 Isabelle Stengers and Penelope Deutscher [trans.], 'Another Look: Relearning to Laugh', *Hypathia* 15, no. 4 (Autumn 2000): 41–54, 53.

28 Ibid.

29 bell hooks, 'Choosing the margin as a space of radical openness', in *Gender, Space, Architecture; an Interdisciplinary Introduction*, ed. Jane Rendell, Barbara Penner, and Iain Borden (London and New York: Routledge, 2000), 203–209.

30 In architecture, explicit references to interstitial space can be found, for example, in Andrea Mubi Brighenti, ed., *Urban Interstices: The Aesthetics and the Politics of the In-between* (Farnham: Ashgate, 2013); and the work of the Atelier d'Architecture Autogérée, see Constantin Petcou and Doina Petrescu 'Acting Space. Transversal notes, on-the-ground observations and concrete questions for us all', in *Urban/Act, A Handbook for Alternative Practice*, ed. Atelier d'Architecture Autogérée and Peprav (2007), 319–328; and Pascal Nicolas-le-Strat, 'Interstitial Multiplicity', in the same volume, 314–318.

31 For example, Francesco Careri, *Walkscapes: Walking as an Aesthetic Practice* (Barcelona: Gustavo Gili, 2001); Thomas Sievert, *Cities Without Cities: An Interpretation of the Zwischenstadt: Between Place and World, Space and Time, Town and Country* (London: Spon Press 2003); Roger Diener et al. *Switzerland: An Urban Portrait* (Basel: Birkhauser 2006).

32 Mayer, 'First world urban activism', 9–10.

33 Ibid., 11.

34 Christian Schmid, 'Henri Lefebvre, the Right to the City and Mainstream', accessed June 2, 2014, http://inura.wikia.com/wiki/Henri_Lefebvre,_the_Right_to_the_CIty_and_the_New_Metropolitan_Mainstream. The need to cut across the mainstream–critical distinction is also identified by Kurt Iveson, 'Some critical reflections on being critical. Reading for deviance, dominance or difference?', *City* 14, no. 4 (2010): 434–441.

35 AbdouMaliq Simone, 'At the Frontier of the Urban Periphery', in *Sarai Reader 07: Frontiers*, ed. Monica Narula et al. (2007), 469. Accessed June 2, 2014. http://sarai.net/sarai-reader-07-frontiers/.

36 Harvey was referencing the former British Prime Minister, Margaret Thatcher. See David Harvey, 'Is This Really the End of Neoliberalism?', *Counterpunch*, March 13–15, 2009, 7.

37 *Picnic the Streets* was initiated by philosopher Philippe Van Parijs and resulted in 2000 picnickers occupying the Place de la Bourse in June 2012 as a way to remind the Brussels authorities' promises to make this square car-free. See also De Cauter, 'Van Hôtel Central tot Picnic the Streets'.

38 I would like to thank Laurence Jenard (co-founder and director of Recyclart) for her comments and important corrections on an earlier version of this chapter, which was important in the refinement of my discussion of Recyclart, as provided in this version. I take full responsibility for any possible misinterpretations from my side.

39 *Afvaardiging voor de Ontwikkeling van de Vijfhoek / Délégation au développement du Pentagone.*

40 The initial 100 per cent political representation of the board, was reduced to three members in 2001–2002 (the Brussels Mayor, the Alderman of Urbanism, and the Alderman of Flemish Affairs); and to only one in 2007. See also Laurence Jenard, interview with the author, January 22, 2008. Wim Embrechts is another co-founder of Recyclart.

41 Recyclart have delivered a variety of products including: furniture for Bar Recyclart and for public administrations (for example *Huis van de Vlaamse Parlementsleden*); playgrounds for housing developments; promotion panels for cultural festivals (for example KunstenFESTIVALdesArts); and even street wagons for the Zinneke Parade. See Wim Embrechts, quoted in Anne Brumagne, 'Stadsbanken Bruegelplein binnenkort ingehuldigd', *Brussel deze Week*, April 15, 2014. http://www.brusselsnieuws.be/nl/nieuws/stadsbanken-bruegelplein-binnenkort-ingehuldigd.

42 A fragmentation of funding followed the demise of more stable UPP funding (1996–2001). Socio-professional activities became funded under the federal budget whilst artistic activities fell under the Flemish and/or French Communities. Such a funding landscape means that there is often less room for experimentation because projects depend on specific performances within commissions.

43 See Recyclart.be, accessed May 1, 2014, http://www.recyclart.be/nl/kunstencentrum/architectuur-stedenbouw-en-openbare-ruimte On the opening day in April 2005, one could watch audio recordings and photographic portraits of people using the square. The project won the *Thuis in de Stad* (At Home in the City) award in 2006, see Embrechts in Brumagne, 'Stadsbanken Bruegelplein binnenkort ingehuldigd'.

44 A 'prolonged and tedious fuss or discussion' and '(In Africa) a parley or improvised conference between two sides'; Oxford Dictionaries, accessed May 1, 2014, http://www.oxforddictionaries.com/definition/english/palaver.

45 Embrechts in Brumagne, 'Stadsbanken Bruegelplein binnenkort ingehuldigd'. The texts and sketches had been prepared by children of two local youth institutions, during workshops.

46 Brumagne, 'Stadsbanken Bruegelplein binnenkort ingehuldigd' (Quote translated from Dutch). The square was refurbished within the framework of Beliris, a collaboration between the Belgian Federal State and the Brussels Capital Region, aimed at optimising the image of Brussels as the capital of Belgium and Europe through, for example, renovation projects and urban renewal.

47 The project was realised within Neighbourhood Contract Van Artevelde (2003–2007). See Aglaée Degros and Michiel De Cleene, *Brussel [her]verovert haar buitenruimte: De openbare ruimte in de Duurzame Wijkcontracten* (Brussels: Brussels Hoofdstedelijk Gewest, 2014), 151–164.

48 This is the public administration for environment and energy in the Brussels Capital Region; called *Bruxelles Environnement – Institut Bruxellois pour la Gestion de l'Environnement (IBGE) / Leefmilieu Brussels – Brussels Instituut voor Milieubeheer (BIM)*.

49 See Escaut.org, accessed June 7, 2014, http://www.escaut.org/urban-scale/ursulines-square/.

50 See Parckdesign.be, accessed June 7, 2014, http://www.parckdesign.be/en/content/parckdesign.

51 Parckdesign 2012 was organised by Architectural Workroom, a Brussels-based, architectural and urban think-tank around Berlage tutor Joachim Declerck. See the Architecture Workroom Brussels, accessed June 7, 2014, http://www.architectureworkroom.eu/en/work/g_a_r_d_e_n_parckdesign_2012/. The 2014 edition was curated by a Paris–Brussels-based practice, Taktyk and AliveArchitecture, who specialise in research-driven, social urban design. See Parckdesign.be, accessed June 7, 2014.

52 Subsidised by the French-speaking Community in Brussels, the CIVA was created in 1999 as the result of the integration of a series of foundations including the Archives d'Architecture Moderne, the Fondation pour l'Architecture, and the Fondation Philippe Rotthier pour l'Architecture.

53 Created in 2002, its influence could be felt in Brussels, despite its location in the Flemish region.

54 *Schéma Directeur/Richtschema*, created by the Brussels Capital Region. See Agence de Développement Territorial, accessed June 12, 2014, http://www.adt-ato.be/fr/zones-strat%C3%A9giques.

55 Stengers, 'The Cosmopolitical Proposal', 994–995.

56 Stengers, 'The Cosmopolitical Proposal', 994. Stengers uses the idiot as a conceptual persona in reference to Gilles Deleuze, who borrows the term from Dostoevsky's book of the same name.

57 Ibid., 996–997.

58 Ibid.

59 Asef Bayat, 'From "Dangerous Classes" to "Quiet Rebels": Politics of the Urban Subaltern in the Global South,' *International Sociology* 15, no. 3 (September 2000), 533–557; 550 and 246. Bayat's 'quiet encroachment' is a critique of post-structuralism's 'resistance paradigm' that is inspired by Foucault's decentred notion of power; and tends to 'overlook the crucial fact that these acts [of resistance of agents] occur mostly within the prevailing systems of power' (545).

60 Ibid., 549–550.

61 Ibid., 545.

62 Petrescu also terms convivial practices as co-design (or co-research). See Doina Petrescu, Keynote Lecture, Rencontres à la croisée de l'architecture et des sciences humaines colloquium, Brussels, May 26–27, 2014. The importance of like-mindedness was also stressed by Laurence Jenard (co-founder and director of Recyclart).

63 Neighbourhood Contract Sluis – Sint-Lazarus (2008–2012); Fabrik acted as contractor; Rotor is an architecture collective specialised in the use of waste and recycled materials. See Aglaée Degros and Michiel De Cleene, *Brussel [her]verovert haar buitenruimte: De openbare ruimte in de Duurzame Wijkcontracten* (Brussels: Hoofdstedelijk Gewest, 2014), 137–150.

64 Donna Haraway, *Modest_Witness@Second_Millenium.FemaleMan©_Meets_OncoMouse™* (New York and London: Routledge 1997), 137; and Maria Puig de la Bellacasa, '"Nothing comes without its world": thinking with care', *The Sociological Review* 60, no. 2 (2012): 197–216.

65 Stengers, 'Introductory notes on an ecology of practices', 187. See also Isabelle Stengers, 'Experimenting with Refrains: Subjectivity and the Challenge of Escaping Modern Dualism', *Subjectivity* 22 (2008): 38–59, 48–49.

66 Stengers, 'Introductory notes on an ecology of practices', 187.

67 Isabelle Stengers, *Thinking with Whitehead: A Free and Wild Creation of Concepts*, trans. Michael Chase (Cambridge, MA: Harvard University Press, 2011 [2002]), 328; Didier Debaise, 'The Living and its Environments', *Process Studies* 37, no. 2 (2008): 2.

68 Isabelle Stengers, 'Penser les sciences par leur milieu', *Rue Descartes*, no. 41 (August 2003): 41–51.

69 Debaise, 'The Living and its Environments', 2. The work of British mathematician and philosopher A.N. Whitehead (1861–1947), an important contributor to the philosophy of science and process philosophy, has received recent interest through the work of Isabelle Stengers, Bruno Latour, Donna Haraway, Steven Shaviro, and Brian Massumi. In relation to the interstice Shaviro, Stengers, and Debaise's work is particularly instructive.

70 Didier Debaise, 'A philosophy of interstices: Thinking subjects and societies from Whitehead's philosophy', *Subjectivity* 6, no.1 (2013): 101–111: 102.

71 This and the previous citation are taken from Debaise, 'The Living and its Environments', 2 and 12; see also Debaise, 'A philosophy of interstices', 108.

72 Debaise, 'The Living and its Environments', 12; and 'A philosophy of interstices', 108.

73 Donna Haraway, *The Haraway Reader* (London and New York: Routledge, 2004): 315; quoted in Donna Haraway and Nicholas Gane, 'When we have never been human, what is to be done? Interview with Donna Haraway', *Theory Culture & Society* 23, nos. 7–8 (2006): 135–158, 155.

74 'They [living societies] let themselves be transformed by what lurks in their interstices and in return integrate these elements into their historical trajectory.' Debaise, 'The Living and its Environments', 10.

75 Ibid., 7.

76 Steven Shaviro, 'Interstitial Life: Substractive Vitalism in Whitehead and Deleuze', *Deleuze Studies* 4 (2010): 110.

77 For Whitehead *everything* (even ordinary objects) that has temporal endurance, or 'temporal thickness', is a society. See Debaise, 'A philosophy of interstices', 103, 104.

78 Brussels has two national theatres; one for the Dutch-speaking community (the Koninklijke Vlaamse Schouwburg) and one for the French-speaking community (the Théâtre National).

79 Offices were developed on the former location of the theatre. See Carole Schmidt and François Thiry, 'Architecture, Theatre, and Tertiary Realism', in *Visions: Architectures publiques, volume 3, Le Théâtre National*, ed. Matthias Langhoff et al. (Brussels: La Lettre Volée, 2005), 72–79.

80 Ibid., 78.

81 Ibid.

82 Maurizio Cohen, 'Théâtre National Brussel', *A Plus* 189, 50.

83 In 1997, The Fondation Légumen (Nathalie Mertens) created a vegetable allotment on what was then a derelict site under speculation, which triggered public awareness and

debate (see http://www.citymined.org/LAB/katarsis.php). Previously in 1995, Mertens had created a sunflower garden on another *terrain vague* in central Brussels (near Place Fontainas).

84 Philippe van Kessel, in Nancy Delhalle 'A Theatre for the City: the new Théâtre National in Brussels. Interview with Philippe van Kessel and Jean-Louis Colinet', in Langhoff et al., *Visions*, 68.

85 Isabelle Stengers, '"Another science is possible!" A plea for Slow Science', Inaugural lecture as Chair Willy Calewaert 2011-2012, Vrije Universiteit Brussel. December 13, 2011, 11. Accessed June 13, 2014, http://threerottenpotatoes.files.wordpress.com/2011/06/stengers2011_pleaslowscience.pdf.

86 Stengers refers to neopagan contemporary witches and other US activists, such as Starhawk; Stengers 'Experimenting with Refrains', 51 and Isabelle Stengers 'Reclaiming Animism', *E-flux Journal* 36 (July 2012): 1–10, 6.

87 Jonction.be, accessed January 7, 2015, www.jonction.be.

88 The Agence de Développement Territorial ADT / Agentschap voor Territoriale Ontwikkeling ATO was created by the Brussels Regional Government, in 2008, and charged with territorial development and the development of a detailed knowledge of the territory's characteristics. Accessed December 30, 2014, http://www.adt-ato.irisnet.be/sites/default/files/ADT%20Brochure%20EN%20DEF_light_SMP.pdf.

89 The collective Congres, ADT/ATO, Recyclart, and the Brussels Master Architect bMa.

90 The exhibition took place between December 7, 2012 and February 10, 2013 with a symposium on December 7, 2012; BOZAR Brussels; see Jonction.be, accessed June 13, 2014, http://www.jonction.be/2012/11/06122012-21012013-expo-4-x-4-bozar/?lang=nl.

91 Nicholas Gane, 'When We Have Never Been Human, What is to Be Done? Interview with Donna Haraway', *Theory, Culture & Society* 23, nos. 7–8 (December 2006), 135–158, 139.

92 As in Stengers, 'Experimenting with Refrains'.

93 The *4 x 4* symposium was organised by the bMa and hosted by the prestigious BOZAR.

94 Stengers, 'Experimenting with Refrains', 40. This follows Bruno Latour's claim that the moderns thrived on a separation from all non-modern cultures but also from their own past; which Latour called the 'great divide'; see *We Have Never Been Modern* (Cambridge, MA: Harvard University Press, 1993).

95 Debaise, 'A philosophy of interstices', 106–107.

96 Ibid., 106.

97 Ibid., 106–107.

98 Ibid., 108.

99 Ibid., 108.

100 Stengers argues that this is what living societies do; namely to seek out rather than avoid being affected; because it informs them about their partiality 'what is food or poison for it, what will allow it to reproduce, what will provide it the opportunity to survive, what will kill it' (Stengers, *Thinking with Whitehead*, 425).

4

Participatory Challenges

Confronted with the political ambiguities and democratic contradictions of the practice turn (as discussed in the first and third chapter of this book) it is now largely accepted that oppositional, dichotomist approaches are no longer suitable for evaluating and understanding architecture. Alongside such recognition, a whole series of previously deployed analytical vehicles, most notably ideology, grand narratives, and theory, were dismissed. In the discussions of participation in architecture, and notwithstanding the numerous innovations of the formats, purposes and outputs of participation, oppositional pairs prevail: between architect and user, top-down and bottom-up, and high and low culture. Several of the long-standing tensions in participatory architecture are, moreover, magnified under the practice turn, such as between democratic decision-making and individual authorship, and between social empowerment and material solutions. It became evident that neoliberal politics celebrated virtues that had previously been part of participation's oppositional activism: inclusiveness, individual freedom, creative appropriation. Not only were these virtues now incorporated into a politics of consensus and appeasement, democratic participation and resistance were now positioned within rather than outside-and-against mainstream politics. Because this position had become perceived as paramount and unavoidable, one can assume that participatory efforts are urged to imagine forms of political activism from-within rather than tap into the dichotomist pairs and radical oppositions that had served so well in the past. In reality, however, this re-imagining has often been reduced to either the radicalisation of practice based on the affirmation of oppositional pairs, or a fatalist relinquishing of any hope for critical practice. Further, as a design profession, architecture's democratic programme can never be fully disconnected from its aesthetic ambitions. Under the practice turn, this double ambition has become complicated. In this chapter, some of these complications will be unpacked in order to demonstrate that the oppositional pairs around which participatory discourse still largely evolves are no longer workable. The current status of the debate on architecture and participation will be introduced, before a closer examination of the democratic and aesthetic intricacies of participation in architecture is undertaken. In doing so, some tentative suggestions for imagining participation beyond dichotomist readings will be formulated.

ARCHITECTURE AND PARTICIPATION: THE CURRENT STATUS OF THE DEBATE

In 1986, in an episode of the BBC documentary series Architecture at the Crossroads, the narrator Andrew Sachs observes, in relation to Neave Braun's 1977 Alexandra Road project in London, that 'as so often before, the aspiration of the architects and those of the tenants were not the same'.[1] The documentary series investigates the tensions within 1980s architecture as an outcome of its attempts (and failures) to come to terms with the modernist legacy. At the heart of the discussion is architecture's failure to account for the needs of users and its tendency to underestimate the effects of appropriation of buildings by their users. The postmodern alternative, formulated in the 1980s, did not, however, manage to avoid these tensions either. The longing for signature architecture often outweighed a genuine architecture 'for the people', and true participation was reduced to populist rhetoric. With their pastiche styles and tendency toward monumentality, the buildings created were often a far cry from the everyday living reality of the occupant. Despite the intentions of postmodern architects and urban designers to create more humane environments – whether through a reconstruction, or evocation, of the past to engender a sense of belonging, or through the choice of materials such as brick rather than concrete – sterile and orderly environments where 'history had been dry-cleaned', nevertheless often resulted.[2]

These postmodern instances demonstrate that, in architecture, the democratic efforts of participation cannot be disconnected from architecture's aesthetic and projective nature. Nevertheless, the history of participatory architecture shows the disjunction of politics and aesthetics, imputing a choice for architects between either a democratic or aesthetic gesture. This disconnection was reinforced under the practice turn of the 1990s when architects were seemingly confronted with a choice between a revived radical practice and one that was unavoidably complacent with late-capitalism.[3]

The discourse on participatory architecture remained, under the practice turn, largely faithful to its political–democratic roots, and continued its work on the empowerment of the users, inclusiveness, and democratic decision-making. This is evidenced by the recent architectural discourse on participation such as the edited volumes *Architecture and Participation* (2005) and *Architecture, Participation, and Society* (2010), which focuses on the critical debates around participation as well as concrete practices, and the participation trilogy edited by Markus Miessen.[4] Due to its political imperative, the architectural discourse on participation is indebted to a wider disciplinary field. In urban planning, a 'participatory turn' occurred in the wake of Paul Davidoff's 1965 article 'Advocacy and Pluralism in Planning', and centred on issues of democratic decision-making and empowerment.[5] The resistance to the all-encompassing expertise of the state planner, and to the dominance of the singular master plan, signalled a shift, in planning theory, from a positivist to post-positivist approach to planning.[6] Post-positivist planning called for normative planning and, thus, for the ethical–political position of the planner. It was a call for collaborating with local communities, advocating the marginalised and excluded, and, in reference to the development of more than one plan, pluralism. This was in contrast to the unitary, comprehensive plan made by the state planners.[7] The impact on participatory design discourse was significant in that it prioritised communication techniques and design methods.[8] Important inspiration can also be found in development studies. Here community involvement is considered a key precondition for dealing with policy making, poverty reduction and informal urban development.[9] In more recent times, the work of political theorists and critical human geographers including David Harvey, Erik Swyngedouw, Neil Smith, Maria Kaika, and Neil Brenner, has had a significant impact on critical architectural discourse, not the least in their discussions of the demise of democracy under the neoliberal and post-political turn. Brenner, for example, connected the European participatory movement of the 1990s with important changes in political governance. The choice of the neighbourhood as an important urban policy level for fighting social exclusion coincided with the replacement of state-led welfare with bottom-up initiatives operated by neighbourhood and community-based associations, and by quasi-nongovernmental organisations (quangos).[10]

The architectural discourse on participation resonates with a broader, interdisciplinary preoccupation with the democratic and emancipatory challenges of design. Architecture, however, differs from disciplines such as critical geography in that it also develops alternative projects and designs. Whilst this is also the case in the discipline of planning, which is equally connected to the design profession, architecture's projective nature is distinct in its celebration of authorship and explicit aesthetic and stylistic imperative. These aesthetic preoccupations have infiltrated participatory debates only tangentially; namely, through discourses on the vernacular, the everyday, popular taste, and kitsch. In Robert Venturi and Denise Scott Brown's *Learning from Las Vegas* and Bernard Rudofsky's *Architecture Without Architects* architecture's high culture and elitist taste is challenged.[11] Rudofsky, in 1964, does so by introducing the 'unfamiliar world of nonpedigreed architecture […] so little known that we don't have a name for it'.[12] By emphasising not as much the 'work of the individual architects […] [but] communal enterprise' Rudofsky draws lessons from architecture 'before it became an expert's art'. The protagonists are here not architects but 'the untutored builders in space and time […] who demonstrate an admirable talent for fitting their buildings into the natural surroundings'.[13] For Venturi and Scott Brown, it was a matter of challenging the distinctions between highbrow and lowbrow tastes, formal and informal, 'heroic and original architecture', and 'ugly and ordinary architecture'.[14]

Appreciations of popular taste, and the mundane, are also found in the recent rediscovery of the everyday in architecture: works such as *The Architecture of the Everyday* (Harris and Berke), *What People Want: Populism in Architecture and Design* (Shamiyeh), *Strangely Familiar. Design and Everyday Life* (Blauvelt), and *As found. The discovery of the Ordinary* (Lichtenstein and Schregenberger), call for a re-evaluation of the familiar, the ordinary, and popular taste in architecture.[15] With their scepticism vis-à-vis celebrity-architects and signature-building, these works form an important departure from the more compliant and aestheticised celebrations of the everyday in the 1980s.[16]

In the specific setting of a design profession like architecture, participatory efforts unavoidably involve issues related to politics and aesthetics. These issues are, however, often kept separate: democratic ambitions can overshadow any move towards a participatory style, yet emancipatory rhetoric can help ease the acceptance of designers' aesthetic preferences. Either way, it is clear that some of the longstanding tensions related to participation in architecture have been reinforced under the practice turn.

PARTICIPATION AS A DEMOCRATIC ACT

> *Usually, the idea of participation connotes that, if everybody were included and would participate, then consensus could be reached and full democracy realized.*[17]

Involving the user in the production of architecture may be considered a threat to an architect's creative autonomy and control over the design process. Consequently, when architects do encourage user participation, it signals a democratic act. It combines the empowerment of the user with a critical questioning of the architect's power relationships, be they with public clients or private developers. This democratic dimension runs through most of the history of participatory architecture. As was highlighted in the second chapter of this book, an important participatory moment coincided with the countercultural mood of the 1960s and 1970s. For participatory architects such as Giancarlo De Carlo and Lucien Kroll, architects were to build for the people. De Carlo famously stated that 'architecture has become too important to be left to architects [...] therefore all barriers between builders and users must be abolished'.[18] For followers of De Carlo, the users of architecture, and of cities, were thus to be involved in the imagination and creation of the built environment. Whilst architects typically saw themselves in charge of the coordination of consultation processes and the translation of ideas into buildings, users could advise, imagine, change, and appropriate the environment. In the case of 'self-building', users could even take part in construction.[19]

Since the 1990s, a revival of participation can be observed as part of a wider recovery of a socially engaged architecture.[20] It was manifest through design practices emphasising the creativity of users, and the self-organisation and (re-) claiming of space. Parallels can be drawn with the 'ethical turn' which occurred in the arts in the early 1990s. In *Artificial Hells. Participatory Art and the Politics of Spectatorship*, art historian Claire Bishop relates this turn to the European legacy of the early-twentieth century avant-garde, the neo-avant-garde of 1968, and to the 1989 fall of communism which, respectively, represented the triumph, heroic last stand, and collapse of collectivist thinking.[21] Unsurprisingly, the post-cold-war city of Berlin has also proved to be a point of reference for user creativity and the temporary use of space. Suggesting an alternative form of so-called 'open source urbanism', urban development was envisaged as a match-making exercise between the possibilities created by abandoned and vacant spaces that are considered unsuitable for and/or await mainstream development; the temporary activities developed for these spaces by users; and policy makers facilitating such activities.[22] More generally, the revival of collectivity can be seen as a response to the transition from state-led to flexible, neoliberal politics. The introduction of 'the market' as a full-blown actor, reshuffled the power-relations in citizen participation. Whilst in the state-versus-the-people model, citizens had challenged the dominance of the all-encompassing state planner they were now up against the exclusions and entrepreneurialism of market liberalism. In this new setting, degrees of control in planning no longer trickled down from state-control to citizen-empowerment, but from state-control to market-control.[23] Neoliberal policies reclaimed the local as a new 'scalar niche' where social inclusion was propagated, and, rather than serving democratic purposes, the local formed an important precondition for (global) competitiveness; termed *glocal*.[24] With the introduction of 'glocal' measures, along with a variety of quasi-nongovernmental organisations (quangos) that adopted ambiguous institutional positions, previous bottom-up ideals of empowerment were felt to be compromised.[25]

The ambiguities of this political climate were reflected in the participatory practices of the 1990s. Previously such practices occupied clear-cut counter-positions, and were propagated through oppositions between the state and the people, the expert and layperson, and empowerment and oppression. However, in the climate of the 1990s, these practices occupied radical positions as much as they operated from-within the all-encompassing power of what Michael Hardt and Antonio Negri called *Empire*.[26] Participatory models promoting active forms of citizen participation through, for example, co-production and collective action were now adopted. This was seen as a way to counter democratic policies using citizen consultation for mere appeasing or legitimising purposes.[27] In contrast to the theoretical and ideological impetus of the 1970s counterculture, radical actions now also emerged from architectural *practice*, and operated at the intersections of theory, professional practice, and architectural education. Architectural education, for example, has seen to a demonstrable revival of critical practices blending radical, anti-neoliberal theories with project proposals and material investigations often emerging from collaborations between academic lecturers and practitioners.[28] Such initiatives demonstrate how the former 'idealistic phase' was complemented, and sometimes replaced, by a practical, 'entrepreneurial phase' which emphasised the feasibility of a project alongside its critical and political aspects.[29] However, the transformation of participatory architecture did not eradicate long-standing tensions, rather it magnified them. These tensions can be summarised in terms of the relationship between the architect and the user; the consensual basis of participation; and the opposition between local and global scales (or agency and structure).

Despite new ideals of co-production over consultation, the relationship between the architect and the user (or the expert and layperson) is still largely theorised in oppositional terms and around rhetoric of power and empowerment. This may be explained by the reinforcement of the role of the expert in neoliberal decision-making: participation is limited to a select group of professionals (architects, planners, and economists), whilst the non-professional sector and less-powerful social groups are largely excluded. As a result, as Rodriguez, Swyngedouw, and Moelaert state, 'the mystique of an inclusive non-hierarchical, and participatory network approach towards planning is undermined by the realities of a network based on the primacy of the expert'.[30] The opposition between expert and layperson was also evident in Sherry Arnstein's conception of the 'ladder of participation', whereby user-involvement was discussed in terms of the redirection of power from the expert to the community.[31] The image of the 'ladder' suggested degrees of participation between 'non-participation' (participation as manipulative, phoney, arrogant) and 'citizen power'.[32] Conforming to the ladder, participatory models were often expressed in terms of degrees of emancipation, and the extent to which a community resisted official planning.[33] In architecture, this somewhat coincided with a portrayal of the architect as elitist, and of the user as innocent; a stigmatisation that was reinforced by the widespread phenomenon of 'pseudo-participation'.[34] Pseudo-participation occurs when participation is used to legitimise and enforce the acceptance of projects, or when designers misuse consultation processes to impose stylistic and ideological preferences. Pseudo-participation was also the cause of the Belgian architectural critic, Geert Bekaert's skepticsm of Lucien Kroll's participatory project *La Mémé*, or *Maison Médicale* (1970–1972), a hostel for medical students at the University of Louvain, near Brussels. Here, not only was the project developed with its future users – the students – in mind, the design team was subdivided and placed in charge of different parts of the project. To avoid the designers becoming 'too fond of a particular element and assume authorship' they were routinely moved around.[35] This resulted in a building which is famed for its 'anarchic and anti-hierarchical image'.[36] Bekaert, however, condemned Kroll's attempts to hand over architecture to the users, as an illusion: 'In fact, Kroll designed everything himself and the celebrated anarchy was simply simulated.'[37] The American architectural theorist Charles Jencks, whilst appreciating the building's 'complexity and richness of meaning', felt it suffered from an aesthetic bias: 'The aesthetic is everywhere picturesque, as if normality and the silent majority have been rigorously snubbed.'[38]

Maintaining an opposition between architect and user has, under the practice turn, become increasingly questionable. Critical discourses, for example, tend to polarise the valuing of creativity: it is celebrated as an empowering virtue for the user – allowing for (re)appropriating and (re)claiming space – but dismissed, when applied to the architect, as a source of decadence and frivolity. Such polarisations conveniently ignore that neoliberalism thrives on the celebration of individual creativity as part of its uneven, profit-driven model of development. Moreover, the empowerment of those operating 'at-the-bottom' over those ruling 'at-the-top' is, unhelpful when resolving the question of *how* to look from below. Donna Haraway, the philosopher of science and technology and feminist thinker, whilst promoting situated knowledge, also warns for having blind faith in and romanticising subjugated viewpoints: 'to see from below is neither easily learned nor unproblematic even if "we" "naturally" inhabit the great underground terrain of subjugated knowledges.'[39] Radical theorists have, more generally, challenged the act of 'giving voice', by exposing the divergences that are at work *within* the category of user, community, or margin, and proposing different methods and styles of knowledge gathering such as story-telling, blues, rap, poetry, and songs.[40] The opposition between centre and margin, and their respective association with power and oppression, distracts from the realisation that marginality may occur in the centre as much as the margin. As was shown in the third chapter of the book, actors may go unnoticed, not necessarily because they are purposively oppressed, but because they operate through registers that are not (yet) intelligible.

Another tension, as the opening quote of this section suggests, relates to the fact that participatory models, unwittingly or not, thrive on a political model based on consensus. This is augmented under the post-political turn whereby consensus-driven, democratic decision-making risks becoming a peacemaker for the neoliberal city.[41] In the context of participatory art, Bishop argues that ideals of social inclusion, creativity, and collectivity are important virtues of politically and socially engaged art. But these virtues are equally promoted by European neoliberal politics, interpreting creativity in terms of entrepreneurialism, risk-taking, self-interest, and performance, and positing even the artist as a model of flexible labour.[42] The challenge for participation is to rethink the model of consensus into one that is more open to conflict, and valuing of disagreement, risk, and uncertainty as intrinsic parts of the negotiation process.[43] Political theorist Chantal Mouffe's proposal for 'conflictual consensus', part of her post-consensual, 'agonistic model of democracy' is particularly instructive in that it does not merely criticise the consensus model of collaboration and its romantic visions of inclusion and democratic decision-making, but offers an *alternative* to the fatalist views of the post-political society – and the third-way politics of Giddens, Beck, and Blair.[44] It is a consensus around principles which, although there may be disagreement about the interpretation of these principles, is nonetheless consensual, because conflict is never entirely avoidable.[45] Conflictual consensus is relevant for participatory practices because it acknowledges that pluralism cannot be achieved through harmony but, by necessity, through conflict and involving moments of exclusion.[46]

A final tension derives from participation's roots in bottom-up developments, posited in opposition to top-down strategies. Occurring in the distinction between tactics-from-below and strategies-from-above, and between agency and structure, it implies a choice of scale, that is local over global. The recent fascination amongst architects and urban designers for the uncontrolled urbanisation of the global south seems to reinforce the local scale as the preferred level for intervention; processes of self-organisation, self-help, and informality justify the growing attention for bottom-up empowerment centred on the local scale. However, the literature on informality also suggests rethinking the traditional distinction between bottom-up (local) versus top-down (global) into a multi-scalar approach. In the context of urban informality, Ananya Roy, for example, exposes the opposition between local and global as a 'false dichotomy': 'Globalization is viewed as disempowering while local communities are seen to be a force for change [...] global and local are presented as mutually exclusive categories.'[47] Instead Roy proposes that we 'contemplate action and agency as *multiscaled*, nimble enough to jump scales and work in multiple theatres of action'.[48] These multiple theatres of action suggest that activist practices operate across multiple scales, contexts, and institutional settings. Arjun Appadurai also calls such activism 'deep democracy', and argues that activist grassroots movements are not necessarily just operating vertically – local versus global, oppressed versus power – but that they now also operate horizontally. In organising their actions around, for example, issues (AIDS, the environment) or identities (feminist, indigenous), grassroots movements operate in the form of 'transnational advocacy networks'.[49] Because of this cross-border networking, so Appadurai argues, activist movements may combine typical grassroots features relying on roots, local anchoring, and proximity, with the construction of a wider, horizontal reach which does not hamper them, but becomes *part of* their depth. Whilst working vertically on the local scale (often in opposition to institutional partners), their *horizontal* sharing of ideas and expertise enables activists to develop into stronger community-based partners that are in a position to 'engage in partnerships with more powerful agencies'.[50] By combining local activism with global strengthening, 'the global and the local can become reciprocal instruments in the deepening of democracy'.[51] Deep democracy, in my view, suggests a form of activism from-within. It recognises that certain forms of local activism have the capacity to mediate and mobilise globalisation's geographies of governmentality *despite* the engrained contradictions and inequalities of these geographies.[52] The multi-scalar workings of deep democracy, therefore, demonstrate how activism can operate from-within and, operating on several scale levels, can be oppositional yet institutional, anti-establishment yet collaborative.

THE AESTHETICS OF PARTICIPATION

> *One can either have participation or Architecture (with a capital A) but not both.*[53]

In his foreword to Paul Jenkins and Leslie Forsyth's *Architecture, Participation, and Society*, Jeremy Till argues that the involvement of users is perceived as spoiling the pure creativity and meaning of architecture; rather than impacting on architecture's core values, participation is seen as a 'worthy other'.[54] The tension between participation and aesthetics can be brought back to architecture's established and protective ideas on aesthetics, which are generally considered incompatible with the political and democratic aspirations of participation and presumed to complicate the creative autonomy and signature authorship of the architect. Consequently, the aesthetics of participation occurs in various degrees between the two extremes of formalism and anti-aesthetics, and between articulated authorship and the favouring of democracy over form.

Under postmodernism, the interest in use and the user, whilst triggering excitement, also generated anxieties amongst architects due to a perceived loss of formal and aesthetic control. Because use can never be fully anticipated, anxiety also accompanied the difficult task of designing the unplanned.[55] Such anxieties triggered a stabilisation of form through the use of types or symbolic meanings, with architects tending to favour the *rhetoric* of pluralism over proper participation. As is evident from the discussions around Lucien Kroll's *La Mémé*, architects were, rightfully or not, blamed for reducing their buildings to participatory 'signs'.[56] This seems, at the same time, a harsh criticism at the address of architects working in the spirit of Kroll. One senses that for these architects, participation was neither a style, nor a method; instead, it was a way of living and an attitude vis-à-vis society; not as an architect but as a human being. One therefore wonders whether their architectural shortcomings had more to do with a lack of experience (at that time) for translating participatory endeavours into form. Two excerpts of an interview with Lucien Kroll are, in combination, quite telling about the architect's role in participation. When interviewed by Judith Lemaire and Irene Lund, and asked whether, even when not resulting in a project, participation can be considered an achievement, Kroll firmly states:[57]

> *For Ita Gassel [ethnologist and action-researcher, with whom Kroll elaborated], yes [...]. For me, it is not; because I would not have done my job. My job is not to create groups; but to help creating meaningful envelopes for them. [...] Why does the architect want to do it? What is participation? It is some sort of politico-moralo-spirituel that makes that you want to live life in one way and not another, with some types of client; not others. So you have to try it, even if it often fails. One needs some experience to avoid clashes from happening.*

At the same time, Kroll seems to have fond memories of the participatory experiences of, for example, *La Mémé*:[58]

> *Do you see that green plant over there? The amaryllis that is too big for its pot? It dates from 1972. The medical students gave it to us. We had fifty students here. And my wife, Simone, had made dinner for them. She has participated a lot in this whole adventure. They brought the plant as a gift. And this amaryllis felt so good here that we have had to keep on cutting and splitting it. I believe we must have made thirty plants out of it. They are everywhere across the garden. And we have donated some to our friends. But originally, it is the plant of the students. These are the things you cannot dream of when confronted with an engineering client with a white sheet of paper. Thus, participation, as a way of making things more personal, more human, is the concern of the architect. My colleagues, who do not like me, do not know this, and I cannot explain it to them because they do not want to know. It has no impact.*

These quotes express, in my view, a far more genuine democratic desire for user involvement in design than is the case in, for example, the participatory designs of Community Architecture. Community Architecture is associated with stylistically traditional architects championed by the Prince Charles Foundation in Britain and by the New Urbanism in the US.[59] Here, an elaborate participatory model of 'charettes' coincides with the use of 'design guidelines' which serve to reinforce the designer's aesthetic control.[60] The ideology of inclusiveness hides the fact that the moralistic and stylistic preferences of the architect are, at times, prioritised over community-interests, and that community is, largely limited to white, middle-class (and in the case of New Urbanism: suburban) values. This prompted Charles Jencks to argue that the ongoing conflicts between Modern Architects and Community Architects were 'taste wars', rather than moral disputes.[61] Further, Kroll advised against choosing either a Walter Gropius or Prince Charles-type figure, for both represent an equal form of domination.[62] In response to the de-politicised community architecture of the 1980s, whereby the notion of community grew increasingly homogenised, Jeremy Till suggests it should be replaced with an 'architecture of the impure community'.[63] Rather than clinging onto the ideal of purity, his is a call for accepting 'contingency and the reality of social construction'.[64]

In contrast to the rearticulating of form, one also saw to the emergence of a critical, and largely anti-aesthetic, form of participation that was primarily concerned with the wider conditions of architecture rather than the mere creation of objects.[65] A preoccupation with aesthetics was seen as elitist and/or secondary to more pressing concerns such as, for example, the political or ecological. In the wake of Venturi and Scott Brown's appreciative work on Las Vegas and the Architecture without Architects movement, aesthetics became a matter of choice between high and low culture.[66] The perceived disconnection between architects and the real world encouraged the promotion of popular taste, and the appreciation of the ordinary, the everyday, the banal and the ugly, as productive forces for urban design.[67]

Between the extremes of formalism and anti-aesthetics, various attempts emerged to reconcile participatory decision-making with the needs and requirements of design. Such methods often served as a critique of the top-down attitudes prevalent in planning and architecture. For example, the introduction of complexity theory in planning formed a critique of the systems approach, and proposed a bottom-up understanding of space in terms of complexity, emergence and self-organisation.[68] These efforts to rethink design methods aimed to optimise dialogue between expert and layperson, and render the design process more transparent; thus, more democratic. This is demonstrated by the clear demarcation of scholarly fields such as Design Research and Design Studies, and by the invention of a variety of participatory design tools such as charettes, design games, and urban games.[69] One can also include innovations in mapping which promote a relational approach to space such as a subjective 'view-from-below' as opposed to an objective 'view-from-above'. Such mapping is often characterised by a Situationist reading of the city, or by a relational, multi-layered reading which allows for integrating a multiplicity of knowledge.[70]

Despite such efforts to reconcile the democratic and design dimensions of participation, problems persist. Firstly, because participation is still largely theorised through a presumed disparity between politics and aesthetics (or democracy and design), it is tempting to interpret the architects' insistence of their right-to-design as a reluctance to share authorship and cede control. This is somewhat suggested by Jeremy Till's opening quote of this section: 'participation or Architecture (with capital A)'. Although participatory design games and charrettes recast the designer as an enabler or facilitator, the designer often remains responsible for defining the rules of the game.[71] At the same time, it is, however, important to acknowledge that, in participatory settings, the architect is still held responsible for the final result. Many participatory architects and urban planners that I interviewed in Brussels emphasised that it is the *duty* of the architect to design, not, as is often argued, their *right*. Whilst citizens are expected to tap into their 'experience expertise' in order to gain deeper understandings of a project's context (that is differing usages of a neighbourhood throughout the course of a day), architects are expected to deploy their design skills for spatially translating these understandings into design proposals.[72] The difficulty of Everyday Urbanism is, therefore evident: whilst offering an excellent and refreshing tool for analysing space, one which is closer to the practices and desires of the users of space, it is not entirely clear how this knowledge can inform design processes. This is demonstrated by the 'dialogic' design for the Chatsworth Metrorail Station and Childcare Centre by John Kaliski whereby the station was constructed, according with the people's wishes, in traditional ranch style, and thus set in dialogue with the adjacent childcare centre which was realised in an 'elegant modernist style' as preferred by the architect.[73]

The disparity between politics and aesthetics is also found under post-modernism, a period when architecture is generally presumed to have gradually de-radicalised in favour of aesthetic preferences. It is not surprising, therefore, that the editors of *Architecture and Participation* prioritise politics over aesthetics, and emphasise the political dimension of participatory architecture as an alternative to evaluating architecture in either functional or aesthetic terms.[74] The struggle between politics and aesthetics was, at the same time, at the very roots of postmodernism. As I have shown elsewhere, architectural students and practitioners were challenged to craft an individual, aesthetic voice amidst the politicised climate of 1970s architecture.[75] Is it therefore not time to let go of the artificial division between a presumed ethical, user-friendly architect and a formalist, elite architect operating in social autonomy?

There is, moreover, a second problem, which relates to the treatment of aesthetics itself. According to the editors of *Architecture and Participation*, the aesthetics that emerges from participatory architecture are of a different kind. They argue:[76]

> Participation, through alternative means of production, leads to alternative aesthetics and spatialities. It is too easy to dismiss some of these aesthetics as 'crude' or 'dirty', because that simply reinforces the presumed superiority of the standard architectural categories of refined and clean.

The validation of dirtiness and impurity over cleanliness, however, still evaluates the aesthetic value of a work *within* aesthetic conventions. Likewise, the democratisation of aesthetics through popular taste, kitsch, the beauty of the ordinary, and even *anti*-aesthetics, nevertheless remain locked within established registers of aesthetics.

POLITICS *AND* AESTHETICS: PARTICIPATION AS EVENT

The current post-critical condition shows, on the one hand, an architectural practice whereby a preoccupation with democratic agendas has perhaps overshadowed the design and material component of participation. On the other hand, one can observe a rediscovery of aesthetics, albeit in a lighter, more de-politicised form.[77] The latter is manifest in the alliance between signature architecture and policies promoting urban regeneration and global competitiveness. Such architecture, however, raises ethical issues. When mobilised as part of an urban regeneration plan, it can contribute to both gentrification and social displacement. Likewise, its dependency on the availability of cheap labour – to compensate for the cost of technological caprice – and on wealthy, but sometimes ethically questionable, clients poses ethical dilemmas that architects are not always prepared to face.

In response, the editors of the 'Aesthetics/Pleasure/Excess' section of the *Architectural Theory Handbook*, called for reconnecting the debates on aesthetics with those on *critical* architecture.[78] Because (critical) theory was severely bruised by the loss of confidence in grand narratives, the editors proposed discussing architectural aesthetics through architectural *criticism*: to determine why some buildings are considered more pleasing than others, they support a 'practical criticism of architectural works'.[79] In this book I explore the remaining merits of theory, albeit reconceptualised in embodied and situated terms (see Chapter 1). Even if practical criticism expands aesthetical judgement, by including popular taste and the appreciation of the everyday and the ordinary, it still centres on the 'pleasing' qualities of buildings. Thus, it hampers the discussion of aesthetics beyond its own registers of evaluation which, as we have seen above, is necessary in order to reconnect it with the political project of architecture.

Efforts to re-engage politics and aesthetics can be found in Bishop's discussions of participatory art; namely, those art practices that emerged since the early 1990s with a particular interest in participation and collaboration.[80] Instead of rethinking aesthetics within its own realm (as denoted in the term 'relational aesthetics'), Bishop searches for the 'creative rewards of participation as a politicised working process'.[81] This search for creative rewards is relevant to architecture for two reasons. Firstly, instead of *relocating* aesthetic–political judgement through a shift from architect to user, aesthetics to anti-aesthetics, or from grand theory to practical criticism, it values creative achievement *as part of* the political merits of the project. Secondly, by emphasising the creative merits of participatory works, it counters the judgement of critical art (and architecture) in solely political and ethical terms. Bishop criticises the fact that, ever since the so-called ethical turn, social art works are judged primarily for their social agency whilst their qualitative artistic gestures are ignored.[82] Bishop's insistence on evaluating social art *as art* is, however, not an attempt to reinstall creative autonomy and authorship. Instead, it is a warning to political art now that its virtues of participation, social inclusion, and user creativity are becoming absorbed into the jargon of post-industrial, neoliberal politics. Bishop argues that, because of the blurring of art and creativity and of critical art practice and cultural policy, it is all the more important to discuss these works not in terms of 'verifiable outcomes' and 'demonstrative impact' (as policies do) but as art.[83] The paradox of social art is, therefore, that whilst it refuses being evaluated *as art*, it does not compare itself with any social work that takes place *outside* the art world.[84]

In order to rethink aesthetics beyond established formats and norm systems, Bishop builds on Jacques Rancière's work on politics and aesthetics. Rancière's critique of the ethical turn in art is not an opposition to ethics, but, instead, a call to reinvent aesthetics; because it 'belongs to a previous model of understanding art'.[85] For Rancière, politics is also a matter of aesthetics and form; and thus aesthetic judgement is also political judgement. Political issues, therefore, should not be discussed in and for themselves, but must challenge the formats and conventions within which political issues are presented; the set conditions under which debate is allowed.[86] For Rancière, works of art can question the formats and conventions through which the world is organised. Art therefore opens up the 'possibility of changing or redistributing that same world'; and they do so not in spite of, but thanks to their aesthetic dimension.[87] Rancière thus redefines aesthetics as 'aisthesis': 'an autonomous regime of experience that is not reducible to logic, reason or morality.'[88] Aisthesis generates a freedom and autonomy of experience of the work by the audience.[89] The meaning of the work is consequently uncertain and unpredictable; it emerges through the creation of the work as much as the experience of it. The aesthetic agency of a participatory work of art no longer resides in either the creative act of the artist or the experience of the audience but, instead, emerges through circulating across such registers.

Bishop demonstrates this through a detailed discussion of Jeremy Deller's *The Battle of Orgreave* (2001); an artwork that re-enacts violent clashes between miners and police in South Yorkshire in 1984.[90] Bishop argues that the decisions taken by the artist during the creation of the work were social as much as artistic in nature. The work's aesthetic–political experience starts with the mobilisation of multiple, even contradictory, audiences. Involved in the performance are people who were originally involved in the battle, locals, and members of the general public, as well as historical re-enactment societies. Deller stages unusual encounters that articulate the political dimension of the work by challenging assumptions relating to class: the miners are not presented as working-class heroes nor do the middle classes become default oppressors.[91] Deller's work juxtaposes the miners and policemen who took part in the original battle with historical re-enactment societies, who are traditionally preoccupied with historical accuracy, style and composition. And thus, Deller's choreography of a political event contains a strong compositional–aesthetic component. In addition, by formatting the work not just as a performance, but also a film, an archive-and-exhibition, and a book, Deller allows the mobilisation of a variety of audiences and creates various outlets for experiencing the work. In line with Rancière, this invites the audiences to question, challenge, and recompose the presented issues. Instead of choosing between politics and aesthetics, or between social engagement and creative autonomy, aesthetics is here presented as part of politics.[92]

There are, of course, important differences between participatory works of art and architecture. In Deller's participatory art, the audience participates in the making *and* the final product of the work. Because the work takes the shape of an event or performance, the participatory moment *is* the work (even if the work also includes products such as an exhibition, book, and film). Architecture, by contrast, informs a sharper distinction between the mobilisation of an audience during the design process (consultation) and around the final product (the use of architecture). Architectural products are, in most instances, physical objects that emerge from a series of actions that are political, aesthetic, but also functional, programmatic, structural, and technical in nature. Works such as Deller's *The Battle of Orgreave* are nevertheless relevant for architecture because they challenge the rejection of aesthetics in participation for being mere signs of formalism and depoliticisation. Also, instead of celebrating (overly) modest authorship by redefining creators as mere enablers or facilitators, Deller's work invites a rearticulation of the authorial role and responsibilities of the creators and choreographers of participatory events; participatory artists are therefore 'directorial instigators' which alludes to an interesting status.[93] On the one hand, the artist (or architect) is considered to be an enabler: one who triggers action, makes things possible, but is never fully in control of the work. On the other hand, the enabling work does not hamper their authorial and directorial role: the capacities of the designer remain essential to the existence of the work.[94] It may seem provocative to reinforce rather than diminish the authorial and directive capacity of the participatory architect. It is, however, a necessary step towards the reconnection of politics and aesthetics. Such a task entails emphasising the responsibility of the architect in using their knowledge rather than blindly following onto the demands of the user. As Jeremy Till states, 'it is irresponsible for architects to *not* use their knowledge'.[95] And this is the case *especially* in participatory projects. The architect's skills to imagine, visualise,

4.1 Les Vignes Blanches, Cergy-Pontoise, France. 1976–1979. Copyright: Lucien Kroll. Used with permission.

integrate, and translate ideas into material and formal solutions allow for building bridges between expert and non-expert.[96] The challenge becomes to take design responsibilities seriously without falling into formal dogmatism or domination. There is a telling anecdote of how such can be achieved: a Japanese journalist called Lucien Kroll's office because he could not find the project he was visiting, Les Vignes Blanches in Cergy-Pontoise (Paris), which was a new town designed by Kroll (1976–1979). It turned out the journalist had indeed been there but he had not recognised it as architecture (Figure 4.1, see Plate 14).[97]

A POST-DICHOTOMIST ACCOUNT OF PARTICIPATION?

Participation under the practice turn has been discussed around two main concerns that continually appear in theories and discourses on participation: democratic decision-making and the aesthetics of participation. I argued that many of those concerns have, since the radical moment of the 1960s and 1970s, remained largely the same; and that participation still tends to be discussed through dichotomist pairs such as expert versus layperson, use versus design, and hard interventions versus soft measures. Many of these tensions have intensified under the practice turn's consensual politics thus paradoxically forming a threat to the democratic integrity of participation. In response, this chapter re-imagines participation beyond oppositions and dichotomies by considering participation as a simultaneously political and aesthetic event, and by re-thinking its democratic programme through practice. Appadurai's notion of 'deep democracy' is interesting here because it imagines a form of activism from-within, one that operates across scale levels, is oppositional yet institutional, and is anti-establishment yet collaborative. Bishop's analysis of Jeremy Deller's *The Battle of Orgreave* inspires a role for the architect in terms of 'directorial instigator' where politics and aesthetics are shared rather than mutually exclusive agendas; and aesthetics is revalorised in participatory practice not in addition to but as *part of* its political agenda. This leads me to suggest a post-dichotomist understanding of participation which considers conflict, consensus, local, global, political, aesthetic, design, and use as equally part of participatory projects. Moreover, in concentrating on the political–aesthetic tension, I have eschewed other aspects of participation that are equally important; such as, for example, its financing, programming, and regulation. This raises a different series of questions that deserve attention: how can *numerous* forces be included in the discussion of participation? Can a post-dichotomist understanding of participation inform a more complex and realistic account of participation? And, if so, how? These questions are the starting point of the next chapter.

NOTES

1 Architecture at the Crossroads. 'Houses Fit for People', BBC2, March 2, 1986. Accessed February 17, 2014, http://www.bbc.co.uk/programmes/p01rk3x0.

2. Architecture at the Crossroads. 'Stop the Bulldozer' BBC2, February 23, 1986. Accessed February 17, 2014, http://www.bbc.co.uk/iplayer/episode/p01rk26h/architecture-at-the-crossroads-7-stop-the-bulldozer. The documentary makes, for example, reference to the *Les Halles* Shopping Centre in Paris and its failure to recreate the genuinely buzzing spaces of the market it replaces.

3. It is worth mentioning exceptions such as OMA/AMO and Dogma (Pier-Vittorio Aureli), both of whom distinguish radical statements (research and paper architecture) from everyday architectural production.

4. Peter Blundell Jones, Doina Petrescu and Jeremy Till, eds, *Architecture and Participation* (Abingdon: Spon Press, 2005); Paul Jenkins and Leslie Forsyth, eds, *Architecture, Participation and Society* (London: Routledge, 2010); Markus Miessen and Shuman Basar, eds, *Did Someone Say Participate? An Atlas of Spatial Practice* (Cambridge, MA: The MIT Press, 2006); Markus Miessen, ed., *The Violence of Participation* (Berlin: Sternberg, 2007); Markus Miessen, ed., *The Nightmare of Participation* (Berlin: Sternberg, 2010).

5. Paul Davidoff, 'Advocacy and Pluralism in Planning', in *The City Reader*, ed. Richard T. Le Gates and Frederic Stout, 2nd edition (London and New York: Routledge, 2000), 423–433. Originally published in the *Journal of the American Institute of Planners*, 3, no. 4 (1965): 331–338.

6. Clara Greed, 'Planning Theory in Retrospect', in *Introducing Planning* (London: Athlone, 2000), 235–256, 240; following E. Guba and Y. Lincoln's categorisation in 'Competing Paradigms in Qualitative Research', in *Handbook of Qualitative Research*, ed. N. Denzin and Y. Lincoln (Newbury Park, CA: Sage, 1992). The positivist paradigm that had been dominant until the late 1950s was challenged by a post-positivist and pluralist planning (in reference to Davidoff's advocacy and pluralist planning), having more attention for reality and inclusiveness.

7. The planner was not just seen as an advocate of marginalised groups, but also 'an advocate for what he deems proper', consequently bringing in their own values too. See Davidoff, 'Advocacy and Pluralism in Planning', 425–426.

8. Key events include the 1970 Design Participation conference, co-organised by Nigel Cross (see Jeremy Till, 'The Negotiation of Hope', in *Architecture and Participation*, ed. Peter Blundell Jones et al. [London and New York: Spon Press, 2005], 23–41) and the 1980 Design Science Method conference (see Mary Comerio, 'Community Design: Idealism and Entrepreneurship', *Anarchitektur* 20 [2008 (1984), 37–47]). Key writings include Henry Sanoff, *Design Games* (Los Altos, CA: William Kaufman, 1979) and *Community Participation: Methods in Design and Planning* (New York: John Wiley and Sons, 1999), and the practical design guidelines offered by Christopher Alexander, Sara Ishikawa, Murray Silverstein, *A Pattern Language: Towns, Buildings, Construction* (New York: Oxford University Press, 1977).

9. In development studies, participation is characterised by a strong emphasis on poverty reduction, and a growing literature stressing informality and self-organisation as important assets in community development. See for example Uma Kothari and Bill Cooke, eds, *Participation: The New Tyranny?* (London: Zed Books, 2001).

10. Neil Brenner, *New State Spaces: Urban Governance and the Rescaling of Statehood* (Oxford: Oxford University Press, 2004).

11. Robert Venturi, Denise Scott Brown and Steven Izenour, *Learning from Las Vegas: The Forgotten Symbolism of Architectural Form* (Cambridge MA, and London: The MIT Press, 1998 [1972]); Bernard Rudofsky, *Architecture Without Architects: A Short Introduction to Non-Pedigreed Architecture* (Albuquerque, NM: University of New Mexico Press, 1998 [1964]).

12 Rudofsky, 'Preface', in *Architecture Without Architects*, no page nos.

13 Ibid., this and previous citation.

14 Denise Scott Brown, 'Everyday', in *Crucial Words: Conditions for Contemporary Architecture*, ed. Gert Wingardh and Rasmus Waern (Basel: Birkhauser, 2008), 74; Venturi, Scott Brown and Izenour, *Learning from Las Vegas*, 129.

15 Steven Harris and Deborah Berke, eds *The Architecture of the Everyday* (Princeton, NJ: Princeton Architectural Press, 1997); Michael Shamiyeh, ed., *What People Want: Populism in Architecture and Design* (Basel: Birkhauser, 2005); Andrew Blauvelt, ed., *Strangely Familiar: Design and Everyday Life*, exhibition catalogue (Minneapolis, MN: Walker Art Center, 2003), exhibition shown within Lille's year as European Capital of Culture, 2004; Claude Lichtenstein and Thomas Schregenberger, *As Found: The Discovery of the Ordinary* (Baden: Lars Müller Publishers, 2001).

16 See Matthew Turner, 'The Future of Trivial Design', *Daidalos* 40 (1991): 102–111, 103; and also Peter Bürger, 'Aporias of Modern Aesthetics', *New Left Review* 184 (November–December 1990): 47–56.

17 Chantal Mouffe, 'Democracy revisited (in conversation with Chantal Mouffe)', in *The Nightmare of Participation (Crossbench Praxis as A Mode of Criticality)*, ed. Markus Miessen (Berlin: Sternberg, 2010), 105–159, 123.

18 Giancarlo De Carlo, 'Architecture's Public', in *Architecture and Participation*, ed. Peter Blundell Jones, Doina Petrescu, and Jeremy Till (London and New York: Spon Press, 2005), 3–22, 13. Originally published as 'Il Publico Dell'architettura/Legitimizing Architecture', in *Parametro* 5 (1970), 4–11.

19 The examples discussed in Peter Blundell Jones, 'Sixty-eight and After', in *Architecture and Participation*, ed. Peter Blundell Jones, Doina Petrescu and Jeremy Till, 127–139, include Walter Segal's work with 'self-builders' in the UK; Eilfried Huth and Guenther Domenig and the New Graz Architecture (Enschensiedlung in Deutschlandsberg), and Peter Sulzer and Peter Huebner (Bauhausle in Stuttgart).

20 See, amongst others, the practices collected in Nishat Awan, Tatjana Schneider, Jeremy Till, eds, *Spatial Agency: Other Ways of Doing Architecture* (London: Routledge, 2011); Miessen and Basar, *Did Someone Say Participate?*; Bryan Bell, *Good Deeds, Good Design: Community Service Through Architecture* (New York: Princeton Architectural Press, 2004).

21 Claire Bishop, *Artificial Hells: Participatory Art and the Politics of Spectatorship* (London: Verso, 2012), 3. Most of these practices emerged in the EU, due to a generous funding context (p. 2). The term 'ethical turn' was coined by Peter Dews 'Uncategorical Imperatives: Adorno, Badiou and the Ethical turn', *Radical Philosophy* 111 (2002): 33 (quoted in Bishop, *Artificial Hells*, 25).

22 Philipp Misselwitz, Philipp Oswalt, and Klaus Overmeyer, 'Urban Development without Urban Planning: A Planners Nightmare or the Promised Land?', in *Urban Pioneers: Temporary Use and Urban Development in Berlin*, ed. Klaus Overmeyer and Senatsverwaltung für Stadtentwicklung Berlin (Berlin: Jovis, 2007), 102–109.

23 With the market having entered planning as full-blown actor, citizens now needed protection, rather than against the all-encompassing State planning, against the exclusions and entrepreneurialism of market liberalism; Tim Brindley, Yvonne Rydin and Gerry Stoker, *Remaking Planning: The Politics of Urban Change*, second edition (London and New York: Routledge, 1996), 170–172. In their 'six styles of planning in practice' the authors no longer opposed regulative (state) planning to citizen empowerment and control but, instead, to private-management planning.

24 Neil Brenner, *New State Spaces*, 272.

25 See Neil Brenner, 'Globalisation as Reterritorialisation: The Re-scaling of Urban Governance in the European Union', *Urban Studies* 36, no. 3 (1999): 431–451; Patsy Healey, 'Transforming Governance: Challenges of Institutional Adaptation and a New Politics of Space', *European Planning Studies* 14, no. 3 (2006): 299–320; Willem Salet, Andy Thornley and Anton Kreukels, eds, *Metropolitan Governance and Spatial Planning: Comparative Case Studies of European City-Regions* (London and New York: Spon Press, 2003); Patrick Le Galès, *European Cities: Social Conflicts and Governance* (Oxford: Oxford University Press, 2002).

26 Michael Hardt and Antonio Negri, *Empire* (Cambridge, MA: Harvard University Press, 2000).

27 In art, Bishop observed how the collective actions of the 'multitude' were seen as a resistance to both art's single authorship and the individualist stance of neoliberalism. See *Artificial Hells*, 12.

28 Examples include the Rural Studio at Auburn University; Urban Asymmetries Studio at the Delft School of Design; Shigeru Ban's natural-disaster recovery work at Keio University; Teddy Cruz at UC San Diego; Eyal and Ines Weizman at the London Metropolitan University; The Contested Urbanism studio at UCL London; Matthias Heyden's participatory work at the TU Berlin, the Contested Peripheries Studio at the Manchester School of Architecture; and the Agency Group at Sheffield School of Architecture.

29 Comerio, 'Community Design: Idealism and Entrepreneurship', 45.

30 Arantxa Rodriguez, Erik Swyngedouw and Frank Moulaert, eds, 'Urban Restructuring, Social-Political Polarization, and New Urban Policies', in *The Globalised City – Economic Restructuring and Social Polarisation in European Cities* (Oxford: Oxford University Press, 2003), 29–45, 41–42.

31 Sherry Arnstein, 'A Ladder of Citizen Participation', in *The City Reader*, ed. T. Le Gates and Stout (Abingdon: Routledge, 2000), 240–252 (based on the 1969 publication in *The Journal of the American Institute of Planners*).

32 Ibid.

33 Leonie Sandercock identified six forms of planning, several of which are corrections of the Advocacy model, see *Towards Cosmopolis: Planning for Multicultural Cities* (Chichester: John Wiley and Sons, 1998). Sanoff distinguishes (referring to Deschler and Sock, 1985) between genuine participation and pseudoparticipation (*Community Participation*, 8). Eric Corijn identified four degrees of participation: 'closed planning', co-production, conflict-based planning, and participation 'from the margins', see 'Deelnemen is belangrijker dan winnen', in *Inzet / Opzet / Voorzet: Stadsprojecten in Vlaanderen*, ed. Boudry et al. (Antwerp and Apeldoorn: Garant, 2006), 164–181.

34 Carole Pateman, *Participation and Democratic Theory* (Cambridge: Cambridge University Press, 1970), quoted in Till, 'The Negotiation of Hope', 27.

35 Peter Blundell Jones, 'Sixty-eight and after', in *Architecture and Participation*, ed. Peter Blundell Jones, Doina Petrescu, and Jeremy Till (Abingdon: Spon Press, 2005), 127–139, 134–135.

36 Ibid., 135.

37 Geert Bekaert, 'Operating Instructions for Architecture. A Century of Architecture in Belgium', in *Horta and After: 25 Masters of Modern Architecture in Belgium*, ed. Mil De Kooning (Ghent: University of Ghent, Department of Architecture and Urban Planning, 1999), 6–43, 35.

38 Charles Jencks, *The Language of Post-Modern Architecture*, fifth rev. edition (London: Academy Editions, 1987 [1977]), 105–106.

39 Donna Haraway, 'Situated Knowledges: The Science Question in Feminism and the Privilege of Partial Perspective', *Simians, Cyborgs and Women: The Reinvention of Nature* (New York: Routledge, 1991), 183–201, 191.

40 This is particularly evident in gender, race, feminist, and queer theories; see Sandercock, *Towards Cosmopolis*, 107–125; bell hooks, 'Choosing the Margin as a Space of Radical Openness', in *Gender, Space, Architecture; an Interdisciplinary Introduction*, ed. Jane Rendell, Barbara Penner, Iain Borden (London and New York: Routledge, 2000), 203–209; Nancy Fraser's 'subaltern counterpublics' in 'Rethinking the Public Sphere. A Contribution to the Critique of Actually Existing Democracy', in *The Cultural Studies Reader*, ed. Simon During (London and New York: Routledge), 518–536, 527.

41 See Jeremy Till, 'Architecture of the Impure Community', in *Occupying Architecture, Between the Architect and the User*, ed. Jonathan Hill (London: Routledge, 1998), 61–75, 67.

42 Bishop, *Artificial Hells*, 13, 16; and see BAVO, *Too Active to Act! Cultureel activisme en het einde van de geschiedenis* (Rotterdam: Valiz, 2010).

43 This is also suggested by Peter Blundell Jones, Doina Petrescu, and Jeremy Till, 'Introduction', in *Architecture and Participation*, ed. Peter Blundell Jones, Doina Petrescu and Jeremy Till (London and New York: Spon Press), xiii–xvii, xiv.

44 Mouffe, 'Democracy Revisited', 106. Mouffe makes reference to her book *On the Political* (Abingdon and New York: Routledge, 2005). Mouffe emphasises the importance of formulating alternative futures because right-wing parties usually thrive in a political situation of loss of belief in alternative futures ('Democracy Revisited', 118).

45 Ibid., 109; 'the ever-present possibility of antagonism: an antagonism that is ineradicable' (107).

46 Ibid., 125–126. Instead of presumably harmonious notions such as 'we, the People', Mouffe acknowledges the fact that participatory processes also include moments of exclusion (128).

47 Ananya Roy, 'Urban Informality, Toward an Epistemology of Planning,' *Journal of the American Planning Association* 71, no. 2 (2005): 147–158, 154.

48 Ibid., 154; my italics. Roy here refers to David Harvey, *Spaces of Hope* (Edinburgh: Edinburgh University Press, 2000).

49 Arjun Appadurai, 'Deep Democracy: Urban Governmentality and the Horizon of Politics', *Environment and Urbanization* 13, no. 2 (2001): 23–43, 26. Appadurai borrows the term from Margaret E. Keck and Kathryn Sikkink, *Activists Beyond Borders: Advocacy Networks in International Politics* (Ithaca: Cornell University Press, 1998).

50 Ibid., 42.

51 Ibid., 26.

52 Ibid., 25.

53 Jeremy Till, 'Foreword' in *Architecture, Participation, and Society*, ed. Paul Jenkins and Leslie Forsyth (Abingdon and New York: Routledge, 2010), xi–xii, xii.

54 Ibid., xii.

55 This point is also made by Michael Guggenheim, 'From Prototyping to Allotyping. The Invention of Change of Use and the Crisis of Building Types', *Journal of Cultural Economy* 7, no. 4 (2014): 411–433, 244.

56 Architects attempted to regain power by stabilising form, not use. Ibid., 412.

57 Translated from French. Judith Lemaire and Irene Lund, 'Le Psychodrama, Les Langues de Chat et L'amaryllis. Interview de Lucien Kroll *'De la participation urbaine: La Place Flagey, Les Cahiers de La Cambre Architecture*, no. 3, ed. Jean-Didier Bergilez et al. (Brussels: La Lettre Volée, 2005), 133–149, 137–138.

58 Ibid., 144. Translated from French.

59 I refer to the British Community Architects of the 1980s, around the work of Nick Wates and Charles Knevitt, and connected to the Prince of Wales (Charles). Some of the work can be considered to be a depoliticised version of the original radical movement of the 1960s, see Till, 'Architecture of the Impure Community', 66.

60 Community Architecture formed the flagship of a 'moral movement in planning' led by Rod Hackney (when he became RIBA president in 1987), and supported by the Prince of Wales and the Church of England (Brindley et al., *Remaking Planning*, 180). Well-known urban design projects include Poundbury in Dorset.

61 Charles Jencks, *The Prince, the Architects, and New Wave Monarchy* (London: Academy Editions, 1988), 7.

62 Lucien Kroll, 'Animal Town Planning and Homeopathic Architecture', in *Architecture and Participation*, ed. Peter Blundell Jones, Doina Petrescu and Jeremy Till (London and New York: Spon Press), 183–186, 186.

63 Till, 'Architecture of the Impure Community', 65. See also Jeremy Till, 'The architect and the Other', http://www.opendemocracy.net/ecology-landscape/architecture_3680.jsp, 26/6/2006 [accessed September 16, 2009]. See also Nan Ellin, *Postmodern Urbanism* (Princeton Architectural Press, 1999 [1996]), in particular chapter 7, 'Crisis in the Architectural Profession', 234–266.

64 Till, 'Architecture of the Impure Community', 65.

65 John Macarthur and Naomi Stead, 'Introduction: Architecture and Aesthetics', in *The SAGE Handbook of Architectural Theory*, ed. C. Greig Crysler, Stephen Cairns and Hilde Heynen (London: Sage, 2012), 123–135. One can think of practices prioritising political, ecological, and social engagements over the development of a style, such as, for example, Earthships.

66 Venturi, Scott Brown and Izenour, *Learning from Las Vegas;* Rudofsky, *Architecture Without Architects.*

67 This was manifest in the revitalised discourses on the everyday since the 1990s. In addition to the references included in note 15, see also Margaret Crawford, John Chase, and John Kaliski, *Everyday Urbanism*, first published in 1999, and, expanded edition, in 2008 (New York: The Monacelli Press); and Michel Provoost and Wouter Vanstiphout, *Wimby! Welcome in My Backyard: International Building Exhibition Rotterdam-Hoogvliet* (Rotterdam: NAI Publishers, 2000).

68 Through urban modelling; it operated as a tool for analysis and for predicting the effects of planning interventions. See, for example, Michael Batty, *Cities and Complexity, Understanding Cities with Cellular Automata, Agent-based Models and Fractals* (Cambridge, MA: The MIT Press, 2005); Patsy Healey, *Urban Complexity and Spatial Strategies: Towards a Relational Planning for Our Times* (Abingdon and New York: Routledge, 2006); and see, in urban and architectural design, the work of Space Syntax and, more recently, also parametric design.

69 Charettes are most known in the community design movement; design games in the advocacy tradition (for example Sanoff's *Design Games*); and urban games in, for example, CHORA/Raoul Bunschoten, eds, *Urban Flotsam: Stirring the City*, Rotterdam: 010 Publishers, 2001.

70 Examples include the Eclectic Atlases by USE/Multiplicity/Boeri; Eyal Weisman's Vertical Territories; and James Corner/Field Operations. These examples are discussed by Arie Graafland who speaks of mapping techniques in terms of 'drift', 'layering', and 'rhizome' in 'Mapping Urban Complexity: Understanding the Socius through Creative Mapping Techniques', DSD Future Cities Project, accessed December 15, 2014: www.ariegraafland.eu. Graafland is building upon the work of James Corner, 'The Agency of Mapping: Speculation, Critique and Invention', in *Mappings*, ed. Denis Cosgrove (London: Reaktion Books, 1999), 213–252.

71 Graafland, 'Mapping Urban Complexity'.

72 This was implicit in several interviews conducted by the author, with architects and planners with an experience in participatory design.

73 Margaret Crawford, in *Everyday Urbanism, Margaret Crawford versus Michael Speaks*, ed. Raoul Mehrotra (Ann Arbor: University of Michigan, 2005), 27.

74 Blundell Jones, Petrescu and Till, 'Introduction', xv.

75 See Chapter 2 in this book, and also Isabelle Doucet, 'Architecture between Politics and Aesthetics. Peter Wilson's "ambivalent criticality" at the 1970s Architectural Association', *Architectural Theory Review* 19, no. 1 (2014): 98–115.

76 Blundell Jones, Petrescu and Till, 'Introduction', xv.

77 Antoine Picon, for example, questions the political stakes in the recent return of ornament architecture; through animated façades: moulded, printed, and textured thanks to digital technologies (*Ornament: The Politics of Architecture and Subjectivity* [Chichester: Wiley, 2013]).

78 Macarthur and Stead, 'Introduction: Architecture and Aesthetics', 135.

79 Ibid., 135.

80 Claire Bishop, *Artificial Hells*, 1. Since the early 1990s, community-based art gradually became a genre in its own right (2).

81 Ibid., 2. Bishop is critiquing Nicolas Bourriaud, *Relational Aesthetics* (Paris: Les Presses du Réel, 1998).

82 The ethical turn was coined by Peter Dews, 'Uncategorical Imperatives: Adorno, Badiou and the Ethical turn', *Radical Philosophy* 111 (2002): 33; see Bishop, *Artificial Hells*, 25. It referred to the growing preoccupation, in 1990s art, with the other, difference, human rights, and emphasised the social over the artistic.

83 Bishop, *Artificial Hells*, 17–18.

84 Ibid., 19; 22–23.

85 Ibid., 28; even the anti-aesthetic is, for Rancière, still part of that regime (29).

86 Jacques Rancière states that 'the frame within which we sense something is given', in *Dissensus: On Politics and Aesthetics* (London and New York: Continuum, 2010); quoted in Bishop, *Artificial Hells*, 29.

87 Bishop, *Artificial Hells*, 27; in reference to Rancière, *Dissensus*.

88 Ibid., 18.

89 Ibid., 27.

90 Ibid., 30 onwards.

91 Ibid., 36.

92 This aesthetic dimension of politics is recognised when politics is theorised in terms of conflict and dissensus; as in Rancière, and also Chantal Mouffe, 'Artistic Activism and Agonistic Spaces', *Art and Research* 1, no. 2 (2007).

93 Bishop, *Artificial Hells*, 37.

94 Bishop calls this 'a trigger for (rather than the final word on) an event that would otherwise have no existence'. Ibid., 37.

95 Till, 'Architecture of the Impure Community', 72.

96 This bridging role of the architect was emphasised by Dag Boutsen (Interview with the Author, January 10, 2008). Boutsen is architect, project leader, and director at the Atelier d'Urbanisme d'Architecture et D'Informatique (AUAI; Lucien Kroll), where he has worked since 1987. Boutsen argued that, in participatory settings, the architect does not need to let go of control but rather needs 'total control'.

97 Ibid.

5

Learning from Things

> *Architecture is more than a set of objects with which we come into occasional contact. It constitutes the very processes, practice, and spaces that make up the physicality of life […] Architecture is then part of the conflicting and contradictory struggle of differing forces, interest groups and movements […] a turbulent dynamic.*[1]

This 'turbulent dynamic' of architecture, discussed in Iain Borden and David Dunster's book, *Architecture and the Sites of History*, is often evident in participatory settings where the tensions between multiple forces can be magnified. It is surprising, therefore, that the discussion of participatory architecture is often construed through oppositional pairs. Such readings tend to polarise discussions between use and design, democratic decision-making and aesthetics, or software and hardware.[2] This, however, can distract from the fact that such forces are often *simultaneously* at work. For example, when reducing participation to communication issues or power games, much of the action is left out. In order to access the 'turbulent dynamic' of participation, I propose to develop richer, more complex accounts through the study of 'participatory artefacts' such as neighbourhood plans, urban policies, or buildings. The ambition of this chapter is to think citizen participation through the numerous actors and networks that are mobilised by 'participatory artefacts'; and to explore how this allows for richer, more complex, and, therefore, more realistic accounts of participation. As a way to access this 'turbulence dynamic', I will propose methodologies from the fields of Science and Technology Studies (STS) and Actor-Network-Theory (ANT).[3] The merits of STS and ANT, and more specifically the study of artefacts, and 'things', will be considered, as will the challenges posed in translating their findings into architecture. In the second part of this chapter, I will focus upon a 'participatory artefact' that is particularly important in Brussels, the Neighbourhood Contract (NC). As a well-established urban planning tool, the NC is an important actor in Brussels.[4] These official contracts, between the Brussels Capital Region (hereafter called Region) and local municipalities, aim at revitalising deprived neighbourhoods through housing renovation, urban design, and socio-cultural initiatives. Because they are developed through an elaborate participatory process, NCs are instructive for studying participation.

But let us begin with an important source of misunderstanding and frustration in participation: the tension between 'hard' and 'soft' measures, here called the hardware and software of space. The hardware of space is typically associated with buildings and construction whilst software solutions typically relate to the human dimension and can include public space interventions and/ or that which does not involve construction but, nevertheless, contributes to spatial quality, that is street cleaning, crime prevention, or noise reduction.[5]

CITIZEN PARTICIPATION BETWEEN DESIGN AND USE

In June 2013, the Brussels newspaper *Brussel Deze Week* published a reader's letter titled: 'Invest in people, not in concrete'.[6] The letter brings to attention the needs identified by the citizens for their neighbourhood (safety, cleanliness, and green space) and the solution provided by the 'friendly boys and girls of the architectural office' (an office tower).[7] In doing so, the tension between the social and physical dimension of space, or between software and hardware, is demonstrated. The problems associated with this tension, particularly the prioritising of hardware over software, was the subject of a 2010 campaign by Engineers without Borders, which declared:

> *Sponsor an African ~~child~~ spreadsheet. It's not sexy. It works.*[8]

With this slogan, Engineers without Borders drew attention to the importance of software solutions in international aid (Figure 5.1). They criticised the fact that aid programmes (and donors) often favour hardware, which is tangible and real, whilst the importance of software, including maintenance, training, planning, and logistics, is often underestimated. One co-founder of Engineers without Borders claimed: 'when you think about people donating to charities it makes you feel a lot better to know that your money went to something tangible: like a well or a school or giving a family a goat. It's not sexy to tell your friends that you helped fund a water committee or pay for teachers' salaries.'[9]

In architecture, the tension between software and hardware is manifest in the presumed division of labour between the designer and the user of space. Whereas the designer is responsible for the structural, material, and technical aspects (hardware), the user engages with space through use and appropriation (software). This division has informed numerous attempts to redirect power to the user in the shaping of space. For example, in John Habraken's structure-and-infill model for housing, users are invited to impose their own orders within the 'structures' and 'grids' provided by the architects.[10] Within a fixed structural basis, users could personalise the design of a housing unit and adjust them according to their changing needs. On an urban scale, design experiments have been explicitly informed by the performance, freedom and creativity of the users of space; such was the case with Constant Nieuwenhuys's New Babylon, Yona Friedman's Superstructures, and Archigram's Plug-in City. Elsewhere, architects

5.1 Engineers Without Borders campaign poster.
Copyright: Engineers Without Borders, Canada division.
Used with permission.

have tried to include everyday use in their design by re-inserting, for example, the close-knit street life of cleared neighbourhoods into the mass housing schemes that replaced them.[11] However, the organisation of the use of space too often remained in the hands of designers, affirming the distinction between hardware and software.[12] This is also reflected in participatory settings where citizens are often excluded from technical discussions, whilst architects, by contrast, are challenged to translate user needs into form.

This distinction between hardware and software, expert and user, became further compromised under the post-Fordist, globalised economy of the practice turn. Just-in-time delivery and outsourced manufacturing left cities with vast areas of abandoned warehouse space and industrial wasteland. Subversive practices, such as urban exploration and guerrilla urbanism, saw political potential in the re-claiming of space through creative appropriation.[13] So too, however, did the neoliberal developers who mobilised spatial tactics and creative appropriation, such as those of 'urban pioneers' or 'creative classes', for boosting the development of commercially unattractive sites.[14] Matthias Heyden, an architect connected to the Institute for Strategies of Participative Architecture and Spatial Appropriation (ISPARA), asks: 'If architects increasingly collaborate with people from all kinds of (sub)cultural fields, shouldn't they also engage more intensively with politics and law, economics and ecology in order to have an impact on the city as a whole?'[15]

In the context of global urbanism, designers have also drawn inspiration from the informal urbanisation of cities in the global south, adopting processes of self-organisation, improvisation, informality, and order-through-chaos. Whilst useful for re-integrating software and hardware, these processes risk getting reduced to mere formal or morphological experimentations; or to what Ananya Roy calls the 'aestheticization of poverty'; the preference to upgrade the built environment, rather than intervene in social and political structures.[16] In such cases, designers fail to see that the software of space has less to do with creative use and reclaiming than with urban policy, such as property regulation, employment and the regulation of informal activities.

TOWARDS A COMPLEX ACCOUNT OF CITIZEN PARTICIPATION

How, then, can software and hardware be reconciled? In architecture, attempts can be found in those theories which emphasise the mutual dependency of design and use. Everyday Urbanism, for example, investigates how users transform and appropriate the spaces made available to them, and how, in turn, designers can learn from these transformative actions.[17] Likewise, recent theories around notions such as agency, contingency, uncertainty, co-production, and the 'dependent' status of architecture (as opposed to 'independent'), propose a reading of architecture that is based on how it is practiced rather than what it means.[18] The architectural theorist Hilde Heynen's suggestion to approach space as a 'stage' is an attempt to integrate physical and social aspects of space. It offers an alternative to both the over-emphasis of spatial measures (intended to orchestrate use; 'space as instrument'; and the undervaluing of space (whereby it is seen as a mere background for social actions; 'space as receptor').[19] These studies are an important step towards the theorisation of the *mutual* influence of design and use, but they, nevertheless, still consider space through oppositional 'pairs', such as design and use, social and physical space. One way to move towards a more complex reading is by studying architectural concerns, or issues, in terms of artefacts or 'things' that gather *numerous* networks of agencies (not just design and use).

The theorisation of things and artefacts is, in STS and ANT, part of a long-standing effort to develop more complex accounts of technological objects and the interaction between design and use, the social and the engineered. Instead of studying objects as either scientific–technological products or products of human, social, and cultural practices, STS and ANT study objects as simultaneously social and technological, factual and symbolic. To theorise the agency of artefacts across design and use, Madeleine Akrich, a sociologist with a particular interest in the users of technology, uses the notion of 'script'. Akrich defines the script as a 'scenario' or 'programme of action', something which involves an attempt to 'predetermine the settings that users are asked to imagine for a particular piece of technology and the pre-scriptions (notices, contracts, advice, etc) that accompany it'.[20] The designer negotiates with both a 'projected user' and a 'real user', and provides the manuals, contracts, and other support to help guide use.[21] This is further developed in Bruno Latour's analysis of the Berlin Key, an object designed in such a way that it restricts use. The Berlin Key is used for the front door separating the public street from the *hinterhof*, typical of the Berliner *mietskaserne* housing typology, whereby the entrances to apartment blocks are not located on the street but are to be found off a semi-public courtyard. At certain times of the day and night, one can only retrieve the key from the door once it is locked. At other times of the day, the key can only be retrieved when the door is left unlocked; for example to allow access for postmen or dustmen. The key operates in such manner thanks to its particular design and shape, but also through the attentiveness of the building concierge (who programmes the lock), and the compliant behaviour of the users. In other words, rather than depending on either design, ideology, programming, or use, the key's performance depends on all of these, something which Latour calls a 'chain of mediation'.[22] This 'chain of mediation' connects design and use and, therefore, is at the basis of each artefact. Because it produces 'a specific geography of responsibilities',[23] the questions asked are: Who gets to write, un-write, and re-write the scripts? Who can be held responsible: the designer, the users, the concierge, or, indeed, the key?

Translating such readings of the artefact into architecture does not come without challenges. Architectural artefacts include not just buildings, but also drawings, plans, models, or diagrams. These representational artefacts differ from technological artefacts in that they operate more intricately between the existing and the imaginary; and across technical, social, and artistic–aesthetic registers. They reflect an existing state of affairs whilst being projective, simultaneously depicting and predicting. Projective drawings can fix one interpretation over and above another. And depictions and predictions change with each new reading of the drawing or when the context of the drawing changes; for example, when the drawing's imaginary status becomes used as a blueprint. Drawings, like buildings, therefore 'stabilize *imperfectly*'.[24] In other words, as Hilde Heynen argues, there is an important productivity in architectural (representational) artefacts that is not always fully recognised in STS literature.[25] This productivity hints at the ethical and critical agency of artefacts, a tense meeting point for STS and architectural–critical theory. Whereas critical theorists are interested in the critical agency and meaning of architectural things, as inscribed by the designers, STS tends to discuss the agency of architecture largely in terms of a social technology.[26] However, with architecture being more than a 'piece of technology', scripts also contain the visions, meanings, and ideologies of the script-writer (the architect). Furthermore, a script's predetermination of use is always contingent: users may disobey the script.[27] This was demonstrated by Michel Foucault's discussion of architecture as *techne*, in 'Space, Knowledge, and Power'. Through the examples of Godin's Familistère and the work of Le Corbusier, Foucault shows that architecture cannot simply be declared as either oppressive or liberating, because oppression and liberation are only effective when exercised: 'liberty is a *practice*'.[28]

Notwithstanding such translational challenges, several studies of artefacts in STS and ANT remain relevant for developing complex accounts of participation. Particularly in ANT, convincing accounts of architecture have been offered through the writings of, amongst others, Albena Yaneva and Bruno Latour. Particularly relevant are the studies of objects not as autonomous, authorial, well-delineated entities, but as 'things' that exist through their attachment and entanglement with socio-technical networks. In addition to Latour's description of architectural projects as 'dishevelled, hairy, networky "things"', a whole range of new terms emerges depicting the re-conceptualisation of objects into 'things'.[29] These include 'object-in-flight', 'hybrid', 'quasi-object', 'actant', 'fluid object', 'matter of concern', or 'controversy'.[30] Despite their differences, these notions share the belief that 'things' act through their networks, and that these networks include human, as much as non-human, agencies. Objects are understood as assemblages, or as 'entanglements of interactions'.[31] Because networks and attachments change over time, objects can only have a 'momentary association'.[32] They cannot be fixed, and can be understood only through processes of reconfiguration and of de- and re-assembling.

Articulating the 'thingy' nature of objects is particularly relevant for participation, because it challenges the reduction of participation to the human dimension only, that is to communicative games of power. Instead, one is invited to treat participatory objects as 'things' around which numerous actors gather. Describing these networks of actors, allows for an expanded and complex understanding of participation.[33] For this purpose, two notions taken from ANT/STS are particularly relevant: the 'fluid object' as developed by Annemarie

Mol and Marianne de Laet, and Bruno Latour's object-oriented democracy, or *Dingpolitik*. Latour's *Dingpolitik* can be seen as an effort to redirect the discussion of democracy around the issues that are at stake rather than focusing on the processes of negotiation:

> *It's not unfair to say that political philosophy has often been the victim of a strong object-avoidance tendency. From Hobbes to Rawls, from Rousseau to Habermas, many procedures have been devised to assemble the relevant parties, to authorize them to contract, to check their degree of representativity, to discover the ideal speech conditions, to detect the legitimate closure, to write the good constitution. But when it comes down to what is at issue, namely the object of concern that brings them together, not a word is uttered.*[34]

With *Dingpolitik*, Latour asks the question: 'What would an object-oriented democracy look like?'[35] It starts from the observation that each object or issue, known as a *Ding*, 'gathers around itself a different assembly of relevant parties [...] [and] triggers new occasions to passionately differ and dispute'.[36] The space that is mapped out by such gatherings is the political, or *politik*.[37] In *Dingpolitik*, 'politics is no longer limited to humans and incorporates the many issues to which they are attached', whilst 'objects become things, that is, when matters of fact give way to their complicated entanglements and become matters of concern'.[38]

To describe the entanglement of things, Mol and de Laet introduce the term 'fluid object'. In their analysis of the Zimbabwe 'B' type Bush Pump, a type of pump designed for the provision of clean water in local villages in Zimbabwe, instead of defining what the pump *is*, de Laet and Mol, study how the pump *acts*, and how it is entangled in a variety of worlds.[39] Fluidity depicts the adaptability, flexibility, and responsiveness that a thing needs in order to act in changing circumstances: design, conception, implementation, performance, and maintenance.[40] Fluidity allows for a thing to engage with changing networks, actors and relationships. The delivery of clean water depends on a series of actions, including finding the right spot for finding water, drilling the hole, assembling the pump, installing the headworks correctly as to avoid wastewater flowing in, and ensuring its maintenance and survival in unpredctable circumstances (for example breakdown; changed institutional setting).[41] Many of these actions are collective actions whereby the community plays a key role. For example, the decision where to drill the hole is supported by GIS systems and engineers as much as by the advice of the village's spiritual leader.[42] Also, an improper installation of the pump can result in wastewater flowing into the system. Because the community makes a difference in the implementation, functioning and maintenance of the pump, the villagers are not portrayed as mere users of the pump; they are, instead, included within the pump's boundaries. The designer of the pump, by contrast, made a difference by *not* being central to the pump. By not claiming authorship the designer placed the pump in the public domain, keeping the technology affordable.[43]

What can be learned for 'participatory artefacts'? *Dingpolitik* shows the importance of analysing democracy and participation in terms of the networks of human and non-human actors that gather around 'things'. Fluidity in turn demonstrates that the democratic gathering around 'things' is determined by the fluidity of its boundaries. Because making-a-difference does not necessarily imply being central to a thing's actions (such as the Zimbabwe 'B' type Bush Pump designer not claiming authorship) fluidity accounts for those actors and networks that 'matter' in the actions of 'participatory artefacts'.

THE BRUSSELS NEIGHBOURHOOD CONTRACT

The 'participatory artefact' I chose to follow is the Brussels Neighbourhood Contract. It is an instrument for urban renewal created in 1993.[44] Through NCs, the Brussels Capital Region aims to revitalise its most deprived neighbourhoods. They are designed and allocated by the Region, but locally applied at municipal level. In what follows, I refer to the organisation of NCs at the time of analysis; the structure and organisation of NC's has meanwhile undergone significant changes. Each year the Region allocates a number of NCs and makes a 'contract' with the municipalities on whose territory these are located. A budget of roughly 10,000,000 euros was provided by regional, federal, municipal, and European resources, and was to be spent over a period of four years. The participatory moment of NCs, at the time of analysis, took place primarily in the first year, which was dedicated to the planning and programming of interventions. This programming cohered with the wider ambitions of the Brussels Capital Region, as formulated in its City Project – part of Brussels' Regional Development Plan, approved in 1995 and revised in 2001. NCs formed, together with Municipal Development Plans, local implementations of the City Project.[45] Compared to the statutory planning of the Regional Area Destination Plan, the Regional Development Plan was more visionary and aimed at an holistic, integrated approach to Brussels' problems.[46] These problems related to a shortage of social housing, the poor status of the housing stock in impoverished quarters, and the continuing urban exodus of higher income groups, with Brussels' central areas, and post-industrial neighbourhoods along the canal, particularly affected. The City Project combined the renovation of residential quarters, in order to re-attract tax payers, with socio-spatial policies directed at the most vulnerable citizens. For this purpose, the Region delineated a territory dedicated to Housing and Renovation; from which NCs were drawn.[47] This combination of spatial and socio-economic measures used to be reflected in the thematic organisation of NCs. Of the five thematic groups (in French: *volets*), three focused upon housing: social, public, and private-public (*volets* 1–2–3). In addition, one group was dedicated to public space projects (*volet* 4), and another to socio-economic and socio-cultural initiatives (*volet* 5).[48]

In terms of participation, NCs signalled an important change. Citizen consultation had been part of official planning since the *Plan Secteur* of 1979;

a significant achievement of the 1970s activism of the ARAU (see Chapter 2). However, whereas the *Plan Secteur* allowed citizens to react against planning proposals, NCs involved citizens in the *creation* of the city, setting a new precedent for Brussels' participatory planning.[49]

The participatory procedures of NCs were part of a contractual agreement between Region and municipality, and were organised through a Local Commission for Integrated Development (LCID) and a General Assembly (GA); each created at the start of a new NC.[50] The LCID offered a platform for discussing the renewal programme amongst regional and municipal public stakeholders, planners, citizens and civil society partners. It then reported back to the General Assembly (GA), where proposals were discussed with a larger group of citizens and organisations. The LCID and GA were most active during the first year, when projects for the neighbourhood were being identified. These projects were collected in a *dossier de base* (action plan) which was then finalised by a private planning consultant, or *bureau d'étude*, who, in turn, was actively involved in leading the discussions in the LCIDs and GAs. Through the action plan, therefore, participation became part of the legal contract between the Region and municipality.[51] Once finalised, the action plan needed to be approved by the Region. Once the implementation phase started, LCID and GA meetings were held less frequently.

Despite this elaborate participatory framework, participation in NCs was not always perceived as a success. From observations of different LCID and GA meetings at the start-up of new NCs, and from interviews with planners, administrators, and other actors involved in NCs, it became apparent that debates tended to pit the planners and politicians against inhabitants leading to frustration and irritation on both sides.[52] Citizens became frustrated during meetings when, for example, they felt their suggestions were not being taken into consideration. Planners and authorities, by contrast, could become irritable and come across as aloof. It is tempting, therefore, to evaluate participation in terms of communication issues and power games. However, from the interviews I conducted with planners, officials, and socio-cultural organisations involved in NCs, it became clear that frustrations often originated outside the boundaries of the LCID and GA meetings, and that many other actors were at work in participation than the ones visible during the meetings. Planners, for example, expressed frustration with having to operate in challenging administrative and political circumstances and justify why certain suggestions by inhabitants were not possible. Similarly, public administrators expressed frustration with the limitations of NCs to respond to the genuine needs of a neighbourhood.

So, apart from planners, citizens, and public administrators, which other forces *act* in the NCs? To identify these 'other' actors, I approach the NC as a 'thing', a 'participatory artefact' that exists in its entanglements. By unpacking these different networks a more realistic account of participation than the ones offered by the analysis of communicative issues and conflicts alone may be achieved.

NEIGHBOURHOOD CONTRACTS IN ACTION: BRING ON THE ACTORS!

From interviews with planners and civil servants involved in NCs, it became apparent that more actors 'acted' in NCs than was obvious from participatory meetings. Several issues appeared with such regularity that it was clear that these were having a major impact on those meetings. Not immediately visible, these elements nevertheless 'acted' in NCs, and became actors.

When NCs were implemented in a municipality, the generic, contractual framework drawn up by the Region (the *Cahier des Charges* or Book of Specifications) entered the specific setting of a neighbourhood. The Book of Specifications is a set of instructions that determines who can participate in the discussion of NCs, what can be discussed, and when. As soon as NCs 'land' in a specific neighbourhood, the generic script of the Book of Specifications is played-out in specific circumstances. At this moment, previously dormant or mundane actors can become protagonists, but this does not mean that they also become visible in the participatory meetings. Is it possible that these actors, and the fact that they are not openly recognised as such, feed into the performance and frustrations of participation in NCs?

One such actor was *time*; or, more specifically, a lack thereof. With few exceptions, planners and officials identified time as one of the protagonists in the participatory success, or failure, of NCs. Just ten months were dedicated to the discussion and finalisation of a programme of actions for a neighbourhood, but, in reality, this period could even be shorter due to delays such as appointing and approving a *bureau d'étude*.[53] Despite such delays, the planner of the *bureau d'étude* was still obliged to deliver a plan of action, informed by the discussions and suggestions formulated during the different LCIDs and AGs, on time.[54] Planners often voiced regret that such time restrictions did not allow for thorough participatory debates, or for exploring interesting ideas that emerged from participatory meetings. Planners, therefore, were forced to opt for stereotypic themes and solutions instead of experimenting with specific solutions for specific neighbourhoods. With their demanding programme, multi-layered decision-making, and administrative complexity (for example procedures for expropriation), the planning of NCs proved time-consuming. The time made available for this planning was generally believed to be too short, and no matter how well-spirited and participation-minded planners were, they felt obliged to measure time-efficiency against participatory ideals. Some planners recognised a practical challenge of doing just enough without, however, doing too much. Some would even go as far as to claim that a NC commission was time-consuming and not financially profitable.

Apart from time, there were other actors which emerged when a NC was activated within a municipality. The Book of Specifications prescribed a certain number of actors or stakeholders who were allowed to participate in the discussion of NCs. Whilst categorised as 'inhabitant', 'local organisation', 'municipal administrator', 'local businesses', and 'planner', once these categories entered practice, the categories became specific individuals. These individuals would bring character, ideologies, and political colours which contributed to the mood and atmosphere within NC meetings. Some political actors and civil servants, for example, would be greater enthusiasts of participation than others, and that enthusiasm may have changed along with shifts in government throughout the course of a NC. Also, the NC's Book of Specifications prescribed a minimum number of participants to be included in each stakeholder category, that is 'inhabitant'. More often, however, a maximum number was applied for practical reasons; namely, because large groups of participants were seen as more difficult to manage. Limiting the number of participants proved to complicate the selection procedure, and could heighten tensions. For example, one NC that I observed, was located in an area with a well-established socio-cultural network. Hence, a higher than normal number of socio-cultural organisations was active in the area. Of the nine organisations that applied, only a few could be included in the NC negotiations. The final selection of participants was informed by the location of these organisations, in order to allow for a more or less even geographical distribution. It was not informed by the thematic or demographic diversity of these organisations.[55]

And so, we can see that the geographical perimeter also becomes a decisive actor in the discussion of NCs. The perimeter, drawn by the Region before the start of a NC, proved to be a powerful actor in determining who was, and, perhaps more importantly, who was not included in the negotiation of a given NC. The perimeter could not be adjusted, even if this seemed justified during the course of the NC negotiations. For example, it was unlikely that organisations that had a strong activity base within a neighbourhood, but were located outside the perimeter, would be included in the negotiations. Despite its power, the perimeter could also prove weak when confronted with a NC's taxon;[56] so weak that certain actors *within* the perimeter could still be excluded from negotiations. For example, in one NC, a controversy occurred around the refusal to include a large federal reception centre for asylum seekers in the LCID. Despite being located within the NC's perimeter, the reception centre was excluded. During the participatory meetings, it was argued that the reception centre was an important actor in the neighbourhood; it housed several hundreds of asylum seekers who, after all, lived in the neighbourhood, and used its infrastructure and public spaces. However, the controversy was less ideological and ethical–political than assumed: the reception centre could not be included for legal reasons. Neither an inhabitant nor an association, and a *federal* public stakeholder instead of a regional or municipal one, it simply did not fit the categories of the Book of Specifications. This demonstrates how the democratic frustrations that often mark participation do not necessarily originate in power games or ideological disputes. They are, as likely, to originate in a stubborn taxon or script.

Not only do inhabitants feel frustrated with powerful actors such as perimeters or scripts, planners do too. During one participatory meeting, when local associations and inhabitants complained that their proposals had not been included in the programme, the planner of the *bureau d'étude*, rather empathetically, responded: 'You have to understand that the Neighbourhood

Contract is based on an ordinance that is very, very strict. We are aware ... we know that there are many things that could contribute to the well-being of a neighbourhood, but these initiatives *cannot* be integrated within the frame of a Neighbourhood Contract.'[57]

A different type of actor in NCs was *experience*. Earlier experiences can 'act' in NCs in a beneficial way. For example, municipalities who are regularly allocated NCs (such as the City of Brussels and Schaerbeek) have created specialised administrative departments dedicated to the coordination of NCs and other urban renewal initiatives.[58] Under the impetus of such coordinative bodies, NCs can accumulate experience which often leads to a knowledge transfer from one NC to the next. This accumulation of knowledge can, in turn, mobilise new actors. For example, to optimise the communications in and around NCs, an information point was created, and project leaders or participation 'animators' appointed. Such information points could be a Neighbourhood House (*Maison de Quartier*) where general information about the NC can be found, or it could be something tailored to meet the specific needs of a neighbourhood: in the City of Brussels, an information point was created specifically for guiding citizens through the complex administrative procedures for obtaining renovation grants. Perhaps surprisingly, experience can, as an actor, also disrupt. One of the planners I interviewed explained how, when starting a new NC, they received 'for free' the conflict-ridden experience of the previous NC; setting a negative mood from the very outset.

Another important actor was the so-called *promenade diagnostique*, a walk in the neighbourhood in which the different participants of a NC took part. It gave the planner an opportunity to clearly communicate their intentions whilst being 'on site'. Planners who organised such walks claimed that it may not have been an appropriate tool for performing a diagnosis of a neighbourhood (making the term a little misleading), but it did afford an opportunity for communication with all the participants. This was considered important for setting the mood and for inviting people to point to problems that they would not necessarily mention in the indoor participatory meetings.

For optimising the visibility of the activities of the NCs within the wider neighbourhood, a newsletter could also be created, and/or, in some instances, a logo was developed. These additional actors, when performing successfully, may also be written into the NC regulations, and thus become, for better or worse, part of the *all* NCs.[59]

A final actor that has proved important in NCs, but was absent during the participatory meetings, was *finance* via the renovation grant.[60] Throughout the duration of a NC, residents could apply for individual grants for renovating the façades of their properties. Aimed at supporting citizens' private investments into their neighbourhoods, these well-intentioned grants, however, did not always perform well in practice. In poor neighbourhoods, such grants could act counterproductively: covering only a percentage of the overall cost, not only did they require that residents make up the difference, renovation grants also prescribed that the works start immediately upon allocation of the funding, even if the actual payment had not come through yet. This forced the applicant to pre-finance the construction works which was a problem for economically vulnerable citizens. Further, in order to be eligible for a renovation grant, all construction work had to be done through official channels, and should have been properly invoiced and taxable. This could, once again, be a challenge for vulnerable communities who were otherwise also reliant on informal support networks. In other words, the socio-economic measures that accompanied NCs were at odds with the reality of the neighbourhoods they aimed to revitalise.

Those actors discussed so far emerged from within NCs, and were dormant and inactive until the NC found implementation in the specific circumstances of a neighbourhood. In addition to these actors, there seemed to be other forces 'at work' in NCs, which were coming from further afield and were seemingly unrelated to NCs. These actors may have been puzzling or mysterious, but they nevertheless played a part in the performance of NCs and deserve our attention.

One such actor is Brussels' urban history. Participation in NCs is somewhat overshadowed by Brussels' legacy of urban traumas which instigated the participatory turn of the 1970s. As some planners have pointed out during interviews, Brussels' history can bias contemporary planning practice, because, for example, bad references tend to survive better than good ones.

Language can itself prove to be an actor in NCs. In the official French-Dutch bilingual setting of Brussels, it is a versatile and agile actor, but also a source of irritation. In the participatory meetings of NCs, for example, despite Brussels' unwritten rule that, during meetings, everybody speaks their own language, French was still predominant; and French and Dutch versions of documents were not always identical, or were poorly translated. I remember, for example, an instance of where the French word *suggestions* (suggestions) was translated into the Dutch word *voorstellingen* (imaginations, representations) instead of *voorstellen* (suggestions or proposals).[61] In this bilingual setting, abbreviations could also have unexpected agency. For example, The Local Commission for Integrated Development (LCID) is called *ca-el-da-ee* in French (CLDI), and *pa-ca-ga-oo* in Dutch (PCGO). Likewise, the Brussels International Development Plan is the *pa-da-ee* (PDI) in French, and the *pee-oo* (PIO) in Dutch. When meetings are interlaced with such abbreviations, confusion may arise.

Another actor seemingly unrelated to NCs was the *setting* for participation. Some set-ups reinforced the speaker–audience relationship, such as when officials and experts used microphones and projection screens with inhabitants and local organisations positioned as an 'informed' audience, whilst other set-ups avoided polarisation by organising negotiations as round-table discussions.[62] PowerPoint presentations become uncooperative actors when their graphic quality is poor or when images are poorly scanned. When curtains that fail to darken the room sufficiently are added to these temperamental projectors it becomes clear that participatory scenes are crowded with action.

Yet, whilst time, perimeter, taxon, experience, and finance were barely visible in the participatory meetings of NCs, compared with projectors, curtains, and language, their vitality may be underestimated. Giving due voice to these actors helps to understand how the democratic deficits experienced in those meetings do not necessarily originate in power games, but in all sorts of forces activated outside the participatory setting. Nonetheless, time, perimeter, taxon, finance, history, and language are all part of the *Dingpolitik* of 'participatory artefacts'. They each play a part in the democratic performance of NCs; a performance that is informed not only by ethical reasoning but also practical reasoning. What is and what is not taken into account in NCs depends on whether it matters to a specific neighbourhood (ethical reasoning), and also on whether it fits the taxon and it is feasible to address within a limited time frame (practical reasoning). Therefore, when the urban planner appeared to trivialise or ignore issues that had been raised by the citizens, or came up with hasty solutions, this was not necessarily to be interpreted as a dismissive act. The planner's decision-making was often co-performed by time, financial, and regulatory constraints, allowing very little 'room to manoeuvre'.[63] Likewise, when authorities offered seemingly lame excuses such as 'but the Ordinance simply does not allow us to …' during participatory meetings, they were in fact referring to genuine legal constraints.

THE TANGLE OF PARTICIPATION

So how can we gain access to the 'turbulent dynamic' of participation? This was the starting point of this chapter. I argued that dichotomist approaches thriving on oppositional pairs, and approaches that reduce participation to communicative power games fall equally short. Instead, I proposed that we develop entangled accounts of participation through a focus on 'participatory artefacts'. Approaching Neighbourhood Contracts as 'participatory artefacts' demonstrated that the many actors mobilised in participation can be human or non-human; wanted and unwanted; cooperative and obstructive; in proximity yet remote; and visible or invisible. Participatory artefacts are, therefore, 'entanglements of interactions' that can only be understood by including *more* rather than *less* actors.[64] Studied in terms of 'fluid objects'; the boundaries of NCs were stretched to include as much of the 'turbulent dynamic' of participation as possible. This allowed for analysing, as open-mindedly as possible, the networks and actors that are mobilised by NCs which, in turn, gives access to the *Dingpolitik* of an artefact. Compared to the analysis of communication and power games, *Dingpolitik* tells us so much more about the democratic tensions inherent with participation.

Firstly, the analysis of NCs showed that participation can only be understood through the 'chains of mediations' that connect the model of participation (its more or less generic script) with the practices that take place in specific situations. I have shown that by studying *only* the script of participation, or *only* the participatory meetings, would be to miss out on much of the action. When participatory models enter practice, several dormant actors, such as time, perimeter, and experience become protagonists with a capacity to stabilise, reinforce, or disrupt. The Brussels NCs demonstrate, in addition, the surprises that accompany participatory practices. Actors that do not have an allocated role in participation, such as history, language, or abbreviations, nevertheless enter the participatory scene. In the specific setting of Brussels, these actors matter. They participate because they have the capacity to obey, disrupt, reassemble, or reconfigure relationships. Giving voice to these other actors allows them to enter the discussions on participation. This is essential for understanding the workings of participation, its frustrations, and tensions.

The task, therefore, is twofold. In order to include the actors that matter in participation, as opposed to the ones that fit the taxon, the boundaries of participatory artefacts should be kept as fluid as possible. The researcher has to become attentive to the voices of participatory practices, and accept that actors come in various shapes, colours, and sizes, which requires a degree of 'methodological naiveté'; a level of curiosity that will allow the researcher to be lured into unfamiliar territory.[65]

Secondly, the study of NCs showed that participatory practices can operate on moral, as much as practical, grounds, neither of which can be evaluated in isolation. What appears as democratic deficit or political stubbornness may well originate in practical necessities or limitations. Participatory artefacts combine practical reasoning with the imagination of alternative futures, which resonates with Foucault's definition of *techne* as 'a practical rationality governed by a conscious goal'.[66] Consequently, the democratic dimension of participation depends on how participation is practised in specific circumstances, not on how great the model is. Instead of optimising and perfecting participatory models, is it not more instructive to account for the contradictions, controversies, and struggles that these models encounter in practice?

To better understand the irritations, misunderstandings, and conflicts prevalent in participatory processes, I have allowed myself some methodological naiveté'.[67] By becoming sensitive to mundane actors such as regulations, taxon, and perimeters, I have gained insights into the hopes, as much as the realities, of participation, its models and ideals, and its messy and uncertain practices.[68] This 'methodological naiveté' has consequences for architectural theory in that it enables us to access accounts of how participation, or architecture more generally, is intended to work, and how it actually works. In doing so, the mundane actors exposed through this methodological curiosity become relevant to architectural theory and, therefore, worthy of greater attention.[69] In the next, and final, chapter of the book, I will push this curiosity for the mundane even further, and put the elasticity of architectural theory to the test.

NOTES

1   Iain Borden and David Dunster, 'Architecture and the sites of history', in *Architecture and the Sites of History: Interpretations of Buildings and Cities*, ed. Iain Borden and David Dunster (Oxford: Butterworth Architecture, 1995), 1–22, 4.

2   Some of these tensions were unpacked in Chapter 4.

3   For a wider discussion of STS and ANT and their relevance for architecture, see Chapter 1.

4   The importance of neighbourhood contracts as actors is demonstrated by publications dedicated to them. For example: Annabelle Guérin, Luc Maufroy, and Frédéric Raynaud, *Brussel verandert…! 10 jaar stedelijk beleid in het Brussels Hoofdstedelijk Gewest 1995–2005*, Gewestelijk Secretariaat voor Stedelijke Ontwikkeling – Luc Maufroy, 2007; Label NV and Fabrice Cumps, eds, *Leven in het hart van de wijken: tien jaar wijkherwaardering in het Brussels Hoofdstedelijk Gewest 1993–2003*, Brussels Hoofdstedelijk Gewest, 2004; Mathieu Berger and Pauline Beugnies, *Brussel Getoetst op Inspraak: De wijkcontracten als oefeningen*, Brussels Hoofdstedelijk Gewest, 2008; and Maurizio Cohen, *Brussels on our Doorstep: Architecture in Neighbourhood Contracts* (Brussels: Brussels Capital Region, 2007).

5   Kush Patel, Karen Franck, and Peter Aeschbacher (*EDRA 43 Seattle: Emergent Placemaking: Proceedings of the 43rd Annual Conference of the Environmental Design Research Association*, 2012) distinguish material space (hard) from the social coding of space (soft). In *Flexible Housing* (Oxford: Architectural Press, 2007) Tatjana Schneider and Jeremy Till define soft elements as those that allow adaptation through use and hard ones as those that 'more specifically determine the way that the design may be used' (7).

6   Jo Breda, 'Buurtbewoner Fontainaspark: "Investeer in mensen, niet in beton"', *Brussel Nieuws*, June 28, 2013, accessed February 10, 2014, http://www.brusselnieuws.be/nl/nieuws/buurtbewoner-fontainaspark-investeer-mensen-niet-beton.

7   Ibid., translated from Dutch.

8   Engineers without Borders (Canada), last accessed April 1, 2014, http://legacy.ewb.ca/en/whatsnew/success/3.html.

9   Cited in Tim Lewis, *Land of Second Chances: The Impossible Rise of Rwanda's Cycling Team* (Boulder, CO: Yellow Jersey Press, 2013), 234.

10 John Habraken, *Supports: An Alternative to Mass Housing* (London: Architectural Press, 1972); originally published in Dutch in 1961 as *De Dragers en de Mensen: Het einde van de massawoningbouw* (Amsterdam: Scheltema & Holkema, 1961).

11 Demonstrated notably by the post-war housing schemes; and perhaps most famously through the street-in-the-sky concept developed in the work of Alison and Peter Smithson; and which found realisation, for example, at Park Hill (1957–1961) in Sheffield, designed by the architects Jack Lynn and Ivor Smith.

12 There are many notable exceptions, including Cedric Price's integration of technology, use, profession, regulations in design. In addition, there is the self-build tradition in architecture whereby users take part in design and construction.

13 These practices adopted a specific terminology around appropriation, re-claiming, space explorations, guerrilla, and tactics; and express an interest in alternative ways of reading, experiencing, and designing space (often inspired by Situationist readings of space).

14 Klaus Overmeyer and Senatsverwaltung für Stadtentwicklung Berlin, eds, *Urban Pioneers: Temporary Use and Urban Development in Berlin* (Berlin: Jovis, 2007); Richard Florida, *The Rise of the Creative Class: And How it's Transforming Work, Leisure, Community and Everyday Life* (New York: Basic Books, 2002).

15 Mathias Heyden, 'Evolving Participatory Design: A Report from Berlin, Reaching Beyond', *Field Journal* 2, no. 1 (October 2008): 31–46, 34.

16 Ananya Roy, 'Transnational trespassings. The geopolitics of urban informality', in *Urban Informality: Transnational Perspectives from the Middle East, South Asia and Latin America*, ed. Ananya Roy and N. AlSayyad (Lanham, MD: Lexington Books, 2004), 289–317, quoted in Ananya Roy, 'Urban Informality, Toward an Epistemology of Planning', *Journal of the American Planning Association* 71, no. 2 (2005): 147–158, 154.

17 Margaret Crawford, John Chase and John Kaliski, *Everyday Urbanism*, second and expanded edition (New York: The Monacelli Press, 2008).

18 See, for example, the practices collected in Nishat Awan, Tatjana Schneider, and Jeremy Till, *Spatial Agency: Other Ways of Doing Architecture* (Abingdon: Routledge, 2011); Isabelle Doucet and Kenny Cupers, eds, 'Agency in Architecture: Rethinking Criticality in Theory and Practice', Special Issue, *Footprint Journal* 4 (2009); 'Agency: Alternative Practices and Alternative Worlds', Special Issue, *Architectural Research Quarterly* 13, no. 2 (2009); and Jeremy Till, *Architecture Depends* (Cambridge, MA: The MIT Press, 2009).

19 Hilde Heynen, 'Space as Receptor, Instrument or Stage: Notes on the Interactions between Spatial and Social Constellations', *International Planning Studies* 18, nos. 3–4 (2013): 342–357. This notion of space as a stage resonates with recent historiographies that study architecture through use and the user, for example: Kenny Cupers, ed., *Use Matters: An Alternative History of Architecture* (Abingdon: Routledge, 2013); Schneider and Till, *Flexible Housing*; Jonathan Hill, ed., *Occupying Architecture: Between the Architect and the User* (London: Routledge, 1998).

20 Madeleine Akrich, 'The De-scription of Technical Objects', in *Shaping Technology / Building Society*, ed. Weibe Bijker and John Law (Cambridge, MA: The MIT Press, 1992), 203–214, 208.

21 Ibid., 209.

22 Bruno Latour, 'The Berlin Key or How to do Words with Things', in *Matter, Materiality and Modern Culture*, ed. P.M. Graves Brown (London: Routledge, 1991), 10–21, 21. See also Bruno Latour, 'Where are the Missing Masses? The Sociology of a Few Mundane Artefacts', in *Shaping Technology / Building Society*, ed. Weibe Bijker and John Law (Cambridge, MA: The MIT Press, 1992), 225–258.

23 Akrich, 'The De-scription of Technical Objects', 207.

24 Thomas F. Gieryn, 'What Buildings Do', *Theory and Society* 31, no. 1 (2002): 35–74, 35; original italics.

25 Heynen also sees parallels between her notion of 'architecture as stage' and Latour and Yaneva's study of buildings as 'moving projects' which equally considers the social and the spatial as 'mutually entangled'. See Heynen, 'Space as Receptor, Instrument, or Stage', 353; in reference to Bruno Latour and Albena Yaneva, 'Give me a Gun and I Will Make All Buildings Move: An ANT's View of Architecture', in *Explorations in Architecture: Teaching, Design, Research*, ed. Reto Geiser (Basel, Boston, Berlin: Birkhauser, 2009), 80–89.

26 Cupers, 'Introduction', 4. Exceptions include Cristiano Storni, 'Unpacking Design Practices: The Notion of Thing in the Making of Artifacts', *Science Technology & Human Values* 36, no. 1 (2012 [2010]): 88–123; the Politics of Design conference, The University of Manchester, June 2010; and the call for papers for a special issue of *Co-Design*, on Designing Things Together: Intersections of Co-Design and Actor-Network Theory (forthcoming 2015).

27 See also Michael Guggenheim, '(Un-)Building social systems. The concrete foundation of society', in *Communicaciones, semanticas y redes: Usos y desvaciones de la sociologia*

de niklas Luhmann, ed. Ignacio Farias and Jose Ossandos (Mexico City: Universidad Iberoamericana, 2011), 245–277.

28 Michel Foucault, 'Space, Knowledge, and Power', in *The Foucault Reader*, ed. Paul Rabinow (London: Penguin Books, 1991 [1984]), 239–256, 245.

29 Not as 'bald objects'. Latour asks for architecture: do we show the finished object disconnected from the numerous assemblages that have made it (these are bald, black-boxed objects, as found in modernist architecture) or do we show a building's networks of fabrication (these are hairy buildings, entangled knots that can only be understood through their networks). Bruno Latour, 'Is There a Non-Modern Style?', *Domus*, no. 866 (January 2004).

30 For 'object-in-flight' see Latour and Yaneva, 'Give me a Gun and I Will Make All Buildings Move'. For 'quasi-object', see Michel Serres, 'Theory of the Quasi-object', in *The Parasite* (Baltimore, MD: The Johns Hopkins University Press, 1982); and Bruno Latour, *We Have Never Been Modern* (Cambridge, MA: Harvard University Press, 1993). For 'fluid object' see John Law and Annemarie Mol, 'Boundary Variations', *Environment and Planning D: Society and Space 23* (2005): 637–642; Annemarie Mol and Marianne De Laet, 'The Zimbabwe Bush Pump: Mechanics of a Fluid Technology', *Social Studies of Science* 30, no. 2 (2000): 225–263. For 'controversy', see Albena Yaneva, *Mapping Controversies in Architecture* (Farnham: Ashgate, 2012). For 'matter of concern' see Bruno Latour, 'From Realpolitik to Dingpolitik or how to Make Things Public', in *Making Things Public: Atmospheres of Democracy*, ed. Bruno Latour and Peter Weibel (Cambridge, MA: ZKM and The MIT Press, 2005), 4–31; and Bruno Latour, 'Why has Critique Run out of Steam: From Matters of Fact to Matters of Concern', *Critical Inquiry* 30, no. 2 (2004): 225–248.

31 Bruno Latour, *Re-assembling the Social: An Introduction to Actor-Network-Theory* (Oxford: Oxford University Press, 2005): 64–65.

32 Ibid.

33 For examples of STS discussions on architecture and the user, see post-occupancy studies and user-based design, Stewart Brand, *How Buildings Learn: What Happens After They're Built* (New York: Viking 1994); Gieryn, 'What buildings do'; and Michael Guggenheim, 'From Prototyping to Allotyping. The Invention of Change of Use and the Crisis of Building Types', *Journal of Cultural Economy* 7, no. 4 (2014): 14.

34 Latour, 'From Realpolitik to Dingpolitik', 5–6.

35 Ibid., 4.

36 Ibid., 5. Latour refers to the original English meaning of 'Thing' or the German 'Ding'; which designates a certain type of archaic assembly (12).

37 Ibid.

38 Ibid., 31.

39 de Laet and Mol, 'The Zimbabwe Bush Pump'. The term 'fluid' was introduced by John Law and Annemarie Mol, 'Regions, Networks and Fluids: Anaemia and Social Topology', *Social Studies of Science* 24 (1994): 641–671. See also Isabelle Doucet '[Centrality] and/or Cent][rality: a matter of placing the boundaries', in *Urban Landscape Perspectives*, ed. G. Maciocco (Berlin and Heidelberg: Springer, 2008), 93–121.

40 de Laet and Mol, 'The Zimbabwe Bush Pump', 226.

41 Ibid., 246. The Zimbabwe Bush Pump is so designed that one can take it to pieces and repair it locally, without involving specialised teams.

42 Ibid., 231–233; 250–251.

43 Ibid., 249–250. Engineers become facilitators or 'peripheral agents' (251).

44 In French, called *Contrat de Quartier;* in Dutch *Wijkcontract*. Ordinance of October 7, 1993 *Houdende de organisatie van de herwaardering van de wijken* (Brussels).

45 Municipal Development Plan: in Dutch, called *Gemeentelijk Ontwikkelings Plan;* in French *Plan Communal de Développement*.

46 Regional Development Plan (*Gewestelijk Ontwikkelingsplan* GewOP I – *Plan Régional de Développement* PRD I); Ordinance of March 3, 1995; and GewOP/PRD II approved in 2001. The NC originates in the participatory planning and urban renewal of the late 1970s (for example Residential Core Renewal Programme of the *Brusselse Executieve*, 1978); and the 1980's narrowing down of urban renewal efforts to deprived areas. See also the Ordinance of August 29, 1991 entitled *houdende de organisatie van de planning en de stedebouw*. For more information, please see Françoise Noël, 'Het stadsvernieuwingsbeleid in de wijken: op de kruising van stedenbouwkundige en sociale actie', in *Brussel over 20 Jaar*, ed. Pierre Dejemeppe et al. (Brussels: ATO, 2009), 213–233; and Stefan De Corte, Wijkontwikkeling met wijkcontracten? Stadsvernieuwing in Brussel', in *In de ban van stad en wijk*, ed. Pascal De Decker, B. Hubeau, S. Nieuwinckel (Antwerpen: EPO, 1996), 209–217.

47 The Ruimte voor Versterkte Ontwikkeling van de Huisvesting en Renovatie RVOHR – Espace de Développement Renforcé du Logement et de la Rénovation EDRLR. More details see Guérin, Maufroy, and Raynaud, *Brussel verandert…*, 13.

48 The NCs anno 2015 have only three *volets* (instead of five, as was the case at the time of analysis).

49 The 2002 Director Schemes (*Schéma Directeur / Richtschema*) were introduced for the development of Leverage Areas (*Hefboomgebied / Zone Levier*) and Sites of Regional Interest (*Zone van Gewestelijk belang / Zone d'Intérêt Regional*). They include an official participatory component.

50 Called, in French, *Commission Locale de Développement Intégré* CLDI and *Assemblée Générale* AG; and in Dutch, *Plaatselijke Commissie voor Geintegreerde Ontwikkeling* PCGO and *Algemene Vergadering* AV.

51 A planner of a *bureau d'étude* who has been involved in numerous NCs claimed that the *dossier de base* served originally as a form of 'juridical security' to the Region; but has gradually developed into a genuine tool for negotiation (Interview with the author, December 12, 2007).

52 The analysis in this chapter is based on the attendance of several meetings during the start-up phase of NCs in two different municipalities (made possible thanks to the kind permission of the respective planning and urbanism departments), and on interviews conducted during the period 2006–2008. The observation of NCs in this period offers an instructive snapshot of participatory practice, even if the more recent updates and changes in regulation have not been taken into account in this chapter. I interviewed thirteen planners and officials, and three socio-cultural organisations involved in NCs. Several planners have been active in Brussels since the 1970s; and share their experience in urban renewal and participatory planning with their younger colleagues. Some planners collaborate with sociologists and anthropologists for participatory purposes. I also interviewed, in addition, ten architects and planners, in Brussels and abroad who were not involved in NCs but had specific experience in participation. The interviewees for this portion of the research have been kept anonymous.

53 In the set-up of NCs anno 2015, the four years are complemented with an additional year before the start of the NC, to develop the programme, and two years after the NC, for completing the works.

54 The *bureau d'étude* is appointed by the Region at the start of a NC; but this appointment is based on a shortlist provided by the municipality. This process of shortlisting and approval, by two different administrative bodies, often delays the appointment of the planner.

55 Author's observation notes of a participatory pre-meeting at the start of a NC, March 2006.

56 The use of the notion of 'taxon' is inspired by Donna Haraway's reference to the figure of the 'inappropriate/d other' (by Trinh Minh-ha): 'To be inappropriate/d is not to fit the *taxon*.' See Donna Haraway, 'The Promises of Monsters: A Regenerative Politics of Inappropriate/d Others', in *Cultural Studies*, ed. Lawrence Grossberg, Cary Nelson, Paula Treichler (London: Routledge, 1992), 295–337: 299.

57 Translated from author's observation notes of a GA in October 2006.

58 *Coordination Contrats de Quartier et Rénovation Urbaine* (Municipality of the City of Brussels) and RenovaS (a non-profit organisation or *association sans but lucrative* asbl to whom the Municipality of Schaerbeek delegates the management of neighbourhood contracts), respectively.

59 Examples include the logo and information point for NCs. During interviews conducted by the author, some architects with experience in participation, warned however that turning good experiences into a 'best practice' would be missing the point as situatedness is essential to participatory success.

60 This actor emerged in interviews with administrators of municipalities involved in NCs and neighbourhood renewal more generally. Several municipal administrations have undertaken efforts to optimise the situation. For example, the *Coordination Contrats de Quartier et Rénovation Urbaine* (Municipality of the City of Brussels) created an information point for guiding citizens through the complex bureaucracy of renovation grants; and negotiated the set-up of prefinancing funds with private banks and other administrations.

61 Author's observation notes of a LCID meeting, March 2006.

62 The first LCID meeting of a NC took place in the main space of a prestigious cultural centre. This location, combined with large projection screens, and the use of microphones gave a certain seriousness to the meeting. The following meeting took place in a more modest meeting room in the same building. In another NC, meetings took place around a large oval table. On the impact of spatial arrangements in participation, I refer to the research by Mathieu Berger; see for example Berger and Beugnies, *Brussel Getoetst op Inspraak*.

63 The sense of frustration caused by the limited *marge de manoeuvre* appeared in several interviews with planners.

64 Latour, *Reassembling the Social*, 64–65.

65 Jane Bennett, *Vibrant Matter: A Political Ecology of Things* (Durham, NC and London: Duke University Press, 2010), 17.

66 Foucault, 'Space, Knowledge, and Power', 255.

67 Bennett, *Vibrant Matter*, 17.

68 This resonates with Jeremy Till's observation that architectural practice is more about uncertainty than about purity, and that architects would therefore benefit from accepting messiness and insecurity as part of their work. See Jeremy Till, 'Architecture of the impure community', in *Occupying Architecture, Between the Architect and the User*, ed. Jonathan Hill (London: Routledge, 1998), 61–75.

69 Such attempts are starting to emerge in architectural theory; see for example the Further Reading Required: Building Specifications, Contracts, and Technical Literature conference, The Bartlett School of Architecture, 2011; Mark Dorrian, 'Regulating Architecture', *Architecture Research Quarterly* 16, no. 3 (2012): 200–204 (and see also the other contributions in this special issue on 'Building with Words'); and the 2014 Architectural Humanities Research Association (AHRA) Annual Conference, Newcastle University, on the theme Industries of Architecture: Relations, Process, Production.

6

Unsung Heroes

In 1998, the Brussels Municipality of Schaerbeek organised an architecture competition for a House of the Citizens (*Maison des Citoyens*). Dedicating a new building to citizens sent an important message that the Schaerbeek authorities took the dialogue with their citizens seriously.[1] In architectural culture, the competition's encouragement of contemporary design was valuable because it challenged the common perception of Brussels 'decorative shallowness'.[2] The winning entry by Atelier d'Architecture Pierre Hebbelinck, realised in 2004, combined a participatory symbolism – the building as a large table around which citizens can gather – with contemporary design features – clean-cut geometry, exposed concrete and transparency. A u-shaped concrete slab symbolising a table is the backbone for the different programmes and activities that gather around it. A video-documentary shows the architect sketching, on beermats, how the building aims to evoke a 'local atmosphere' (Figure 6.1; and Figure 6.2, see Plate 15).[3]

It is tempting to draw parallels with Charles Jencks's symbolic and stylistic reading of architecture's meaning and his observation of a 'disparity between popular and elitist codes'.[4] Jencks recognised 'slips-of-the-metaphor' in Herman Hertzberger's *De Drie Hoven* residential complex for the elderly (1975), in Amsterdam, for example, where the casbah-like organisation of small-scale, interlocked spaces was intended to induce feelings of care and humanism. Jencks argued that such subtle analogy was overshadowed by the, perhaps unintended, façade arrangement. With its structure of individual black rooms sitting within a concrete grid, 'each room looks like a black coffin placed between white crosses' and the architect is thus 'inadvertently saying that old age, in our society, is rather fatal'.[5] A similar disparity occurred in Brussels, when inhabitants of the popular quarters of Molenbeek referred to a brand new apartment building as *boîte de conserves*, which translates as a tin can, evidently failing to appreciate the architect's hope of expressing the industrial past and an 'optimistic vision for the future' through the building's shiny aluminium façade.[6]

It is equally tempting to evaluate the House of the Citizens in terms of its reception, use and appropriation. The building's symbolic representation of openness and accessibility, reinforced by the generous use of glass, struggled to convince local communities. A social worker claimed that, in a neighbourhood

6.1 Model of the *Maison des Citoyens* by Atelier d'Architecture Pierre Hebbelinck. Copyright: Pierre Hebbelinck. Used with permission.

6.2 *Maison des Citoyens* by Atelier d'Architecture Pierre Hebbelinck. Photograph by Marie-Françoise Plissart. Copyright: Pierre Hebbelinck. Used with permission.

where illicit activities take place, the transparency of the building risked being read as a means of surveillance, rather than the supposed accessibility.[7] Over the years, the building was vandalised; resulting in its premature aging. And yet, this did not signal a complete dismissal. The architect continued to speak with building users and seemed to accept their disgruntlement as growing pains typical of catalyst projects in fragile neighbourhoods.[8] Not all users were so negative: a group of asylum seekers, who had been forced to sleep rough in cold winter conditions, found shelter in the building's outdoor spaces and underpasses.[9]

But is there something else at work in the House of the Citizens; something other than the symbolic analogies of this building or its performance through use or rejection? This book started from the premise that cities and buildings emerge through an assemblage of numerous actors and stakes; and these are of diverse plumage. Throughout this book, I have shown that such actors can be non-human as much as human. Cities are fabricated through the actions of professionals, politicians, citizens, and visitors; but they are equally produced through plans, buildings, infrastructures, ideas, imaginations, everyday practices, and even, as Chapter 5 shows, regulations, time, perimeters, abbreviations, and language. The involvement of such actors changes over time; actors come and go. Rather than reducing the evaluation of architecture to a single aspect or meaning, I suggest that we bring to the fore the de- and re-assembling of all the colourful actors that make-city.

This chapter pushes an understanding of architecture and cities as practices a little further. By focusing on an even wider net of actors that tend to get overlooked, the discussions of 'what counts' in architecture expand. It is worth returning to Bruno Latour's definition of what it means to 'act'.[10] Latour defines a participant in action as 'any thing that modifies a state of affairs by making a difference […] in the course of some other agent's action'.[11] Whether human or non-human, something *acts* not because it is acknowledged as an actor in the categories of the researcher, but because it makes a difference; because it matters in the course of action. Consequently, many actors that enact and co-fabricate the city go unnoticed, not because they are invisible or because they are deliberately excluded or oppressed, but because they do not seem to make a difference to the city. Such actors can appear as mundane and trivial. They can be unwanted or even uncooperative. The task at hand is to reinsert and revalue such actors in urban and architectural thinking. Isabelle Stengers aptly described such a task as the 'decolonisation of thought'.[12] It is a disobedient task of 'healthy disrespect'[13] vis-à-vis the exclusionary, authoritative, and generalising tendencies of architectural theory when limited to masters, oeuvres, and canons. It is a task of accepting what Donna Haraway called the 'surprises and ironies at the heart of all knowledge production'.[14]

I have sought the company of three actors that, in my view, deserve to be included in making-city: a public urinal, situated icons, and derogatory words. While these actors may seem an odd, or even arbitrary selection, and significantly different in action and appearance, they equally make a difference, and hence act, in Brussels.

The first actor is often considered to be banal and unflattering: the public urinal. I was initially drawn to two particular urinals because they frequently appeared in meeting reports that I consulted relating to an urban renewal project for the Quartier Brabant, known for its window prostitution. Persistent discussions on these urinals peppered the reports which mostly contained systematic details on the progress of all sorts of hardware projects in the Quartier Brabant such as housing renovations. Rather than a mere by-product of an urban renewal initiative worth 10 million euros, the urinals turned out to make an important difference to this neighbourhood.

A second, very different type of actor are what I call 'situated icons'. Situated icons are design projects that do not take part in a global architectural discourse driven by landmark buildings and seminal projects but are important actors in local urban contexts. One such project is the refurbished Place Flagey in Brussels (2008), celebrated for its collaborative design process and for its catalytic effect on subsequent architectural competitions. Whilst not a stylistic landmark, Flagey nevertheless proved to be an important milestone in Brussels' architectural culture, and therefore deserves due attention. Situated icons also include design projects that *are* explicitly iconic but cannot be fully understood without reference to their local context, such as the project for the Place Rogier by Xaveer De Geyter Architects, currently in construction. This project shows how the iconic emerges equally from a strong formal–individualistic statement and from Brussels' tangle of practices, uncertainties, and contingencies. The Rogier project is an important actor in re-connecting Brussels' growing enthusiasm for landmark architecture with a realistic understanding of its local situation. It helps to realise global ambitions that suit Brussels rather than relying only on the mere import of global success formula.

The third actor returns to a question posed earlier, namely: whether there is something else at work in the performance of the House of the Citizens besides symbolism and use? The House of the Citizens cannot be disconnected from its geographical location. It is situated at the Place Gaucheret, which forms a transition between the vast *terrain vague* of the unfinished Manhattan Plan – the large-scale Central Business District planned in the 1960s – and the old residential fabric that had escaped demolition (Figure 6.3). The Place Gaucheret contains daily reminders of a failed urbanism. New constructions here seem to be unavoidably haunted by Brussels troubled past. Is it just as possible to consider the general haunting of Brussels' architectural culture by the traumas of the past? To explore this, I look not at plans and buildings but rather follow two popular derogatory words in the Brussels language: *architek* and *Bruxellisation*. Despite dating from different periods, both words decry the harassment of a population through destructive architectural and urban projects. By following the numerous traces left behind by these words, it will become clear that, rather than merely transmitting meaning, words act. These words make a difference to architectural and urban debates in Brussels: both words travelled swiftly through popular culture, nurtured Brussels' fear of the new and, consequently, the negative connotation that the architect had with the public.

6.3 The *Maison des Citoyens* in context: outlook onto the Quartier du Nord office area, including the realised towers of the Manhattan Project. Photograph by the author, 2015.

THE EXTRAORDINARY JOURNEY OF PUBLIC URINALS

On January 24, 2013, the Brussels TV station Télé Bruxelles announced that the Municipality of Schaerbeek had made 40, 000 euros available for improving the Rue d'Aerschot, Brussels most notorious street for window prostitution. The plan included the 'replacement of the [existing] urinals with more hygienic models that are maintenance-friendlier'.[15] An accompanying video featured a rather modest brick urinal with a sloped roof. It is covered with snow and the attached signboard reads *ceci est un urinoir* (this is a urinal).[16] What here follows is a biography of these public urinals, from their early conception in 2002, up to their inauguration in 2005 and subsequent performance.

The urinals originated in the 2001–2004 Neighbourhood Contract (NC) for Aerschot-Progrès / Aarschot-Vooruitgang.[17] NCs, as they were organised at the time of analysis, were publicly funded urban renewal programmes for the renovation of deprived neighbourhoods and they were thematically organised in five groups or *volets*. NCs focused primarily on renovating often old and run-down, housing stock (*volet* 1–3) but they also involved the refurbishment of public spaces (*volet* 4) and socio-cultural actions (*volet* 5). NCs typically ran for four years whereby the first year was used for planning and discussing the project proposals in a participatory manner (see Chapter 5).[18] That is, dialogue between planners, authorities and residents was organised through regular meetings of a Local Commission for Integrated Development (Commission Locale de Développement Intégré – Plaatselijke Commissie voor Geïntegreerde Ontwikkeling). The meetings of this Commission were systematically minuted and approved in a *procès-verbal* (PV).[19] The minutes keep track of the progress of different housing projects in the shape of regularly updated tables, reporting on communications with owners, proposals for renovation, and expropriation procedures.

NC Aerschot-Progrès aimed to optimise the living conditions surrounding the Rue d'Aerschot, including the residential, perpendicular streets connecting it with the Rue de Brabant. The Rue de Brabant is a busy shopping street that forms the central axis of this neighbourhood, called Quartier Brabant. It is popular for its Turkish and Moroccan food, furniture, fashion, and music.[20] As a supra-local ethnic shopping street, it attracts national and international consumers, and is particularly busy during the weekends. The neighbourhood is, as a whole, bounded by the Brussels' inner ring road, the North Railway Station, the Rue Royale and the Rue des Palais (Figure 6.4). It is located in the administrative areas of the municipality of Schaerbeek and Saint-Josse-ten-Noode. The area underwent important transformations between 1919 and 1952, when the North Station was moved 300 metres to create the underground North–South railway junction. This resulted in the morphological, functional, and visual isolation of the quarter; and its disconnection from the Brussels city centre. In addition, due to developments on the other side of the North Station (in the wake of the Manhattan Plan), the Quartier Brabant, now at the 'rear' of the station, became gradually marginalised in social, economic, and political terms.[21] As the neighbourhood's infrastructure aged, it was poorly maintained, yet intensely used by customers of the Rue d' Aerschot

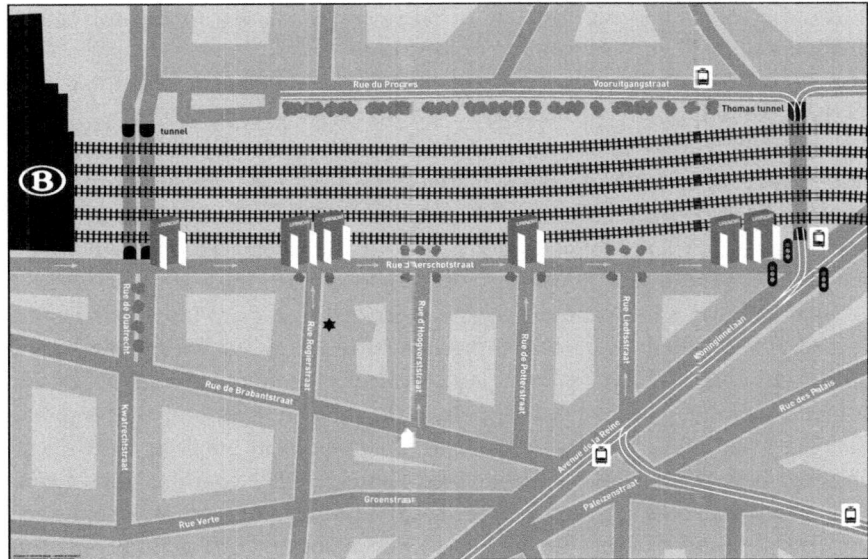

6.4 Map of the area surrounding the Rue de Brabant and the Rue d'Aerschot. The map indicates new urinals that replaced the original ones in brick. Map by VOLTA. Copyright: Samenlevingsopbouw-Brussel vzw. Used with permission.

and Rue de Brabant, by students and commuters crossing the quarter to and from the station, and by its residents.

The Rue de Brabant flourished within trans-national ethnic networks: the window prostitution of the Rue d'Aerschot, moreover, became entangled with criminal and human-trade networks. Together, the Rue d'Aerschot and Rue de Brabant exercised significant pressure on the living quality of the neighbourhood; the streets perpendicular to and in-between the Rue d'Aerschot and Rue de Brabant received the overspill of both. In addition to refuse, discarded food, drugs and sex industry-related litter, these streets put up with crime, noise, and public urination. One of the major challenges of the NC therefore was to restore the residential character and living quality in this area.

In such a context, urban renewal typically requires 'hard' measures as much as 'soft' ones. Hard measures typically include renovation projects and other solutions 'in stone'. Soft measures refer to greenery, public space, security, noise, the use of space, and cleanliness which inhabitants of fragile neighbourhoods such as the Quartier de Brabant emphasise as important. During participatory planning processes, such as the NCs, citizens often display frustration with the fact that experts seem to be more preoccupied with the hard measures than they are with the soft ones. This frustration is reinforced by the common misconception that soft measures are less technical and therefore easier, and quicker, to implement than hard measures.

The hard-soft measures tension was also evident in the Aerschot-Progrès NC. Augmenting the living quality in the streets connecting the Rue d'Aerschot and the Rue de Brabant was an identified priority, with a particular ambition of discouraging the further spread of prostitution bars, also called *commerces de charme*, in these residential streets which required a combination of hard and soft measures. Where possible, the municipality simply prohibited prostitution by refusing commercial permits. In addition, it used hard measures as a way to avoid prostitution creeping into these residential side-streets.[22] As such, the NC aimed to convert corner buildings of the Rue d'Aerschot into residential premises. Vitrines were prohibited and the municipality could opt to either purchase the building, force the owner to convert the property into housing, or, if necessary, expropriate.[23] It also used architectural solutions to optimise and articulate the residential character of these side-streets. For example, to avoid the suggestion of a vitrine, the elevation of street-level windows above eyesight was encouraged.[24] This was successfully achieved at two corner buildings at Rue Liedts, where structures replacing the demolished houses, raised the ground floor windows to avoid levelling the pedestrian gaze.[25]

Such hard measures were not always perceived as successful by inhabitants. One observed that the windows in the side streets were still, for the most part, occupied by *'des filles en petites tenues'*; and it was regretted that much of the planned expropriations had not happened.[26] In addition to renovating the corner buildings, the municipality also planned interventions in public space such as enlarged pavements, bins, and new street lighting. Public space solutions were deployed to reinforce a distinction between the prostitution and residential areas through applying different treatments to pavement and street surfaces.[27] The request for public urinals emerged within this context.

Suggestions for installing urinals in the Rue d'Aerschot had been present at the start of the NC. During consultation meetings, inhabitants had pointed to the fact that the long wall separating the Rue d'Aerschot from the railway tracks, 'is already serving as an improvised urinal'.[28] Inhabitants claimed that all the 'nice proposals' of the NC would be pointless if no action would be taken against the numerous 'soft' problems of the neighbourhood.[29] More frequent street cleaning, more litterbins, more regular waste collection, and the installation of public urinals were mentioned as important, which was confirmed by a public survey held towards the end of 2002.

Implementing the urinals proved more challenging than one would expect because the urinals raised all sorts of discussions and disagreements regarding their location, maintenance, and design. For example, whilst the location of the urinals was, according to experts, dictated by spatial conditions, inhabitants stressed the importance of visibility and access as the only guarantors for the urinals actually being used.[30] Inhabitants challenged the proposed implementation of a urinal at the crossing of the Rue d'Aerschot with the Philippe Thomas Tunnel under the railway tracks, where the urinal could benefit from a more than average pavement width. However, inhabitants noted that the location was dark and unsafe, and thus unlikely to be used.[31] Maintenance arrangements proved to be an even greater stumbling block. Public toilets had rapidly disappeared from cityscapes and public funds rarely provide for public toilet cleaning whilst private outsourcing is expensive.[32] The struggle to secure maintenance for the urinals resulted in extensive discussions and delayed the building process. Between 2002 and 2005, the minutes of the Local Commission for Integrated Development record research into self-cleaning toilets, price tenders for maintenance, and occasional moments of desperation. The latter was particularly the case nearer the conclusion of the NC; 'The municipality must take *urgent measures* [...] and one must proceed to the *immediate installation* of the urinals.'[33] Whilst other public works in the Rue d'Aerschot proceeded, the installation of the urinals was delayed.[34] Deadlines were repeatedly postponed, and ultimatums were enforced and subsequently broken. With the NC approaching its end, the Belgian Federal Public Service of Mobility and Transport, responsible for the public works at the Rue d'Aerschot, declared that during March 2005, the building site would be closed 'with or without the urinals'.[35] The deadline was further postponed to May 2005, then to the autumn of 2005, and finally to late 2005/early 2006.[36] Whilst the works were delayed, there were seemingly petty discussions around the choice for a flat or sloping roof.[37] In November 2005, more than three years after they had entered the discussions, the urinals were finally operational.

The urinals' journey was, however, not quite over. Due to the mounting time pressure at the closure of the NC, the urinals' construction had ultimately been informed by the need for 'urgent measures' and 'provisional solutions'; and thus by compromises.[38] The regional department for public space maintenance and waste collection, Bruxelles-Propreté, had been appointed to do a daily cleaning *au Kärcher*.[39] They must not have anticipated just how well-used the urinals would be and thus the solution became inadequate and unsustainable. Bruxelles-Propreté eventually discontinued the cleaning allegedly because it was considered 'too dirty a job'.[40] In consequence, the municipality was forced to hire a private cleaning service at a monthly cost of 3,500 euros for cleaning the urinals twice a day.[41] Likewise, the hasty decision to commission the urinals' construction to an ordinary contractor (in charge of the other public works in the Rue d'Aerschot) that did not specialise in urinal construction contributed to the urinals' rapid decay. The simple brick construction contained standard bathroom tiles which rapidly eroded under the repeated exposure of urine.[42] In other words, the urinals' performance proved problematic and public urination remained a problem in the neighbourhood. As a result, the urinals triggered numerous neighbourhood initiatives long after the NC ceased. In 2006, local social organisations installed signs in order to better guide people towards the urinals.[43] Some initiatives focused on wider liveability issues in the neighbourhood; not just the urinals. For example, *A Health Portrait of the Quartier de Brabant* was published in 2008 providing a snapshot of the living conditions and problems in the area.[44] Other actions included a door-to-door survey in the streets perpendicular to the Rue d'Aerschot, where problems persisted; and detailed, comparative research into alternative solutions for the urinals, including quotes, budgeting, and technical detailing was undertaken.[45] In 2009, it was followed by a series of humorous actions under the ludic banner 'operation public urination' (*opération pipi sauvage*). These actions included, amongst others, the installation of spatter boards and fake electric strings at popular urination spots, and pavement markings guiding men from these spots to the urinals. A sign stating 'ceci est un urinoir' (this is a urinal) was installed above a urinal whilst popular public urination spots were tagged 'ceci n'est pas un urinoir' (this is not an urinal).[46] In 2009, local social worker Géraldine Bruyneel presented the *Plan hygiénique 2010 rue d'Aerschot Schaerbeek* to the municipality which included a proposal for more appropriate urinals. As a result of the *Plan hygiénique*, the municipality was prepared to create a task force to address the topic. Finally, in 2013, funds were made available for dismantling and replacing the urinals with eight new ones[47] (Figures 6.5 and 6.6; Figure 6.7, see Plate 16; and Figure 6.8, see Plate 17).

6.5 (*left*)   One of the two originally installed urinals. Photograph by the author, March 2007.

6.6 (*right*)   Local social workers applying signs onto the pavement aiming at directing people to the nearby urinals. Copyright: SamenlevingsopbouwBrussel vzw. Used with permission.

6.7   Signs indicating that this location is not a place for urination ('ceci n'est pas un urinoir') whilst directing towards nearby public urinals. Photograph by the author, 2015.

6.8   Example of a new urinal. Eight of those were installed from late 2013 onwards, replacing the original brick ones. Photograph by the author, 2015.

What can be learned from this decade-long journey of public urinals in the Rue d'Aerschot? The urinals hint at common participatory frustrations caused by the misconception that 'soft' problems in space can be solved more easily than 'hard' ones. The urinals also invite approaching architecture beyond mere aesthetic, ideological, or cultural registers; and show the importance of including dirt, unruliness, and messiness in a (modern) planning obsessed with cleanliness.[48] More importantly, the urinals demonstrate that mundane and seemingly negligible artefacts can become full-blown actors in making-city. They become actors because, in this neighbourhood, they matter; they make a difference. The relentless efforts of local authorities and neighbourhood organisations to optimise the urinals' performance demonstrate that, even as a failed construction, the urinals still 'acted'. Within the taxonomy of urban renewal, the urinals were ill-fitting and became the product of numerous compromises; and failed to deliver. But this failure informed an important, and on-going, learning process amongst authorities and local organisations that, moreover, informed novel technical, communicative, and managerial alliances between local associations, experts, authorities, and citizens. This was also the case when experts of the Brussels Institute for Management of the Environment (BIM-IBGE) claimed that acoustic testing was impossible because the noises in this neighbourhood are not standard (that is car-music, screaming as opposed to traffic noise), and one of the local social workers suggested experimental techniques used at Universities.

SITUATED ICONS

I call the second type of actor 'situated icons'. These are projects that do not perform on a global scale as aesthetically pleasing landmarks, thriving on imported success formula from elsewhere (the so-called 'Bilbao-effect').[49] Instead, they derive their iconic status from making a difference in a specific, local situation. Situated icons can act like landmark buildings but are purposively situated and entangled within their location. I follow two situated icons in Brussels: the project for the refurbishing of the Place Flagey and the project for the Place Rogier and its underground spaces.[50] Through a discussion of these projects, I will argue that architectural icons can be understood through their situatedness rather than merely being stylistic, isolated objects.

Contemporary (global) architectural discourse operates, to a significant degree, through the logic of performance and achievement, which is measured by generic categories and award systems such as for the greenest, most sustainable, most beautiful, and even the ugliest (for example the Carbuncle Cup for the ugliest building in the United Kingdom). Global discourse operates through the celebration of landmark buildings, so-called best practices, and 'starchitects'. Even antagonistic works such as squats, temporary urbanism, and experimental neighbourhoods can enter the logic of the iconic; namely when global discourse turns such practices into more or less generic types whose impact and achievements are hoped to find reproduction elsewhere.

Considered in this way, Brussels has barely produced any architectural highlights in recent decades and the city has been reluctant in experimenting when compared to similar cities, such as London's urban regeneration, the metropolitan aspirations of Paris, the cultural laboratory of Berlin, or the architectural promotion of the SuperDutch.[51] Despite important opportunities created by its international function, Brussels' contemporary architectural status is a far cry from the historical heydays of Art Nouveau at the turn of the 19th century – when Brussels occupied a central position on the international architecture scene – and the architectural splendour of the 1958 World Expo including the well-known Atomium and the Philips Pavilion designed by Le Corbusier and Iannis Xenakis.[52] Since then, large commissions have remained in the hands of powerful development consortia and large local architectural firms who are active across the globe and operate within powerful developer circles but feature less in the international vanguard press. It is no secret that such local power frustrates some younger architects who often experience the Brussels' scene as incestuous, lacking in ambition, and mediocre.

The situation seems to be changing. The Brussels authorities are anxious to finally obtain a place on the global architecture map. Upon his appointment in December 2013, the city's Mayor, Yvan Mayeur, announced his ambition to turn Brussels into a metropolis on a par with Berlin and Paris. Referencing ambitious urban renewal projects such as Times Square in New York, Mayeur proposed that Anish Kapoor be commissioned for Place de Brouckère.[53] By renovating central boulevards and creating metropolitan squares, Mayeur hoped to generate a much-needed economic and cultural boost. The question for Mayeur became: if Paris has the Champs-Elysees and Berlin the Kurfürstendamm, then what can Brussels have?[54] In other words, Mayeur's proposals embraced urban regeneration's trickle-down promises and the copy-pasting of generic urban formulae such as iconic architecture. Bold ambitions can also be found in slogans developed for promoting Brussels abroad; 'Brussels: to dare', 'Ambition for Brussels', and 'Brussels capital of Europe / Brussels capital of the world'.[55]

The two projects that I have chosen to discuss challenge this correlation between bold architectural ambitions and architectural icons. Whereas the project for the Place Flagey will show the impact of architectural projects that, according to contemporary standards of the iconic in architecture, are rather mundane; the project for the Place Rogier will demonstrate how iconic architectural objects rely on their situatedness and, thus, cannot be simply imported.

The refurbished Place Flagey was inaugurated in 2008 after five years of participatory design thinking. Aesthetically and formally somewhat underwhelming according to iconic standards, Flagey is nevertheless catalytic in that it instigated changes in Brussels' attitude towards public design commissions. Designed by the German–Belgian team Latz & Partners / D+A International, the project challenged the popular method of urban embellishment according to which public space is considered to be the glue that holds the city together, and is modelled on design types and morphologies of the past (Figure 6.9, see Plate 18; and Figure 6.10, see Plate 19). Urban embellishment was, in Brussels, promoted by the publication of sympathetic urban design manuals that provided detailed

6.9 Place Flagey, Latz & Partners / D+A International. Copyright and photograph by Serge Brison. Used with permission.

6.10 Place Flagey, Latz & Partners / D+A International. Copyright and photograph by Bernard Capelle. Used with permission.

guidelines for the lay-out, furniture, lampposts, and so on, of public spaces, according to the reconstruction logic.[56] These manuals, however, also tend to reduce urban design to a cosmetic treatment of space; based on the simplified contrasting between good and bad formal solutions for the city. Such an approach often results in stylistic conformism rather than creative experimentation; public space design consequently became an important frontline for the struggle for contemporary design in Brussels.[57]

The Place Flagey is a large public square located in the municipality of Ixelles. It houses the architecture school La Cambre and the legendary Flagey recording studios, built in Art-Deco style (1938, Joseph Diongre), and restored in the early 2000s by Philippe Samyn. Place Flagey is located at the crossroads of the affluent area of the Avenue Louise, the European Quarter, and a popular, socially more modest area undergoing gentrification. As such the square is frequented by a diverse public of students, hipsters, families, Eurocrats, and the urban poor. The winning design, rather than beautifying the square and orchestrating its use *à la* urban embellishment, maintained a vast open space that could be freely appropriated by everyday users as well as being capable of hosting large events.

The project was initiated by a collective called Platforme Flagey; a unique collaboration between citizen groups (Parcours Citoyen, Inter-Environnement Bruxelles and Habitat et Rénovation) architects (architecture school ISACF-La Cambre, the Centre de Recherche Architecturale de La Cambre, and the architectural action group Disturb), and the cultural community centre GC Elzenhof. In August 2003, Platforme Flagey organised a Call for Ideas (*Appel à l'idées*) in response to the official proposal for the square, by Agora, for which a planning permission request had been submitted in June. This proposal was deemed too technocratic and a missed opportunity; a mere 'footnote to the contract for the underground infrastructure works'.[58] Moreover, made without public tender or consultation, the planning process was deemed to be undemocratic. The combination of the critique of an existing project with the formulation of alternatives recalled the counter-projects of the 1970s (see Chapter 2). However, comparatively the role of the involved architects was significantly different. The proposed alternatives were no longer designed by a like-minded group of architects and students adhering to a specific style; or, in the words, of Disturb-member Christophe Mercier: '[w]ho are we to determine what should be done with the Place Flagey?'[59] Instead of a counter-project, Platforme Flagey organised an international Call for Ideas. Rather than proposing a project, the call functioned as a participatory catalyst using architecture as its medium. Receiving nearly a hundred entries, accompanied by an exhibition, significant press attention, and numerous neighbourhood actions, the formulation of alternative solutions was embedded in a wider debate.[60] The results of this call convinced the new Minister of Mobility and Public Works, Pascal Smet, to organise an official international architecture competition in 2004–2005. It also encouraged the minister to launch a broader public space policy and to organise architectural competitions. The Flagey project is therefore both a pilot and a catalyst for the organisation of architectural competitions in Brussels.

Flagey also informed a participatory process that, rather than aspiring consensus, recognised the different, often conflicting agendas in design processes. The architects were, similar to the 1970s counter-projects, working at the service of citizen committees. This however, did not imply that their motivations for campaigning had to be identical. Whereas the architects connected to Disturb, for example, campaigned for more thorough debates on the city through architectural competitions, Parcours Citoyen's social activism focused their interest on involving citizens in urban decision-making. This opportunism and divergence between stakeholders was not ignored but, rather, activated. Without the social legwork of Parcours Citoyen, such as the organisation of a large neighbourhood banquet, the local population would not have been as receptive to an international architecture competition. In other words, *all* stakeholders were credited for the design successes of Flagey; not just the architects.[61] The Platforme Flagey, rather than thriving on shared ideologies, worked constructively through the contradicting objectives of the different stakeholders. In addition, Platforme Flagey proved, as a collective, open to change. A Permanent Assembly (*Conférence Permanente*) was created in order to welcome discussions about the use and maintenance of the square. Containing a different set of actors than the Platforme Flagey, namely those more involved in the management and maintenance of the square, the Permanent Assembly can be thought of as a 'reassembled' Platforme Flagey.

The Flagey project can be considered iconic not because of its radicalism, landmark status, or aesthetic features but because it revolutionised the processes and mind-sets of those practicing urban design in Brussels as seen in the subsequent elaborate programme of design competitions. Flagey's iconic status therefore resides more in its processes than in its project status; and in its capacity to recover potential from within Brussels rather than seeking sustenance from global models. Interestingly, in order to act as a catalyst Flagey elegantly reactivated the participatory and transformative legacy of the counter-projects of the 1970s; albeit without retaining the stylistic and formal dogmatism with which these projects were also associated.

Another 'situated icon' is the project for refurbishing the Place Rogier and its underground spaces, including an important metro hub. Located at the edge of city-centre Brussels, Place Rogier is a public space at the intersection of two busy urban boulevards and a popular shopping street, flanked by high-rise offices, hotels and a shopping centre (Figure 6.11). Despite being an important transit space for commuters and shoppers to and from the nearby North Station, it has not been successful in acting as a public space. Place Rogier's renovation stems directly from the Flagey legacy because it originates in an architectural competition organised in 2006.[62] The competition was ambitious in that it encouraged the creation of a metropolitan project with international allure. The winning entry by Xaveer De Geyter Architects (XDGA) explicitly departed from the 'small scale' of Brussels, and emphasised Rogier's metropolitan character.[63] It was argued that, with the selection of XDGA, Brussels seemed to be 'finally getting serious about urban design'.[64] A closer look into the design and on-

6.11 Rogier Project, Xaveer De Geyter Architects: context. The horizontal boulevard coincides with the municipal boundary between the City of Brussels and St. Joost-ten-Node. Copyright XDGA Architects. Used with permission.

going construction of what will become an iconic landmark will, however, reveal that its iconic ambitions cannot be disconnected from the specific situation of Brussels.[65]

XDGA is a firm that has been closely intertwined with Brussels since its creation in 1991, and the office has been an important contributor to metropolitan projects for the city. The Rogier project should be situated within a series of XDGA's metropolitan statements including their collaboration with OMA for Forum Les Halles in Paris (2003); a winning entry for the Schuman Square design competition in Brussels (2010); and Xaveer De Geyter's earlier work, most notably, his contribution to the proposal for the Brussels Carrefour de l'Europe in 1983.[66] Despite XDGA's international reputation, Brussels' city authorities did not easily embrace its radical statements. Many of XDGA's Brussels projects remained on paper; the award-winning Kitchen Tower (a 60 metres high tower for a cookery school) and Rogier being notable exceptions.[67]

The iconic status of the Rogier project is envisaged through a gigantic circular canopy with a diameter of 64 metres. This canopy offers shelter to the square and a new patio opening up the existing underground subway system (Figure 6.12, see Plate 20; and Figures 6.13 and 6.14). This landmark object does, however, not emerge from imported ideas on the iconic. It is instead a product of XDGA's thorough understanding of the local context; as De Geyter argues:

> I do not believe that all urban questions can be treated through icons in concrete and steel and of the most audacious forms […] But that does not mean that we never make emblematic works. Sometimes it is justified by a work's programme or position in the city – as an identification point or symbol.[68]

6.12 Rogier Project, Xaveer De Geyter Architects.
Copyright XDGA Architects. Used with permission.

6.13 Rogier Project, Xaveer De Geyter Architects. Copyright XDGA Architects. Used with permission.

6.14 Rogier Project, Xaveer De Geyter Architects: view of courtyard / entrance to underground space. Copyright XDGA Architects. Used with permission.

The iconic statement of Rogier can be seen as a fitting response to Brussels' metropolitan status and aspirations. In addition, it is a product of XDGA's skilfulness in manoeuvring this iconic statement through Brussels' intricate decision-making and construction processes. This complexity starts with the administrative and financial position of the Place Rogier. It is situated at a municipal border and contains a regional road. As a consequence, the pavements belong to different municipalities whilst the road surface is regional territory. The project therefore needs to juggle the procedures and design preferences of a triple-head client: two municipalities and the Brussels Region. Finance also comes from two regional and one supra-regional authority, thus there are three tenders; not one.[69]

The project was further complicated by the complex underground space. Due to the absence of detailed plans and sections of the underground metro spaces, design and engineering turned into an archaeological endeavour of learning whilst digging and dealing with surprises. When the designers discovered that the underground infrastructure did not allow for planting two straight lines of trees, as was suggested by the original design, they reconceptualised the boulevard of strolls into a landscape of trees.[70] Also, the underground structure turned out being part of the structural basis of the adjacent Sheraton Hotel, which impacted on the structural foundations of the canopy.

XDGA tailored its representational tactics in anticipation of such a complex spatial, administrative, and financial situation. For example, through the use of physical work models that are quick and easy to adjust, the architects could accommodate last-minute adjustments and changes in decision-making.[7] The architects also developed images and diagrams that are flexible, adaptable and resilient enough to survive Brussels' notoriously lengthy building processes. For example, one of the original diagrams survived eight years of reworking into different versions.

Such resilient images are important also for safeguarding the iconic throughout the messiness of Brussels' building practice. They offer a suit of armour protecting the iconic building against numerous threats and invasions. One such threat was formed by the plans of a neighbouring hotel to create its own entrance canopy. This was an independently developed project that potentially disturbed the iconic gestures of the project by XDGA. Moreover, the drawings for this second canopy concealed (through the incorrect use of scales) that, in reality, the two canopies could actually collide.[72] Another threat came from the city's ingrained prejudice to ambitious architectural projects. For example, years into the construction process, it turned out that a technical control agency had not bothered testing certain aspects of the canopy design because it had assumed that, in Brussels, this type of project would never be realised.[73] Another emblematic element in the design – a sculptural staircase connecting the new square with the underground spaces – came under threat when a public administration 'donated' an escalator to the project. This administration can purchase items that are regularly used in public works, such as escalators, without going through a process of price tendering. As a result, the escalator was purchased outside the project tender and its delivery on site was independent from the project planning. The architects had planned to construct this structurally complex staircase first; when the site was still free and easy to manoeuvre. The escalator arrived, however, on site long before the designers had started building the staircase, and so they had to adjust their construction strategy. A gift had somewhat become a burden.[74]

The Rogier project demonstrates how iconic ambitions in architecture cannot be disconnected from the specific practices, circumstances, and threats from which they emerge. This is arguably the case for any translation of design ideas into construction practice; but it is particularly important in the case of the iconic, which is often portrayed as clean-cut and detached objects.[75] This can particularly be seen in the multi-layered, complex situation of Brussels. The Rogier project leaves no doubt as to its iconic ambitions but these ambitions depend on the project's resilience to local circumstances and, thus, on the architects' capacity to navigate the iconic through all sorts of local hurdles. In Brussels, more so than in other cities, any successful realisation of ambitious architectural projects relies on the architect's will to embrace local intricacies.

For different reasons, I have identified the Flagey and Rogier projects as important actors. They equally make a difference to Brussels' architectural culture; thanks to and in spite of Brussels. I called these actors 'situated icons'. Flagey proved iconic not in an aesthetic or formal sense, but because it revolutionised urban design procedures and mind-sets. Rogier proved, as a design and construction process, surprisingly entangled with the city despite its iconic statement. A deeper understanding of the processes behind these projects, invites a study of the iconic beyond the performance of architectural objects on a global scale. Instead I suggest that we value architectural products that may not shine in international discourses, but are nevertheless of great importance in a specific city, as iconic. Equally, I suggest that the evaluation of iconic architecture should be situated in the concrete, specific processes of becoming; and to temper the high expectations that often accompany imported landmarks.

HAUNTED BY WORDS

We are good people; we don't have an architect in the family.[76]

In a city that reluctantly embraces architectural ambition, one cannot help but sense a fear of the new; an everyday scepticism about experimental and innovative architecture. Such scepticism can be explained by Brussels' history of urban destruction and by its traumatised population whose livelihoods were all too often crushed under the pressure of economic development. If Brussels indeed suffered from a fear of the new; does it act in such a way that it also matters? I argue that the fear of the new, similar to situated icons and public urinals, makes a difference to Brussels' architectural culture. The everyday promotion and maintenance of the Brussels' fear-of-the-new is effectuated through two words; *architek* and

Bruxellisation. *Architek* is an insult that allegedly emerged in the local dialect during the 1880s. It was used by the local population to mock Joseph Poelaert, the architect of the Palace of Justice, a building that was so vast (26,000 square metres) that large parts of the popular *Les Marolles* neighbourhood had to be demolished. The word *Bruxellisation* dates back to the 1960s and 1970s and denotes the destruction of a city by profit-driven developers and architects. A notorious symbol of *Bruxellisation* is the Manhattan Plan, mentioned earlier, in which the CIAM-inspired business district caused the demolition of residential neighbourhoods.[77]

These are not just words that hold a derogatory meaning; they also *act*. *Architek* and *Bruxellisation* act because they travel through literature, everyday language, and in physical space. In *How to Do Things with Words*, J.L. Austin calls such words 'performatives' because they involve 'the performing of an action [rather than] just saying something'.[78] Non-representational theories, as developed by Nigel Thrift and others, have, likewise, indicated a shift away from what words symbolise, mean, or represent to how they are practised.[79]

Architek and *Bruxellisation* are indeed 'performatives'.[80] They have travelled well through popular literature, such as city guides, popular history and journalism, exhibition guides, and graphic novels. They travelled equally well through crime novels, films, or short stories that are, entirely or in part, set in Brussels. In such works, *architek* and *Bruxellisation* appear either literally or, as is often the case, under aliases. *Bruxellisation* travels mostly in French, but it also appears in Dutch (*Brusseliseren*) and English (*Brusselisation*). The word also appears in the form of 'massacre urbanism', 'the glory of decay', or 'frenzied destruction party'.[81] In other instances, *Bruxellisation* is somewhat hidden in terminologies describing Brussels in terms of 'funeral architecture', a 'torn apart city', or a city that can be compared to a Bonsai tree which is 'trimmed, mutilated, and mistreated'.[82]

Architek has similarly travelled in different shapes and through different supports. It is often assisted by an exclamation mark (*architek!*) or adjectives such as *smeergen* or *vuilen* architect, meaning dirty or filthy (in the sense of unjust).[83] The most common adjective, however, is *skief* or *skieven* meaning crooked but also, figuratively, 'false and untrustworthy'.[84] It was also argued that *skief* is corrupted English; the English workers on the construction of the Palace of Justice supposedly called Joseph Poelaert the chief architect. The word 'chief' was then allegedly misinterpreted by the local population as *skief*.[85] Whatever the origins of *skief*, it becomes clear that *architek* is likened to a villain. Under the pseudonym Curtio, Georges Garnir, published *Architek!* (1910), a short story that presents the Dutch translation of the French word *fripouille*; meaning a scoundrel; a wily fellow involved in fraudulent practices.[86] *Architek!* was the third volume in a book series called *Baedeker de Physiologie Bruxelloise à l'usage des étrangers*; which is a mixture of a travel guide (as those by German publisher Karl Baedeker) and a *physiologie*, a popular genre in France in the 1840s consisting of small volumes dedicated to a humorous study of professions, such as the doctor, the lawyer, or the journalist. Curtio's story followed in the footsteps of two volumes with equally remarkable subjects: *Zievereer* (1906), which means driveller, and *Krott et Cie* (1907), which translates as Slum & Co.

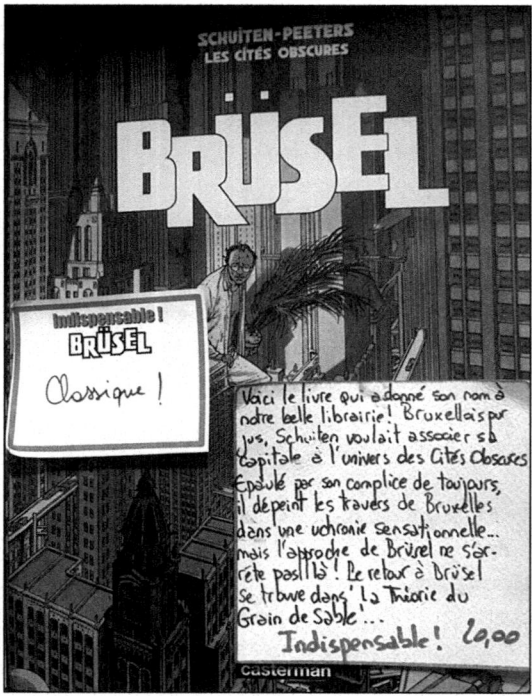

6.15 Cover of the *Brüsel* graphic novel by François Schuiten and Benoît Peeters (2008 [1992]) as displayed in the Brussels shop with the same name: promoted as 'a classic' (classique!) and 'indispensable' (indispensable!). Photograph by the author.

Words moreover perform better when travelling through material means. For example, *architek* has travelled swiftly through several reprints of the short story *Architek!*[87] Words travel faster and further in works that are well known and well-distributed, such as Geert Van Istendael's *Arm Brussel* or, even more so, the graphic novel *Brüsel*, by François Schuiten and Benoît Peeters.[88] *Brüsel* was published in 1992 as the fifth volume in a well-known series of graphic novels about a parallel world of city-states.[89] Despite being a fiction, the story is, not unlike Brussels, one of unbridled modernisation. *Brüsel* captivates the tensions between how city authorities and constructors imagine a new, modern city, and the everyday suffering this causes for citizens. In this novel, both *architek* and *Bruxellisation* perform. *Brüsel*, set in the era of *architek*, alludes to the hygienist planning of the 19th century and features the Palace of Justice; but it also makes reference to the destructive planning style associated with *Bruxellisation*. *Brüsel* moreover travelled well. It is popular, internationally renowned, and has been translated into several languages. *Brüsel* thus does not just demonstrate that words travel in all sorts of shapes and disguises; but that they perform through the allocation of meaning as much as through material practices. This was confirmed when I visited the Brussels bookshop, also called *Brüsel*, which is specialised in graphic novels and popular with tourists. In this shop, the book was promoted on shelf as a classic ('classique!') and as 'indispensable!' (Figures 6.15 and 6.16).

The speed and scope of *architek* and *Bruxellisation* is influenced by other material means. For example, *architek* and *Bruxellisation* travel well through works that are made widely available in libraries; sometimes in several copies and easy to find through search terms such as 'Fiction with Brussels as a theme' or 'Brussels: urbanism'. Book indexes additionally help to mobilise words. For example, the index of the *Dictionnaire de Bruxelles* may include only one direct link to *architek* and *Bruxellisation*; it includes numerous indirect links, through the terms façadism, order, progress, *chantier* (construction site), ruins, and *terrains vagues*.[90] An even more explicit material reminder could be found in the shape of a popular bar in the Marolles neighbourhood, only a few streets away from the Palace of Justice, which was called *Skieven Architek*.[91]

From the performances of *architek* and *Bruxellisation*, one can see that certain words can act. Whilst everyday, popular words may seem irrelevant to architectural debates, an examination of their performance nevertheless enriches the understanding of how a city is made and imagined. In the specific setting

6.16 The Palace of Justice as seen from the Marolles neighbourhood. Photograph by the author, 2015.

of Brussels, the words *architek* and *Bruxellisation* assist in nurturing a mind-set of scepticism vis-à-vis the making of the city. As 'performatives' such words can become powerful forces in consolidating as much as impairing mind-sets.

CELEBRATING THE UNSUNG HEROES OF ARCHITECTURE

In this chapter, I have introduced three types of agency that tend to get overlooked by architectural theory because they do not fit generic, abstract taxonomies.[92] I have argued that these actors should appear in accounts of architecture and the city; because the three actors discussed – a urinal, situated icons, and words – all matter in the *specific* context of Brussels.

The inclusion of non-human actors, such as buildings, policies, legislations, and urban plans and designs, in the making of cities is by now fairly accepted in academia. As discussed in the first chapter of this book, fields such as the Social Studies of Science and Technology, Actor Network Theory, and New Materialism suggest that cities should be researched through humans and non-humans; through the social and material; design and use. One can witness a growing enthusiasm for including humans and non-human on an equal par within architectural studies. However, it is not suffice to simply include non-humans next to humans; to include *more* actors. The challenge is in deciding *which* actors to include. The urinal, the Flagey and Rogier projects, and the words *architek* and *Bruxellisation* all demonstrated the presence of actors that are specific to a city and make a difference, but do not make it into discourse.

These actors show that it is not enough to take into account 'as many voices as there are actors' but to include those that matter most.[93] Actors matter when they make a difference; which is indicated by the traces they leave behind. The urinal, for example, left significant traces in the meeting reports and follow-up actions of a Neighbourhood Contract. These traces may go unnoticed, not because they are invisible, but because they do not fit a priori theoretical categorisations. It is therefore important to become receptive to actors that may, at first, appear as trivial or irrelevant. Because such actors are not identified through external lenses but, instead, emerge from the specific context of a city, they are likely to be dissimilar; that is a urinal, a building, and a word. By implication, comparisons between cities may be discouraged because certain actors only matter in specific contexts; their recognition thus invites a sensitivity to the specificity of cities.

The urinal in the Rue d'Aerschot, the Flagey and Rogier projects and *architek* equally matter in understanding Brussels' architectural culture. These actors create worlds around them and, consequently, they are not to be approached as mere resources but as actors and 'agents'.[94] Things-as-agents are situated as much as they, themselves, situate. Whilst architectural theory may not acknowledge such actors, they nevertheless take part in making-city. I call them architecture's 'unsung heroes' and, as a theorist, I can give voice to these unsung heroes. For me, the recognition of these actors is a critical act. Namely, it is a call for a theory and historiography beyond the discussion of seminal works.[95] This ultimately allows for a more complex, specific, and realistic understanding of cities; one step closer to how cities actually work.

NOTES

1. Other municipalities had similar initiatives but in less expressive settings. For example the House of Participation of the City of Brussels (*Maison de la Participation et de la Citoyenneté*, now called *Bruxelles Participation*), was, at the time of interviewing its coordinator, in January 2008, located within an existing office building; not visible from the outside or publicly accessible.
2. Maurizio Cohen, 'La Maison Citoyen, Schaerbeek', *A plus* 190 (October–November 2004): 68.
3. See Wah!, *La Maison de Citoyens*, 2004, filmed as part of the project LAB 1030 Schaerbeek, http://www.labproject.be/1030/32.html [last accessed 28/11/2014]. The architect first draws a table and chairs; then, on a separate beermat, the building.
4. Charles Jencks, *The Language of Post-Modern Architecture*, 5th rev. edition (London: Academy Editions, 1987), 21.
5. Ibid.
6. Bruno De Meulder, 'Molenbeek, or what became of the welfare state. La Rue, La Fonderie and La Poudrière, labs and credos in the city of industry and squalor', *Archis*, 4 (1996), 34.
7. Philippe Severyns and Frans Steenhoudt, 'Burgemeester bouwt. Architectuur aan de macht', *A Plus* 204 (2007): 72–78; Dominique Pieters, 'Volkskracht. Maison des Citoyens in Brussel (B) door Pierre Hebbelinck', *De Architect* 36 (January–February 2005): 72–75.
8. Cristel Despy, 'La Maison des Citoyens', in *LAB 1030 Schaerbeek, Livret d'Architecture contemporaine à Bruxelles*, by La Société des Architectes Diplômés de Bruxelles and WAH! Studio (Brussels: 180° éditions, 2011), 77.
9. Asylum seekers had been forced to sleep rough after the authorities had removed them from the nearby North Railway Station where they had camped due to a lack of shelter capacity.
10. See the first chapter of this book.
11. Bruno Latour, *Re-assembling the Social: An Introduction to Actor-Network-Theory* (Oxford: Oxford University Press, 2005) 71.
12. Isabelle Stengers 'Reclaiming Animism' *E-flux Journal* 36 (July 2012): 2; quoting Eduardo Viveiros de Castro.
13. Rosi Braidotti, 'Embodiment, Sexual Difference, and the Nomadic Subject', *Hypathia*, 8, no. 1 (Winter 1993): 1–13, 2; quoting François Châtelet, *La philosophie des Professeurs*, 1973 and also in reference to Michel Foucault's *Surveiller et Punir* (1977).
14. Donna Haraway, 'Situated Knowledges: The Science Question in Feminism and the Privilege of Partial Perspective', in *Simians, Cyborgs and Women: The Reinvention of Nature* (New York: Routledge, 1991), 199.

15 Translated from French, interview with Mirabelle da Palma, coordinator of neighbourhood spaces in Schaerbeek; film-report by Anaïs Letiexhe and Jean-Christophe Pessese; http://www.telebruxelles.net/portail/info/schaerbeek/23230-la-rue-daerschot-en-mutation – [last accessed July 17, 2013].

16 Ibid. The sign references René Magritte's *La Trahison des Images* (1928–1929) which pictures a pipe and the statement 'ceci n'est pas une pipe' (this is not a pipe).

17 Two urinals were realised in the Rue d'Aerschot, at the corners with the Rue Rogier and Avenue de la Reine, respectively.

18 Anno 2015, the organisation of NCs has changed significantly. They include only three *volets* (instead of five, as was the case at the time of analysis) and the four years are complemented with an additional year before the start of the NC, to develop the programme, and two years after the NC, for completing the works.

19 The author would like to thank those individuals and organisations who have generously shared their knowledge of the area and granted access to valuable documentation, including the meeting reports relating to NC Aerschot-Progrès and neighbourhood activities. These include, amongst others, Françoise Deville (RenovaS, a non-profit organisation or *association sans but lucrative* asbl to whom the Municipality of Schaerbeek delegates the management of neighbourhood contracts), Géraldine Bruyneel (SamenlevingsopbouwBrussel vzw), Grégoire Kirreef (Projet Rousseau), and Bruno Van Loo (Brabant Bouge project).

20 Research by geographers Tim Cassiers, Christian Kesteloot, and Henk Meert was particularly useful for the understanding of the Quartier Brabant; its socio-economic condition, ethnic entrepreneurship and transnational functioning. See for example the final report for the *Overlegplatform Brabantwijk* (Koning Boudewijnstichting), by Cassiers, Kesteloot, and Meert (2000), *Enkele ideeën voor de toekomst van de Brabantstraat, op basis van bezoeken aan Parijs, Londen en Amsterdam*.

21 Key studies of the area include: Evert Lagrou and Marc Dubois, *Stationssteden: Eurostation, 10 jaar onderweg* (Brussels: Eurostation NV, 2003); Stefan De Corte, *Wijkfiche 1: Brabantwijk* and *Wijkfiche 7: Noordwijk* (Brussels: Cosmopolis Geografisch Instituut VUB, 2001); De Corte and W. De Lannoy, *Brusselse Woontypologie – Inventaris September 1999* (Brussels: Geografisch Instituut VUB, 1999); C. Naegels, *Onderzoek naar de leefbaarheid in de Transitwijk Schaerbeek* (Brussels: Vzw Sint-Lukaswerkgemeenschap, 1994); Lagrou and Geert Willemyns, *Brabantwijk: leven in de schaduw van de grootstad* (Brussels: Vzw Sint-Lukaswerkgemeenschap, 1995); Kesteloot, *Valorisatie Brabantwijk* (Brussels: Koning Boudewijn Stichting, 1995).

22 Meeting Minutes of CLDI of January 19, 2004, 5.

23 Ibid.

24 Meeting Minutes of CLDI of October 21, 2004, 4.

25 Designed by Frédéric Huwaert /3A Architectes. See Maurizio Cohen, *Brussels On Our Doorstep: Architecture in Neighbourhood Contracts* (Brussels: Brussels Capital Region, 2007), 76.

26 Meeting Minutes of CLDI of April 21, 2004, 3.

27 Meeting Minutes of CLDI of December 10, 2002, 3. Public space interventions also included the plantation of trees and the furnishing (greenery, lights) of the railway-embankment that runs alongside the Rue d'Aerschot; carried out by the National Railway Company of Belgium (NMBS/SNCB).

28 Translated from French, Meeting Minutes of CLDI of March 26, 2002, 3.

29   The Meeting Minutes of CLDI of January 23, 2003 report on the *Avis de la Commission de Concertation*, held on January 10, 2003; containing suggestions based on a public survey held between November 24, and December 23, 2002.

30   Meeting Minutes of CLDI of December 10, 2002, 4.

31   *Avis de la Commission de Concertation*

32   From the map 'Fontaines d'eau potable et toilettes gratuites de Bruxelles', 2014 (7th edition), published since 2008 by Infirmiers de Rue asbl / vzw straatverplegers, it is clear that, ever since, public toilets, more so than urinals have, become more common in Brussels (www.straatverplegers.org). These public toilets are managed by the Institut Bruxellois pour la Gestion de l'Environnement IBGE/BIM. The cleaning of the urinals installed from 2013 onwards in the Rue d'Aerschot, as a replacement of the earlier brick constructions, is outsourced to a private company.

33   Meeting minutes CLDI of January 27, 2005, 6; translated from French; emphasis in original, in bold.

34   Meeting Minutes CLDI of February 19 2004, 6; and CLDI of January 27, 2005, 6.

35   CLDI of January 27, 2005, 6; the Service Public Fédéral de la Mobilité et des Transports (SPFMT) had accepted the works provisionally on December 22, 2004, and granted a final extension for March 2005.

36   Meeting Minutes CLDI of March 24, 2005, 6; CLDI of May 3, 2005, 5; CLDI of September 22, 2005, 5; CLDI of November 29, 2005.

37   Meeting Minutes CLDI of September 22, 2005, 5.

38   There was a panic-stricken tenor to the Meeting Minutes of CLDI of January 27, 2005, 6.

39   Decision taken in the CLDI November 29, 2005. This had already been suggested two year earlier, in the *Avis de la Commission de Concertation*.

40   Interview by the author with Géraldine Bruyneel, SamenlevingsopbouwBrussel vzw, November 27, 2009. Each urinal is used more than 5,000 times per week, see the work document by Géraldine Bruyneel, *Plan Hygiénique 2010 rue d'Aerschot, Schaarbeek*, November 2009, 8.

41   Bruyneel, *Plan Hygiénique*, 8.

42   Ibid.

43   Signs had already been suggested during the NC; see meeting minutes CLDI of February 19, 2004, 6; CLDI of November 29, 2005, 6-7; and CLDI of February 28, 2006, 7.

44   Karin Van Zele, Hugo Henneman, Isabelle Doucet, Géraldine Bruyneel, *Gezondheidsportret Brabantwijk beweegt!* (Brussels: Samenlevingsopbouw, 2008). It was based on surveys with local professionals and inhabitants, carried out between September 2006 and September 2008.

45   Bruyneel, *Plan Hygiénique*, 10–11.

46   Participating organisations include SamenlevingsopbouwBrussel vzw, Pléiade Nord and Collectif Brabant Bouge. The actions were supported by the municipality of Schaarbeek and received considerable press coverage.

47   The urinals were installed from late 2015 onwards. Their maintenance is outsourced to a private company, which guarantees cleaning twice a day and an additional, more thorough cleaning, every month.

48 See, for example, the special issue 'Architecture and Dirt', *The Journal of Architecture* 12, 4 (2007); Jeremy Till's work on impurity and messiness, in *Architecture Depends* (Cambridge, MA: The MIT Press, 2009); and Ananya Roy's and Arjun Appadurai's work on urban informality; Ananya Roy, 'Urban informality. Towards an Epistemology of Planning', *Journal of the American Planning Association* 71, 2 (2005): 147–158; Arjun Appadurai, 'Deep Democracy: Urban governmentality and the horizon of politics', *Environment and Urbanization* 13, 2 (2001): 23–43.

49 A discussion on the difference between icon and landmark falls outside the scope of this book. I use the term iconic in reference to recent debates on the iconic in architecture, as used both in architectural discourse (for example Charles Jencks, *Iconic Building*, Rizzoli, 2005) and in the context of urban regeneration: Maria Kaika, 'Architecture and crisis: re-inventing the icon, re-imag(in)ing London and re-branding the City', *Transactions of the Institute of British Geographers* 35, issue 4 (October 2010): 453–474; and Frank Moulaert, Arantxa Rodriguez and Erik Swyngedouw, eds, *The Globalised City – Economic Restructuring and Social Polarisation in European Cities* (New York: Oxford University Press, 2003).

50 I have chosen the Flagey and Rogier projects over other projects that were influential in architectural culture, such as The Berlage's *A Vision for Brussels* project and Rem Koolhaas's *Image of Europe* exhibition (2004). This choice was informed by the consistent appearance of these projects in architectural discourse; and as concrete architectural projects rather than exhibitions or events. For a discussion of *A Vision for Brussels*, see Isabelle Doucet, 'A Vision for Brussels: Fuel to the Urban Debate or, at Last, an End to the Brussels Trauma?', *Footprint Journal* 1 (Autumn 2007): 97–105; and 'Learning from Brussels. An Irreductive Approach to Architectural and Urban Problématiques?' *Belgeo* 1–2 (2011): 29–39.

51 Bart Lootsma, *SuperDutch: New Architecture in the Netherlands* (Princeton, NJ: Princeton Architectural Press, 2001).

52 Brussels' Art Nouveau was represented primarily by its protagonists Henri Van de Velde, Paul Hankar, and Victor Horta, and was formative in the creation of a European avant-garde. See Franco Borsi and Hans Wieser, *Bruxelles: Capitale de l'Art Nouveau* (Brussels: Vokaer, 1971); Mil De Kooning, ed., *Horta and After: 25 Masters of Modern Architecture in Belgium* (Ghent: University of Ghent, 1999); Dario Matteoni, 'Il Belgio di fronte al Movimento Moderno', in *Rassegna* 34 (1988): 24–34; Jacques Aron, *La Cambre et l'Architecture: Un regard sur le Bauhaus Belge* (Liège: Mardaga, 1982). On the 1958 World Fair, see: Rika Devos and Mil De Kooning, eds, *The Architecture of Expo 58* (Brussels: Dexia/Mercatorfonds, 2006).

53 Yvan Mayeur had been inspired by Kapoor's Cloud Gate at AT&T Plaza, Millennium Park, Chicago. See Mathieu Colleyn, 'Yvan Mayeur: "Un Times Square au centre de Bruxelles"', *La Libre Belgique*, December 13, 2013, http://www.lalibre.be/actu/belgique/yvan-mayeur-un-times-square-au-centre-de-bruxelles-52aa903f3570105ef7d2ee42 [last accessed January 7, 2014]; and Marjan Justaert, 'Yvan Mayeur: bijna burgemeester van Brussel. Hopelijk durft zijn entourage hem tegen te spreken', *De Standaard*, December 7, 2013.

54 Justaert, 'Yvan Mayeur: bijna burgemeester van Brussel'.

55 'Twintig slogans voor de hoofdstad', *Het Nieuwsblad*, October 20, 2007, http://www.nieuwsblad.be/article/detail.aspx?articleid=S31IVKOA [last accessed August 7, 2013].

56 Maurice Culot, René Schoonbrodt, IEB, AAM, *Les Espaces Publics Bruxellois: Analyse et Projets* (Brussels: Fondation Roi Baudouin, 1981). Marie Demanet, Jean-Pierre Majot (eds) *Handboek van de Brusselse Openbare Ruimten* (Brussels: Iris, 1995; published in French as *Manuel des Espaces Public Bruxellois*). See also the second chapter in this book.

57 See Cohen, *Brussels On Our Doorstep*, 36; Benoît Moritz, 'Designing and developing public spaces in Brussels', *Brussels Studies*, 50 (June 21, 2011).

58 Joeri De Bruyn, 'Eindelijk een wedstrijd voor de openbare ruimte in Brussel', *A Plus* 196 (October/November 2005): 36.

59 Quoted in Centre de recherche architecturale de l'ISAC – La Cambre, 'L'architecture comme medium de la participation citoyenne. Bilans et perspectives de la Platforme Flagey', in *De la participation urbaine: La Place Flagey, Les Cahiers de La Cambre Architecture*, no. 3, ed. Jean-Didier Bergilez, Taha Bouhassoun, Geoffrey Grulois, Irène Lund (Brussels: La Lettre Volée, 2005), 63; translated from French.

60 About one third were international entries; but proposals by local inhabitants and artists were also received. The competition was coordinated by architecture school La Cambre (Centre de Recherche Architecturale de La Cambre CRACi. See Judith e Maire and Dominique Nalpas, 'Kiezen voor Inspraak', in *Brussel over 20 jaar*, ed. Pierre Dejemeppe, Céline Mouchart, Caroline Piersotte, Frédéric Raynaud, and Dirk Van de Putte (Brussels, ATO, 2009), 128–130.

61 Confirmed by the publication of a manual reporting on the project's activist, participatory and design history: Bergilez et al., *De la participation urbaine: La Place Flagey*.

62 That is, the public space policy of the Minister of Mobility and Public Works Pascal Smet.

63 Véronique Boone and Lars Kwakkenbos, 'Inrichting Rogierplein-Brussel: Strippen of oversteken', *A Plus* (October/November 2006): 29. This metropolitan character was also explicitly present in the runner-up project by SUM.

64 Véronique Boone and Lars Kwakkenbos, 'Square and boulevard strip Brussels', *A10* 12 (2006): 15.

65 At the time of writing, the project was still in construction. This analysis draws also from an interview by the author with Sara Noel Costa de Araujo, from XDGA, in Brussels on December 20, 2007; and conversations with Xaveer De Geyter as part of the preparations for a joint presentation in the context of the *État des Lieux* lecture series, Brussels, September 2014.

66 Xaveer De Geyter, lecture *État des Lieux*, Brussels, September 13, 2014. As part of the Hoogpoort Team (together with Stephane Beel, Arjan Karsenberg, and Willem-Jan Neutelings), De Geyter was responsible for one of the more metropolitan statements within the Bonduelle competition for the Carrefour de l'Europe in 1983 (see also the second chapter in this book). Les Halles refers to the competition entry by OMA, in collaboration with XDGA, for New Forum Les Halles in Paris. In the European quarter in Brussels, The Schuman project was the winning entry for a competition in 2010.

67 Kitchen Tower was commissioned 2000 and completed 2011; it received the 2013 Bigmat Award and the Belgian Architecture prize for the category 'non-residential-public'. Recent recognition can also be evidenced by a retrospective XDGA_160_EXPO. Xaveer De Geyter Architects, Centre International pour la Ville, l'Architecture et le Paysage, November 8, 2013–January 26, 2014.

68 Xaveer De Geyter in Fanny Bouvry, 'Xaveer De Geyter, La ville comme muse', *Le Vif Weekend*, November 19, 2013, http://weekend.levif.be [last accessed 24/11/2014], translated from French. The Rogier project in fact combines two types of XDGA projects: polemical projects and concrete proposals (interview by the author with Sara Noel Costa de Araujo, XDGA, on December 20, 2007).

69 The supra-regional Beliris is a collaboration between the Belgian federal state and the Brussels region, for realising projects that promote Brussels as the capital of Belgium and Europe. I will not focus here on the public debates around this project, for example the citizens meetings organised by Bral and Periferia and the official advisory commission (see ARAU, 'Place Rogier. Commentaires de l'ARAU sur l'avis de la commission de concertation du 13 Juillet 2007. Communiqué de Presse de l'ARAU du mardi 9 Octobre 2007', 1–12).

70 Interview Costa de Araujo.

71 Interview Costa de Araujo. De Geyter's experience with working with models at OMA, is here worth noting; De Geyter in Fanny Bouvry, 'Xaveer De Geyter, La ville comme muse'.

72 De Geyter, lecture *État des Lieux*.

73 Ibid.

74 Conversation with De Geyter.

75 Maria Kaika also referred to 'autistic architecture' to describe the lack of engagement of some iconic architectures with the surrounding city ('Autistic Architecture: The Fall of the Icon and the Rise of the Serial Object of Architecture', *Environment and Planning D: Society and Space* 29, 6 [2011]: 968–992).

76 Jean D'Osta and Louis Quiévreux, *Dictionnaire du dialecte bruxellois*, fifth rev. edition (Brussels: Éditions Libro-Sciences, 1985), 20 [transl. from French]; it makes reference to an alleged 1883 lawsuit, reported in the *Journal des Tribunaux*, whereby it was used as part of the defense of a young woman of the Marolles neighbourhood.

77 Approved in 1967; approximately 11,000 inhabitants were affected. See N. Brasseur, J. Lievens, and A. Martens, *De grote stad: een geplande chaos? De noordwijk van krot tot Manhattan* (Leuven: Davidsfonds, 1975); and A. Martens and M. Vanden Eede, *De Noordwijk: slopen en wonen* (Berchem: EPO, 1994).

78 J.L. Austin (1990 [1962]), *How to Do Things With Words* (Oxford and New York: Oxford University Press), 6–7; based on a lecture in 1955.

79 Nigel Thrift, *Non-representational Theory: Space, Politics, Affect* (London: Routledge, 2008).

80 A fuller discussion of *architek* and *Bruxellisation* as 'performatives' can be found in Isabelle Doucet, 'Making a City with Words. Understanding Brussels through its Urban Heroes and Villains', *City, Culture and Society* 3, 2 (2012): 105–116.

81 Thibaut Vandorselaer and Jean Van Hamme, *Bruxelles dans la BD: Itinéraire découverte* (Louvain-La-Neuve: Versant Sud, 2004), 4–5; Erik De Kuyper, *Een passie voor Brussel* (Amsterdam: Babylon-De Geus, 1995), 24–30 [transl. from Dutch]; Geert Van Istendael, *Arm Brussel* (Antwerpen/Amsterdam: Uitgeverij Atlas, 2002 [1992]), 171 [transl. from Dutch].

82 D. De Bruycker, in Labor, Maison de la Francité, and Brussels 2000, eds, *Dictionnaire de Bruxelles: définition d'une ville par les gens qui y vivent, y passent, ou y travaillent* (Brussels: Labor and Maison de la Francité, 2000), 181; Isabel Wets and Vincent Verhaeren, eds, *Bruxelles, ma belle?* (Brussels: Editons Croiseregard, 2006); A. Duchesne in Labor et al., *Dictionnaire de Bruxelles*, 59 [all quotes transl. from French].

83 Osta and Quiévreux, *Dictionnaire du dialecte bruxellois*, 20.

84 Ibid., and Dirk De Moor et al., eds, *Brusselse Toeren: 10 straffe wandelingen, een fietstocht en een metrotoer* (Tielt: Lannoo, 2006), 62.

85 De Moor et al., *Brusselse Toeren*, 80; Marcel De Schrijver, *Et Brussels Brusselt nog in Brussel!* (Brussels: De Speegelmanne, 2003), 51.

86 Curtio, *Zievereer, Krott & Cie, Architek! Baedeker physiologie Bruxelloise* (Brussels: Éditions libro-science, croquis d'Amedée Lynen et Gustave Flasschoen, 1975), 6.

87 Ibid.; Georges Garnir, *Baedeker de Physiologie Bruxelloise à l'usage des étrangers* (Brussels: Éditions Labor, Bruxelles-Capitale Series, 1994 [1910]); Cypriaan Verhavert, *Brusselsche Typen: Cahiers van het Brussels dialect*, 1, Academie van het Brussels, 1996 [1923], 24.

88 Geert Van Istendael, *Arm Brussel* (Antwerpen/Amsterdam: Uitgeverij Atlas, 2002 [1992]); François Schuiten and Benoît Peeters, *Brüsel – Les Cités obscures* (Tournai: Casterman, 1992).

89 The series has existed since the early 1980s. The first album, *Les Murailles de Samaris*, appeared in 1982; *Brüsel* in 1992 (www.urbicande.be).

90 Labor et al., *Dictionnaire de Bruxelles*.

91 During a visit to Brussels in January 2015, it turned out the bar had closed.

92 They do not fit the taxon, as is the case with the 'inappropriate/d other', theorised by Trinh Minh-ha and used by Donna Haraway: 'To be inappropriate/d is not to fit the *taxon*.' Donna Haraway, 'The Promises of Monsters: A Regenerative Politics of Inappropriate/d Others', in *Cultural Studies*, ed. Lawrence Grossberg, Cary Nelson, Paula Treichler (New York and Abingdon: Routledge, 1992), 295–337, 299.

93 Michel Callon, 'Techno-economic Networks and Irreversibility', in *A Sociology of Monsters: Essays on Power, Technology and Dominance*, ed. John Law (London: Routledge, 1991), 152; taken from Thomas Bender, 'Postscript: Reassembling the City: Networks and Urban Imaginaries', in *Urban Assemblages: How Actor-Network-Theory Changes Urban Studies*, ed. Ignacio Farias and Thomas Bender (London: Routledge, 2010), 319.

94 Haraway, 'Situated knowledges', 198.

95 Moves towards this historiography can be seen in Adrian Forty, *Concrete and Culture: A Material History* (London: Reaktion Books, 2012); and Kenny Cupers, ed., *Use Matters: An Alternative History of Architecture* (London: Routledge, 2013).

7

Conclusions: Towards a Cautious Pragmatism

> 'Learning from' requires encountering, and encountering may indeed imply comparison, but there is no comparison if the encountered others are defined as unable to understand the point of the comparison. We are returned here to the Latin etymology of 'comparison': compar designates those who regard each other as equals – that is, as able to agree, which means also able to disagree, object, negotiate, and contest.[1]

This book emerges from my encounter with a city; Brussels. Through this encounter I have learned something about the workings of cities. But this learning is not innocent. The nature of the encounter is such that one party, most likely the theorist, tends to mobilise the other, Brussels, in ways that reduce it to a mere case in order to test predefined ideas and concepts. I have avoided such a reductive relationship by providing an embodied account informed by the acceptance that the city is not mute; that it may disagree and resist the claims made by theory. I have therefore put up with Brussels' temper; listened attentively to its murmurs; and allowed it to affect my thinking. This confrontation with Brussels challenged my own categories of thought.[2] It allowed me to question theoretical taxonomies, and thus to disrupt architectural theory's dominant 'partition of the sensible'.[3] Brussels invited me to expand the type of actors that is normally allowed to participate in the debates on architecture. Not only have I given voice to unusual actors, such as a urinal or a derogative word like *architek*, I have also added to the visibility of actors that are side-lined by architectural discourse's moral conventions on what is 'good' architecture, such as counter-projects. I have also highlighted actors, such as Recyclart, which operate from-within albeit with a surprisingly disruptive force. Notwithstanding their diversity, these actors equally matter to Brussels.

The central question of this book was how to imagine a critical positioning in architecture that operates through practice. In response, I analysed concrete instances of critical engagement as found in the specific context of Brussels after 1968. Moreover, to gain access to the *specificity* of Brussels' architecture and urban production, I felt challenged to develop novel ways for recollecting the Brussels saga. I did so by bringing an account of Brussels' architectural production as a 'situated practice'; held together by a continuously negotiated assemblage of actors. These actors were as many as they were diverse: architects and urban policy makers as much as activists, social workers, and citizens; architectural movements, urban renewal programmes, theories, plans, projects, and ideologies, works of construction, but also demolitions, urban traumas; mundane constructions and everyday actors, such as a urinal and popular insults. In order to give voice to such variety of actors, I have disentangled the Brussels assemblage through an embodied encounter rather than through mere descriptive accounts. This required slowing down, hesitation, being sensitive to disruptions and surprises, and the willingness 'to live with indigestible intellectual and political heritages', including one's intellectual heritage or a city's past.[4]

The embodied account pursued in this book ultimately challenges a historiography of Brussels in terms of determinate breakages and turns. For example, the study of counter-projects and *Architek* showed that actors travel far beyond their own space-time frames. A city's transformations are, rather than breakages, 'thick continuities'.[5] This re-thinking of the way we recollect the past also opens the possibility for different *future* narratives. Different ways of understanding the past induce also different ways of imagining and thinking the city. As Rosi Braidotti argues, the theoretical effort is a 'quest for alternative figurations'.[6] For example, locating criticality in oppositional activism as much as from-within, as was the case with the interstitial activism of Recyclart (Chapter 3), suggests alternative routes for future urban action. Likewise, the revisiting of counter-projects (Chapter 2) showed how an 'aesthetic turn' can coincide with radicalisation; opening novel ways for imagining the co-existence of politics and aesthetics in radical architecture. In other words, criticality occurred in familiar territory but it also emerged from less explored loci. It proved detached, oppositional, and autonomous, but also situated in the real; immersed in its messiness. As a disruptive force, criticality emerged from the margins as much as the centre. At once stubborn, cunning, lenient, radical, and gentle, criticality turned out to resist categorisation.

By re-engaging with understudied or uncomfortable traditions, novel reinterpretations of a city's heritage emerge. These are not to be confused with a blueprint or set-in-stone solution. They rather 'prompt us to consider this world with other questions', and thereby unleash the possible.[7] I recognised such a productive act of reclaiming in the *Jonction* event, discussed in Chapter 3 of this book. As a situated and digestive act, *Jonction* demonstrates the importance of slowing down in order to identify emergent opportunities, and of the preparedness to 'change gears' in order to grasp these opportunities.[8]

This book offered a series of empirical–conceptual explorations into critical practices in Brussels. These included counter-projects, citizen participation, urban activism, situated architectures, but also mundane actors such as words or urinals that equally make-city. Through the study of such actors, a slightly different account of Brussels emerged. In addition, these explorations were informative for understanding how criticality is practised, how it 'works'.

From these explorations, one learns to envisage critical engagement beyond conventional distinctions, such as between radical opposition and appeasement; autonomy and compliance. Instead, oppositional activism and critical actions from-within turned out to *share* several challenges: to reconcile politics with aesthetics;

to maintain political integrity whilst seeking implementation; and to choose the appropriate tools for critical action. For example, I learned that, despite their explicit autonomous–oppositional critique, the Brussels counter-projects also operated from-within; and not just because of their involvement in on-the-ground political activism. Their most autonomous tools, the drawings-manifestos, demonstrated a conscious choice to attack the architectural establishment from-within *via* the Brussels population. Through the use of a popular graphic language, subtle referencing to real individuals, and the deployment of *zwanze*, a typically Brussels type of mockery, these drawings were deeply entangled with everyday Brussels. Reversely, the interstitial activism of Recyclart taught us that radical action does not need to be oppositional; but can occur from-within and, to a certain degree, may even rely on this within-ness.[9]

It is, however, not enough to simply acknowledge the affinities between oppositional activism and critical actions from-within. The explorations in this book invite to become equally receptive to countercultural, oppositional practices, everyday activities, and the disruptive forces that nag us from-within normalised space. It invites to become receptive to the variety of forces that make up a city, that are *specific* to a city. It thus forces us to radically expand the actors that are normally allowed to participate in the debates on architecture and the city; no matter how mundane, bizarre or unsettling these forces may be. The actions of the fear of the new, of urban mind-sets, perimeters, language, insults, and urinals, call for widening the scope of what we call architecture.

LEARNING FROM BRUSSELS' CAUTIOUS PRAGMATISM

> *Brussels does not have a great reputation regarding contemporary architecture and urbanism. The city lacks a clear vision and the projects that do get realised are often of mediocre quality. And yet, things are noticeably changing.*[10]

Brussels is currently undergoing a rediscovered optimism regarding contemporary architecture; encouraged by the sensitising work by the Brussels Master Architect, urban think-tanks, activities to promote contemporary architecture, and new ambitious projects.[11] However, such optimism bears the risk of being reduced to a mere obsession with iconic architecture, also called *architecture phare*, that would be disconnected from the Brussels reality. I believe that my analysis of architectural emancipation in Brussels is instructive for dealing with such transitional phases. Because this emancipation was piecemeal, fragmented, and, despite its ambition, still rooted in the Brussels socio-urban situation, I identify it with a 'cautious pragmatism'. A result of juggling French and Flemish culture, traditionalism and progression, and global ambition and local reality, this cautious pragmatism is a product typical of Brussels. It engages with generic ambitions as well as situated conditions, it thrives on optimism as much as scepticism. Cautious pragmatism in Brussels is a form of positive enthusiasm, but one that is tempered by keeping close to the everyday reality.

It is significant that in 2013 the elected Mayor of the City of Brussels expressed his commitment towards ambitious urban renewal projects and to 'depart from a logic of "a little bit of support here and then a little bit here and there"'.[12] Whereas such ambition is commendable, this book also supports 'a little bit here and there' because a slow, step-by-step experimentation is what makes Brussels *specific* but also because cities in general could benefit from a slowing down. This means moving to a situated modus operandi as opposed to, for example, imported 'best practices'. Such a situated approach is not to be confused with conservatism, localism, or contextualism. Instead it invites to carefully listen to the cities we study; to their laughter, their struggles, their resistances, and their peculiarities.

This book portrayed Brussels through a close reading of critical practices. Though describing Brussels anew may not offer a 'solution' for the city, I argue that it nevertheless allows for different possible futures to emerge. Such futures are, however, only ever possible; they cannot be guaranteed. The uncertainty triggered by 'mere' descriptions was theorised by Isabelle Stengers when quoting Alfred North Whitehead on the role of thinking: 'The task of the university is the creation of the future, so far as rational thought, and civilized modes of appreciation, can affect the issue. The future is big with every possibility of achievement and of tragedy.'[13] The equal possibility of achievement or tragedy is a considerable concern for the design professions. Scholarly research seems, by comparison, somewhat more sheltered from the risks that come with such contingency. As Stengers argues:

> I understand quite well that when they are called out to a fire, fire-fighters hurry without slowing down and wondering about their own role and subjective stance. But the point is that nobody really calls us [theorists] out.[14]

Whilst theory may not be called out to deal with emergencies, it cannot shy away from responsibilities for the world. The question is not whether or not theory bears such responsibilities; but whether slowing down is justified when confronted with social injustices that require immediate action. How can slowing down be of assistance in a world of acceleration?

With this book I have explored such options for architectural theory. I have tested a different kind of theory practice for architecture that was inspired by Brussels as much as by pragmatist thinkers including Stengers, Braidotti, Haraway, and Latour. These companions have helped me to approach theory as 'category work' in the sense that it reclaims, questions, and digests taken-for-granted ideas and concepts for thinking-city.[15] I approached theory as an act of describing the intricacies of the real and, by doing so, as a quest for alternative configurations and compositions. Theoretical reasoning is, as such, *practised*.[16] Theory is subject to appropriation and can therefore empower but also harm.[17] In other words, theorists may adopt a privileged position that allows them to slow down reasoning and to formulate ideas even when those ideas are not urgently required; this privilege is also a duty. When listening to the practices of making-city and allowing the city to talk back, theory can encourage other questions to be asked and, perhaps, allow for other futures to emerge.[18]

What would architectural theory look like if it no longer chains the real to its concepts and resists strait-jacketing it into its categories? What would architectural theory look like if it welcomed being inspired as much as annoyed by the practices it observes, if it took the city's temperament more seriously? And what possibilities could such a way of approaching theory create for criticality and for Brussels? This book has begun to answer such questions by means of crafting an architectural theory that is affected by the real in order to better understand it. It is an architectural theory that aims to be radically inclusive, situated, and fuelled by a deep care for the real. My hopes for such theory-practice is that, precisely by rejecting the authority to declare what is good or bad architecture, good or bad cities, it also allows other futures to become possible.

NOTES

1 Isabelle Stengers, 'Comparison as a Matter of Concern', *Common Knowledge* 17, no. 1 (2011): 48–63, 63.

2 Isabelle Stengers shows this beautifully in 'Diderot's Egg. Divorcing Materialism from Eliminativism', *Radical Philosophy* 144 (2007): 7–16.

3 Jacques Rancière, *The Politics of Aesthetics: The Distribution of the Sensible* (London: Continuum, 2004), 12–13; quoted in Jane Bennett, *Vibrant Matter: A Political Ecology of Things* (Durham, NC and London: Duke University Press, 2010), 105. For Bennett, following onto Rancière, the partition of the sensible renders some visible as political actors whilst other remain 'below the threshold of note' (105). I take the notion of taxonomy from Donna Haraway who suggests that one needs 'to figure out how to think of the world through connections and encounters that re-do you, not through taxonomies'. See Nicholas Gane, 'When We Have Never Been Human, What is to be Done? Interview with Donna Haraway', *Theory Culture & Society* 23, nos. 7–8 (2006): 135–158, 145.

4 Haraway in Gane, 'When We Have Never Been Human, What is to be Done?', 139.

5 Ibid., 155.

6 Rosi Braidotti, *Metamorphoses: Towards a Materialist Theory of Becoming* (Cambridge: Polity, 2002), 3.

7 Isabelle Stengers, 'The Cosmopolitical Proposal', in *Making Things Public: Atmospheres of Democracy*, ed. Bruno Latour and Peter Weibel (Cambridge, MA: ZKM and The MIT Press, 2005), 994–1003, 998.

8 Simone refers to the 'politics of anticipation', that is: being prepared to change gears is a necessity for certain communities, in order to create opportunity for themselves. See AbdouMaliq Simone, '2009 Urban Geography Plenary Lecture – On Intersections, Anticipations, and Provisional Publics: Remaking District Life in Jakarta', *Urban Geography* 31, no. 3 (2010): 285–308, 294; See also Arjun Appadurai's reference to a 'politics of patience', in 'Deep Democracy: Urban Governmentality and the Horizon of Politics', *Environment and Urbanization* 13, no. 2 (2002): 23–43, 28.

9 This is particularly evident in Recyclart's interstitial activism discussed in Chapter 3. The notion of criticality from-within rather than in opposition also resonates with Mathias Heyden's observations of the K77 Berlin squatter occupation, an example of radical rather than oppositional architecture. Self-managed and self-built, the K77 Berlin

squatter project also benefited from a particular type of available funding, without which it would not have been possible. See Mathias Heyden, 'Evolving Participatory Design: A Report from Berlin, Reaching Beyond', *Field Journal*, no.1 (2008): 31–46, 36. Colin McFarlane also suggests studying oppositional, activist forms of learning as much as the more established ones involving officials, see *Learning the City: Knowledge and Translocal Assemblage* (Chichester: Wiley-Blackwell, 2011), 1.

10   Elien Haentjes, 'Week van de architectuur: Brussels is toekomst, toekomst, toekomst', *Brussel Deze Week*, October 10, 2013. The article contains an interview with Brussels-based architect Nicolas Firket.

11   See, amongst others, the activities of the Agency for Territorial Development (ADT/ATO), ProjetKanal, the Brussels Studies Institute, BOZAR, the Week of Architecture, the CIVA, and new ambitious projects/plans for the Place Rogier (see Chapter 6) and the Citroën site.

12   Mathieu Colleyn, 'Yvan Mayeur: "Un Times Square au Centre de Bruxelles"', *La Libre Belgique*, December 13, 2013, accessed January 7, 2014, http://www.lalibre.be/actu/belgique/yvan-mayeur-un-times-square-au-centre-de-bruxelles-52aa903f3570105ef7d2ee42; translated from French.

13   Isabelle Stengers, '"Another science is possible!" A plea for Slow Science', Inaugural lecture as Chair Willy Calewaert 2011–2012, Vrije Universiteit Brussel, December 13, 2011, 5, accessed June 13, 2014, http://threerottenpotatoes.files.wordpress.com/2011/06/stengers2011_pleaslowscience.pdf.

14   Isabelle Stengers, 'Experimenting with Refrains: Subjectivity and the Challenge of Escaping Modern Dualism', *Subjectivity* 22 (2008): 38–59, 57.

15   Haraway, 'When We Have Never Been Human', 143.

16   Stengers refers to a 'theorizing craft' in 'Experimenting with Refrains', 53.

17   Stengers refers to how Donna Haraway has not been caring for the cyborg carefully enough by considering it being unleashed into the world, which has resulted in it being used as an academic weapon. See Stengers 'Experimenting with Refrains', 51–52.

18   Stengers agrees with the Marxist belief that at stake is to change the world, not to understand it, but she adds that this should also include allowing for the possibility of the world to change our thinking. See 'Experimenting with Refrains', 57.

Appendix: Interviews and Exchanges with Brussels Stakeholders

INTERVIEWS WITH ARCHITECTS, URBAN PLANNERS, OFFICIALS, AND CIVIL SOCIETY

Jens Aerts (Ministerial Cabinet Pascal Smet)
Françoise Allaert and Stijn Thomas (Maison de la Rénovation Urbaine St. Josse)
Olivier Bastin and Nadine Chanvillarc (L'Escaut, Brussels)
Dag Boutsen (Atelier d'Urbanisme d'Architecture et D'Informatique AUAI, Brussels)
Maurice Culot (AAM, Brussels)
Livia De Bethune (SUM, Brussels)
Thomas De Béthune (Ministerial Cabinet Charles Picqué)
Thierry Decuypere (V-Plus, Brussels)
Xaveer De Geyter (Xaveer De Geyter Architects, Brussels)
Aglaee Degros (Artgineering, Rotterdam)
Françoise Deville (RenovaS)
Rients Dijkstra (Maxwan, Rotterdam)
Cédric Erken (Coordination Contrats de Quartier et Rénovation Urbaine, Ville de Bruxelles)
Eloisa Astudillo Fernandez (L'Escaut, Brussels)
Marc Godts (FLC, Brussels)
Michel Jaspers (Jaspers-Eyers Architects, Brussels)
Laurence Jenard (Recyclart)
Christian Lasserre (CLI, Brussels)
Constantin Lazarou (Maison de la Participation, Ville de Bruxelles)
Gilles Ledent (ARIES, Brussels)
André Longin (Coordination Contrats de Quartier et Rénovation Urbaine, Ville de Bruxelles)
Steve McAdam (Fluid Office, London)
Benoit Moritz (MSA, Brussels)
Marianne Mueller (Mueller-Kneer Architects, London)

Sara Noel Costa de Araujo (Xaveer De Geyter Architects, Brussels)
Mati Paryski and Christian Frisque (Coop-Arch RU, Brussels)
Isabelle Pauthier (ARAU)
Jean-Luc Quoistiaux (AGORA, Brussels)
Jim Seghers (City Mine(d))
Guido Steegen (Arsis, Brussels)
Patricia Vermaut (House of Participation, Municipality of Anderlecht)

COLLABORATIONS, EXPLORATIVE INTERVIEWS, AND INFORMAL CONVERSATIONS

Rabeha Afennas (Unizo Brussels)
Mathieu Berger (Université Libre de Bruxelles)
Géraldine Bruyneel (SamenlevingsopbouwBrussel vzw)
Tim Cassiers (Vrije Universiteit Brussel, Cosmopolis)
The members of Constant VZW
Bruno De Meulder (K.U. Leuven)
Stefan Decorte (Vrije Universiteit Brussel, Cosmopolis)
Ivo Ghizardi (Les Halles de Schaerbeek)
Hugo Henneman (LOGO Brussel)
Grégoire Kirreef (Projet Rousseau)
Laurent Michiels (RenovaS)
Ludo Moyersoen (City Mine(d))
Julien Piérart (Université Catholique de Louvain, Gezondheidsportret Brabant Beweegt)
Nicole Purnode (Brussel Gezond Stadsgewest)
Delphine Rigolet (Espace P)
Thierry Timmermans (CPAS/OCMW)
Sofie Van Bruystegem (City Mine(d))
Bruno Van Loo (Limite/Limiet and Brabant Bouge)
An Van Mechelen (BBOT/BNA)
Karin Van Zele (LOGO Brussel)

And possible others who I may have omitted from this list;
and for which I apologise.

Index

Note: page numbers in **bold** type refer to illustrations.

A

A2RC (Architecture et Construction entre Rêve et Réalité) 65
AAM *see* Archives d'Architecture Moderne (AAM)
Aarschot-Vooruitgang *see* Aerschot-Progrès
actants 17–18
action committees 40, 42
activism from-within 92–94, 191–192
Actor-Network Theory (ANT) 16, 17–19, 20, 133, 137, 138
actors 18, 141–144, 146–147, 157–158, 178, 187–188
Aerschot-Progrès 160
aesthetics 54–57, 61, 118–121
agency 15, 17
Agglomérations (Agglo) 43
Agora 168
Akrich, Madeleine 137
anti-industrial resistance 11–12, 57–59, 63, 64
Antwerp 11
Appadurai, Arjun 118, 125
Arabesk-Palaverboom Plate 6, 87, **88**, 93
ARAU *see* Atelier de Recherche et d'Action Urbaines (ARAU)
Archigram 40, 54, 73, 75, 134
architect role 124–125, 132
Architectural Association 54

architectural competitions
  in general 12, 13, 83, 169
  particular competitions 101, 155, 169, 170
architectural culture 10–14, 178
architectural icons *see* situated icons
architectural manuals *see* design manuals
Architectural Theory Handbook 122
Architectural Workroom 107
Architecture and Participation 121
Architecture at the Crossroads 112
architecture rationelle 75
architecture urbaine 45, 75
Architectuurwerking De Singel 10
architek 4, 12, 158, 175–178
Archives d'Architecture Moderne (AAM) 45
  Bulletin 45, 47, 59, 77
  counter-projects 25, 41, 45
  drawing-manifestos **51**
  legacy 64–68
  Rational Architecture: The Reconstruction of the European City 58
Arenberg Cinema 79
Arnstein, Sherry 115
Aron, Jacques 83
Art Nouveau 12, 182
assemblages 16, 19, 22, 53, 68–69

Atelier d'Architecture Pierre Hebbelinck
  Plate 15, 155, **156**
Atelier d'Art Urbain 65
  see also Vizzion
Atelier de Recherche et d'Action Urbaines
  (ARAU) 25, 40–41, 42–45, 49
  aesthetics 55, 57
  alternative Brussels coachtour 52
  Carrefour de l'Europe proposal Plate 2
  counter-projects 54–55, 57, **57**, **58**
  drawing-manifestos **51**
  Hôtel Central 79
  legacy 64–68
  on public participation 72
Atelier Gigogne Plates 10/11, 96, **97**, **98**
Aureli, Pier-Vittorio 126
Avenue Louise 40

B
Baird, George 14, 31
Bar Recyclart 87
Barake Plate 4, 79, **80**
Bastin, Olivier 6, 78, 104
Bastin, Roger 44, 68, 78
Bateau d'Élie 49, **50**, 54–55, **55**, 61
Bayat, Asef 94
Beel, Stéphane 10
Bekaert, Geert 10, 116
Belgitude 6
Beliris 184
Bellacasa, Puig de la 23
Bennett, Jane 191
Berlin 114, 137, 193
Beursschouwburg Theatre 79
Biest, Jacques van der 42
BIM (Brussels Instituut voor Milieubeheer)
  see Brussels Institute for
  Management of the Environment
Birkiye, Séfik 52, 59, **60**, 65–66, 76
Bishop, Claire 114, 117, 122–123, 128
bMa (*Bouwmeester Maître Architecte*) see
  Master Architect (bMa)
Boltanski, Luc 21
Bonduelle competition 68
Book of Specifications 141
Borden, Iain 15, 133

Bourgeois, Victor 12
Boutique Urbaine 44, 72
Boutsen, Dag 132
Bouwmeester Maître Architecte (bMa) see
  Master Architect (bMa)
BOZAR (Brussels Centre for Fine Arts) 13,
  99
Brabant see Quartier Brabant
Braidotti, Rosi 23, 37, 188
BRAL (Brusselse Raad voor het
  Leefmilieu) 43, 79
Braun, Neave 112
Breës, Gwenaël 103
Brenner, Neil 113
Breughel Square 88
Brown, Denise Scott 113, 120
Brusk 89, 91
Brussels Architecture Institute (IBAI) 13,
  82, 83, 92, 93–94
Brussels Centre for Fine Arts (BOZAR) 13,
  99
Brussels Institute for Management of the
  Environment 89, 91
Brussels Instituut voor Milieubeheer
  (BIM) see Brussels Institute for
  Management of the Environment
Brussels International Development Plan
  77, 145
Brusselse Raad voor het Leefmilieu
  (BRAL) 43, 79
Bruxelles Participation 179
Bruxellisation 12, 40, 158, 175–178
Bruyneel, Géraldine 163
bureau d'étude 141, 142, 152
Busieau, Gilbert 59, **60**

C
Cahiers Marxistes 61, 71–72
Carlo, Giancarlo de 114
Carrefour de l'Europe Plate 2, **46**, 58, **58**,
  63, 68, 72, 74, 170
Castells, Manuel 43
Cauter, Lieven De 85
Centre International pour la Ville,
  l'Architecture et le Paysage (CIVA)
  11, 12, 30, 92, 107

Centre International Rogier 96, 98
Chapelle-Kapellekerk 86
charettes 119, 121, 131
Chatsworth Metrorail Station and
    Childcare Centre 121
Chemins de la Ville 67
Cinema Légumen 79
Cinema Nova 79, 98, 103
*Cinq propositions pour le Square du
    Bastion* **50**
citizen participation *see* participation in
    architecture
City Mine(d) 79, 81, 98, 101
City Project 140
CIVA *see* Centre International pour la Ville,
    l'Architecture et le Paysage (CIVA)
CLDI *see* Local Commissions for
    Integrated Development (LCIDs)
co-production 15, 83, 96, 115
Commission Locale de Développement
    Intégré (CLDI) *see* Local Commissions
    for Integrated Development (LCIDs)
Community Architecture 119, 130
conseils de quartier 71
contemporary design 13, 83, 96, 98, 155
Contrat de Quartier *see* Neighbourhood
    Contracts (NCs)
*Contreprojets – controprogetti –
    counterprojects* 41–42, 62
convivial practice 94
*Coordination Contrats de Quartier et
    Rénovation Urbaine* 152
Cosmopolitical Proposal 84, 107
counter-projects 25, 41–42, 44–69
    collaborative approach 45–49
    de-politicisation or radicalisation
        61–63
    drawing as resistant practice 49–54
    first generation 54–57
    learning from 68–69
    legacy 64–68
    as political–aesthetic assemblages
        68–69
    as political *provocateurs* 44–45, 68
    second generation 57–59
    terminology 71

Crawford, Margaret 32, 130
Crépain, Jo 10
Criekingen, Mathieu van 31
critical theory 14, 21, 31
criticality-from-within 21–24, 192–193
Cuisinier, Jacques 98
Culot, Maurice
    and AAM 45
    and ARAU 74, 78
    drawing-manifestos **51**, 52
    and La Cambre 45, 54, 63
    *Les Espaces Publics Bruxellois: analyse et
        projets* **66**
    quotations and views 40, 41, 47, 59, 61,
        62, 63, 67, 75, 83, 104
Curtio (Georges Garnir) 175
Cuyper, Eric de 40

D

D+A International Plates 18/19, 166, **167**
Dassonville, Chantal 31
Davidoff, Paul 112
Debaise, Didier 26, 84, 95, 105
Delbrouck, Dominique **52**, 65
Delegation of the Pentagon 86–87
Deleuze, Gilles 94
Delevoy, Robert L. 40, 45, 63
Deller, Jeremy 123–124, 125
Demanet, Marie 67
democratic considerations 114–118
design manuals 58, 66, 166, 168
design methods 120–121
design practice 14–16
design workshops 12, 13, 82
development studies 113, 126
d'Helft, Brigitte 65
digesting 99, 101
Dingpolitik 139–140, 146
Diongre, Joseph 168
Direction de l'Architecture 13, 31
Director Scheme 92
DistUrb 81, 168, 169
Dogma 126
dossier de base 141, 151
drawing-manifestos 41, 42, 49–54, 69
Dunster, David 133

E
earthly accounts 18
École d'Architecture pour la
  Reconstruction de la Ville 63
École Nationale Supérieure d'Architecture
  et des Arts Visuels de la Cambre *see*
  La Cambre
École Urbaine 44, 72
ecology of practices 22
Engineers without Borders 134, **135**
*Les Espaces Publics Bruxellois: analyse et
  projets* **66**
*Etats généraux de l'architecture et de
  l'urbanisme* (symposium) 40
ethical turn 114, 122, 123, 127, 131
European Award for the Reconstruction
  of the City 64
European Capital of Culture 2000 12, 81, 82
Everyday Urbanism 121, 136

F
Fabrik 87, 91, 94, 107
façadism 67, 69
fenêtre vertical démocratique 63, 76
51N4E 101
Flagey *see* Place Flagey
Flanders 10–11, 29
Flemish Architecture Institute 10, 92
Fondation Légumen 108
Fondation Philippe Rotthier pour
  l'Architecture 64
Fondation Pied de Biche 79
Fondation pour l'Architecture 11–12, 65, 77
Fondation Roi Baudouin 64
Foucault, Michel 138
4 x 4 exhibition Plates 12/13, 99–101, **99,
  100**
France Plate 14, **124**
Fraser, Murray 15–16
Freetown Brussels 79
French Community 13
Friedman, Yona 134

G
Garnir, Georges 175
Gaucheret *see* Place Gaucheret

GC Elzenhof 168
gemeenplaats 10
gentrification 1, 67, 82, 122
Germany 114, 193
Gewestelijk Ontwikkelingsplan (GEWOP)
  see Regional Development Plan
Geyter, Xaveer de 10, 170
Gielen, Bjorn 91
Gillis, Christophe 78
global practice 15, 117–118, 136, 165
global project for the city 58–59
glocal 115, 117–118
Graafland, Arie 14
Grand Boulevard du Nord 76

H
Habitat et Rénovation 168
Habraken, John 134
Hackney, Rod 130
*Handboek van de Brusselse Openbare
  Ruimten* 66–67, **66**, **67**
Hankar, Paul 12
Haraway, Donna 21, 22, 24, 35, 37, 99,
  116, 152, 157, 192
Hardt, Michael 115
Harvey, David 85
Hays, K. Michael 14, 41
Hebbelinck, Pierre *see* Atelier
  d'Architecture Pierre Hebbelinck
Hertzberger, Herman 155
Heyden, Matthias 136, 192
Heynen, Hilde 136, 138, 149
Hill, Jonathan 15
historicism 65, 70, 71
Horta, Victor 12, 39
Hôtel Central 25, 79, 81, 85
House of Participation of the City of
  Brussels 179
House of the Citizens *see* Maison des
  Citoyens

I
IEB (*Inter-Environnement Bruxelles*) 43,
  79, 168
Institut Bruxellois d'Architecture *see*
  Brussels Architecture Institute (IBAI)

Institut Bruxellois pour la Gestion de l'Environnement (IBGE) *see* Brussels Institute for Management of the Environment
Institut Supérieur des Arts Décoratifs de la Cambre (ISACF) *see* La Cambre
Institute for Strategies of Participative Architecture and Spatial Appropriation (ISPARA) 136
Inter-Environnement Bruxelles (IEB) 43, 79, 168
Internationaal Rogiercentrum *see* Centre International Rogier
International Development Plan *see* Brussels International Development Plan
interstitial activism 26, 81, 85
    choosing attachments over autonomy 101
    as a digestive practice 96–101
    empowering from-within 92
    Recyclart 86–91
    as resistance from-within 92–94
    as a space of encounter 94–96
ISACF (Institut Supérieur des Arts Décoratifs de la Cambre) *see* La Cambre
ISPARA (Institute for Strategies of Participative Architecture and Spatial Appropriation) 136
Istendael, Geert van 176
ITT building (proposed) 40

J

Jaspers Eyers Architects 77
Jencks, Charles 49, 61, 116, 120, 155
Jeune Architecture Belge 13
Jonction Plates 12/13, 83, 99, **99**, **100**

K

Kaika, Maria 184
Kaliski, John 121
Karbon 101
Kelly, Patrick 76
Kessel, Philippe van 98
Kino-Trotter 79

Kitchen Tower 170, 183
Knevitt, Charles 130
Koning Boudewijn Stichting *see* Fondation Roi Baudouin
Koolhaas, Rem 19
Krier, Léon 42, 45, 47
    depicted in drawing-manifesto 52
    Luxemburg project 74
    neoclassical work 58, 64
Kroll, Lucien 114, 120, 125
    La Mémé/Maison Médicale 29, 116, 119

L

La Cambre 40
    counter-projects 25, 41, 45, 47, **48**, 54–55, **55**, 58–59, **60**
    drawing-manifestos 49–50, **49**, **50**, **52**, **53**
    Platforme Flagey 168
    project anthologies 61
    projet global sur la ville 58–59
La Mémé 29, 116, 119
La Monnaie theatre 29
Laet, Marianne de 139
Lakense Straat Plate 3, 65, **65**
landmark buildings 4
language communities 6–7, **8**
language issues 29, 145
Latour, Bruno 16, 17–19, 137, 138, 139, 149, 150, 157
Latz & Partners Plates 18/19, 166, **167**
LCIDs *see* Local Commissions for Integrated Development (LCIDs)
Le Corbusier 138, 166
Lefebvre, Henri 15, 43
Legrand, Jozef 87
Lelubre, Daniel 55, **56**
Lemaire, Raymond 57
L'Escaut Plates 10/11, 91, 96, **97**, **98**
Les Marolles 1, **3**, 4, **9**, 40, **177**
    counter-projects 54
    drawing-manifestos **51**
Les Saprophytes Plate 7 **89**
Les Vignes Blanches, Cergy-Pontoise Plate 14, **124**

Local Commissions for Integrated
   Development (LCIDs) 141, 145, 152,
   160
Loeckx, André 57–58
London 112, 166
Loo, Anne van 78
Luxemburg Station 81

M
Maelbeek 49, **49**
*Maison de la Participation et de la
   Citoyenneté* 179
Maison des Citoyens Plate 15, 155–157,
   156, 158, **159**
Maison des Pages 55, 57, 68, 73, 75
Maison du Peuple 39
Maison Médicale 29, 116
Majot, Jean-Pierre **52**, 67
*Man of Thoughts: 5 years Brussels Head
   Architect* exhibition, Sept 2014 6, 14,
   14, 28–29
Manhattan Plan 12, 39, **159**, 175
Manuel des Espaces Publics Bruxellois
   66–67, **66, 67**
MAPRAC 81, 82, 92
marginal space 85
market liberalism 115, 127
Martin, Reinhold 14, 22, 27
Martini Tower 96, 98
Marxism 21, 31, 43, 73, 192
Master Architect (bMa) 6, 10, 13, 82–83,
   99, 104
Maxwell, Robert 62
Mayer, Margit 85
Mayeur, Yvan 166, 182
Meades, Jonathan 1
Mercier, Christophe 168
Mertens, Nathalie 108–109
Miessen, Markus 112
modest witness 24
Moelaert, Frank 116
Mol, Annemarie 138–139
Molenbeek 155
Mont des Art 82
Moritz, Benoît 104
Mouffe, Chantal 117, 129

municipalities 7, **8**
Musée d'Art Moderne *see* Museum of
   Modern Art
Museum of Fine Arts (BOZAR) 13, 99
Museum of Modern Art 44, 55, **56, 57**,
   68

N
Negri, Antonio 115
neighbourhood 61, 113
Neighbourhood Contracts (NCs) 27, 83,
   133, 140–147, 151, 152, 180
   Aerschot-Progrès 160, 161–163
Neirinck, Patrice 59, **60**
neoclassicism 58, 64, 65, 70
neoliberalisation 85, 115
Nesbitt, Kate 14
New Simplicity *see* Nieuwe Eenvoud
New Urbanism 65, 119, 120
Nieuwe Eenvoud 10
Nieuwenhuys, Constant 134
Nimmegeers, Staf 5–6
North–South railway junction Plate 1, 12,
   39, 59, 83, 86, 89, 99, 160

O
object-in-flight 18
OMA/AMO 126, 170
open-air cinema 79, **80**
Open City *see* Studio Open City
oppositional pairs 20, 26, 111
Oproep aan jonge Europese architecten
   65

P
Palace of Justice 1, **3**, 4, 39, 40, 175, **177**
Parckdesign competition 91, 107
Parckfarm 91
Parcours Citoyen 168, 169
Parijs, Philippe van 106
Park Hill, Sheffield 148
participation in architecture 26–27, 71,
   72, 111–132
   see also Neighbourhood Contracts
      (NCs)
   aesthetics of 118–121

degrees of 128
as a democratic act 114–118
between design and use 134–136
Director Scheme 92
politics *and* aesthetics 122–125
post-dichotomist account of 125
pseudo-participation 116
towards a complex account of 136–140
understanding 146–147
participatory artefacts 27, 133, 137–140 146
participatory design games 120–121, 131
pastiche 62, 67, 69
PCGO *see* Local Commissions for Integrated Development (LCIDs)
PDI *see* Brussels International Development Plan
Peeters, Benoît 176
peripheries 85
Pesleux, Marcel 54
Petrescu, Doina 94
Picnic the Streets 85, 106
Picqué, Charles 67
PIO *see* Brussels International Development Plan
Plaatselijke Commissie voor Geintegreerde Ontwikkeling (PCGO) *see* Local Commissions for Integrated Development (LCIDs)
Place Bara 79
Place de Brouckère 166, **167**
Place de Liverpool 94
Place du Jeu de Balle *see* Vossenplein
Place du Musée 55
Place Flagey Plates 18/19, 158, 166–169
Place Gaucheret 158
Place Rogier Plate 20, 158, 169–174, **170**, **171**, **172**
Plan de Développement International de Bruxelles (PDI) *see* Brussels International Development Plan
Plan particulier d'aménagement 45
Plan Régional de Développement (PRD) *see* Regional Development Plan
Plan Secteur 43, 64, 141
Plan voor de Internationale Ontwikkeling van Brussel (PIO) *see* Brussels International Development Plan
planning *see* urban planning
plantrekkerij 6
Platforme Flagey 168
PleinOPENair 79, **80**, 81, 98, 103
Poelaert, Joseph 1, **3**, 4, 39, 175
Port Grimaud 62
Porte de Namur 49
Porthoghesi, Paolo 42, 61–62
post-criticality 15, 22
post-political city 15
post-political turn 113, 117
post-positivist planning 112, 126
postmodernism 11–12, 14, 25, 41, 112, 118, 121
practice turn 14–16
pragmatism 17, 22, 33
praxis 15
Price, Cedric 148
Prince Charles Foundation 119
Prisme Éditions 12, 30
private–public projects 10, 96
Prix Européenne de la reconstruction de la ville see European Award for the Reconstruction of the City
procès-verbal (PV) 160
projective practice 15
Projet d'aménagement de la vallée du Maelbeek **49**
promenade diagnostique 144
public–private projects 10, 96
public space 47
  Place Flagey 166–169
  Place Rogier 169–174, **170**
  reclaiming 79, 81–91
public urinals Plates 16/17, 158, 160–165, **165**

Q
Quartier Brabant Plates 16/17, 158, 160–165, **161**
Quartier des Arts 67, 71
Quartier du Nord 76, **159**

Qui a peur de L'Architecture? 13, 104
Quinlan, Terry 64

R
RAC (Rijks Administratief Centrum) 81
Radisson SAS Royal Hotel 77
Rancière, Jacques 123
Rational Architecture: The Reconstruction of the European City 58
reclaiming 96, 98–99
La Reconstruction de la Ville Européenne conference Nov. 1978 52, 64, 73
Reconstruction of the European City movement 11–12, 42, 45, 47, 62
   aesthetics 61
   contrasted with later activism 82
   drawing-manifestos 52
   legacy 64–68
Recyclart Plate 5, 26, 81–82, 86–91, **86, 87**, 93, 99, 102, 106
   see also Fabrik
Regional Development Plan 140, 151
regional division 7, **7, 8**
regionalisation 43
Rendell, Jane 15, 35
renovation grants 144–145
Right to the City 25, 40, 42–44, 85
Rijks Administratief Centrum (RAC) 81
Rodriguez, Arantxa 116
Rogier *see* Place Rogier
Rogoff, Irit 36
Rossi, Aldo 40
Rotor 94, 107
Roy, Ananya 117, 136
De Roze Verspreiding Plate 7, 89, **89**, 93
Rudofsky, Bernard 113
Rue d'Aerschot Plates 16/17, 160–165, **161**
Rue de Brabant 160–161, **161**
Rue de Montagne 76
Rue du Musée 72

S
Sachs, Andrew 112
Saint-Josse-ten-Noode 160
Samyn, Philippe 168
SCA Architectes Associés Plates 10/11, 96, **97, 98**
Schaerbeek 12, 155, 160
Schoonbrodt, René
   aesthetics 54, 55, 57
   and ARAU 42, 49
   depicted in drawing-manifesto 52
   École d'Architecture pour la Reconstruction de la Ville 63
   Les Espaces Publics Bruxellois: analyse et projets **66**
Schuiten, François 176
Schuman Square 170
Science and Technology Studies (STS) 16, 18, 133, 137, 138
se débrouiller 6
'second turn' in Brussels architecture and urbanism 83, 104
self-build 114, 148
Shaviro, Steven 95
Simone, AbdouMaliq 85
situated icons 158, 165–174
skate park 89, **90**, 91, **91**
Skieven architek 1, **2**, 4
Smet, Pascal 168
Smithson, Alison and Peter 148
social housing 13, 31, 140
soft regeneration 67, 82
Somol, Robert 14
spatial considerations 85, 134, 136, 136–137
spatial planning 44–45, 77
spatial practices 15, 17
Speaks, Michael 14
Spoerry, François 62
Square du Bastion 49–50
Stad-aan-de-Stroom UDP 11
Stengers, Isabelle 19, 21, 22, 36, 37, 84, 93, 95, 98, 105, 109, 157, 190, 192
Steyaert, Floris 91
Stichting Architectuurmuseum (S/AM) 10
Stichting Open Deur 79
Strauven, Francis 10
street furniture 66–67, 87–88, 91

STS *see* Science and Technology Studies (STS)
Studio 012 Secchi-Vigano 101
Studio Open City 11, 12, 82, 104
Supernova Jonge Belgische Architectuur 13, 31, 82
sustainability 15, 19
Swyngedouw, Erik 32, 103, 113, 116
Sykes, A. Krista 14–15

T
taxon 143, 152
Terlinden, François 55
Théâtre National Plates 10/11, 96–98, **97**, **98**
Thrift, Nigel 175
Till, Jeremy 118, 120, 124, 152
traditionalism 12, 25, 41, 64–65, 70
transdisciplines 21, 35
tree house 79

U
underground space 173
United Kingdom 65, 112, 130, 148, 166
University of Louvain 29, 116
urban activism 11, 13, 25–26, 41, 42–44
  see also counter-projects; interstitial activism
Urban Development Agency 99
Urban Development Projects (UDPs) 10, 11
urban embellishment 58, 66, 75, 87–88
urban form 55, 62
  see also spatial considerations
urban games 120–121, 131
Urban Pilot Project (UPP) 86
urban planning 10–11, 12, 112–113, 128
  see also Neighbourhood Contracts (NCs); Plan Secteur
Urban Renewal Act 1988 10–11
Urban Renewal Campaign 10
urban salons 87–89
Urbanistica Alternativa 75
Ursulines Square/Skate Park Plates 8/9, 89, **90**, 91, **91**

user participation *see* participation in architecture
utopian realism 22

V
V+ 101
Vade-Mecum 13
VAI (Vlaams Architectuur Instituut) 10, 92
Vandenhove, Charles 29, 57
Velde, Henri van de 12
Venice Architecture Biennial 19, 42, 61
Venturi, Robert 113, 120
Verdonck, Benjamin Plate 4, 79, **80**
Verliefden, Michel 65
vertical democratic window *see fenêtre vertical démocratique*
Vizzion 52, 65–66, 77
Vlaams Architectuur Instituut (VAI) 10, 92
Vossenplein 1
VrijstadBXLVilleLibre *see* Freetown Brussels

W
Walloon region 7, 29
Wates, Nick 130
Wet inzake Krotopruiming 39
Whitehead, Alfred North 95, 108, 190
Whiting, Sarah 14
Wijkcontract *see* Neighbourhood Contracts (NCs)
World Expo 1958 12, 39, 166
Wynants, Maxime 54

X
Xaveer De Geyter Architects (XDGA) Plate 20, 101, 158, 169–173, **170**, **171**, **172**
Xenakis, Iannis 166

Y
Yaneva, Albena 16, 18, 138, 149

Z
Zaera-Polo, Alejandro 19
zwanze 6